The Wisdom of Aristotle

SUNY Series in Ancient Greek Philosophy

Anthony Preus, editor

The Wisdom of Aristotle

CARLO NATALI

TRANSLATED BY GERALD PARKS

State University of New York Press

The author would like to thank Douglas Hutchinson for his editorial assistance on the translation.

Published by
State University of New York Press, Albany

Printed in the United States of America

For information, address State University of New York Press,
90 State Street, Suite 700, Albany, N.Y. 12207

Production, Laurie Searl
Marketing, Anne M. Valentine

Library of Congress Cataloging-in-Publication Data

Natali, Carlo.
[Saggezza di Aristotele. English]
The wisdom of Aristotle / Carlo Natali: translated by Gerald Parks.
p.cm.—(SUNY series in ancient Greek philosophy)
Includes bibliographical references and index.
isbn 0-7914-4895-9 (alk. paper)—isbn 0-7914-4896-7 (pbk. : alk. paper)
1. Aristotle—Ethics. 2. Ethics, Ancient. I. Title. II. Series.
[B491.E7 N3813 2001]
171'.3—dc21 00-045019

10 9 8 7 6 5 4 3 2 1

To C.

CONTENTS

ABBREVIATIONS

In the notes, and text, reference is made to the works of Greek and Latin authors by the abbreviations of their Latin titles. Capital letters are not normally used. To help the reader identify the works cited, the following list gives these abbreviated titles in alphabetical order, accompanied, where appropriate, by the Latin title in full and an English translation of it. In some cases only the Latin or English title is given. Unless otherwise specified, the works are by Aristotle.

ad. Nic. = *ad Nicoclem* = *To Nicocles* (by Isocrates)
Ag. = *Agamemnon* (by Aeschylus)
antid. = *Antidosis* (by Isocrates)
a. po. = *Analytica posteriora* = *Posterior Analytics*
apol. = *Apology* (by Plato)
a. pr. = *Analytica priora* = *Prior Analytics*
de an. = *De anima* = *On the Soul*
de. cael. = *De caelo* = *On the Heavens*
def. = *Definitiones* = *Definitions* (by Pseudo Plato)
de gen. an. = *De generatione animalium* = *On the Generation of Animals*
de mem. = *De memoria et reminiscentia* = *On Memory and Recollection*
de motu an. = *De motu animalium* = *On the Movement of Animals*
EE = *Ethica Eudemea* = *Eudemian Ethics*
EN = *Ethica Nicomachea* = *Nicomachean Ethics*
Eum. = *Eumenides* (by Aeschylus)
Eutyphr. = *Euthyphro* (by Plato)
Gorg. = *Gorgias* (by Plato)
hist. an. = *Historia animalium* = *History of Animals*
Il. = *Iliad* (by Homer)
in Aristot. top. comm. = *in Aristotelis Topica commentarii* = *Commentary* (by Alexander of Aphrodias) *on Aristotle's Topics*
in Eth. Nic. = *On the Nicomachean Ethics* (by Aspasius)
in Metaph. = *On the Metaphysics* (by Alexander of Aphrodisias)

in Metaph. = *On the Metaphysics* (by Pseudo Alexander)
leg. = *Leges* = *Laws* (by Plato)
mem. = *Memorabilia* (by Xenophon)
Men. = *Meno* (by Plato)
metaphys. = *Metaphysica* = *Metaphysics*
MM = *Magna Moralia*
nem. = *Nemean Odes* (by Pindar)
Nic. = *Nicocles* (by Isocrates)
Od. = *Odyssey* (by Homer)
paneg. = *Panegyricus* (by Isocrates)
Phaed. = *Phaedo* (by Plato)
phys. = *Physica*= *Physics*
pol. = *Politica* = *Politics*
polit. = *Politicus* (by Plato)
Prot. = *Protagoras* (by Plato)
protr. = *Protrepticus*
py. = *Pythian Odes* (by Pindar)
resp. = *Res Publica* = *Republic* (of Plato)
rhet. = *Rhetorica* = *Rhetoric*
Soph. = *Sophist* (by Plato)
Theaet. = *Theaetetus* (by Plato)
top. = *Topica* = *Topics*

The following abbreviations refer to authors:
AESCH. = Aeschylus
ALEX. APHROD. = Alexander of Aphrodisias
ANDOC. = Andocides
ARISTOPH. = Aristophanes
ASPAS. = Aspasius
DIN. = Dinarchus
EURIP. = Euripides
HEROD. = Herodotus
ISOCR. = Isocrates
LYS. = Lysias
PIND. = Pindar
PLAT. = Plato
PROD. = Prodicus
PROTAG. = Protagoras
PS. ALEX. = Pseudo Alexander
PS. PLAT. = Pseudo Plato

SOPH. = Sophocles
THEOGN. = Theognis
THUC. = Thucydides
XENOCR. = Xenocrates
XENOPH. = Xenophon

Other abbreviations used in this book are:
ad l. or *ad loc.* = *ad locum* = at the place (mentioned or under consideration)
BC = Before Christ
cf. = compare
cit. = cited (the work previously cited)
comm. = commentary
contra = against
diss. = dissertation
ed. = edition
ed. or eds. = editor or editors
e.g. = exempli gratia = for example
esp. = especially
et al. = et alii = and others
etc. = et cetera = and other things
et seq. = et sequens or sequentia = and the following (page or pages) (used in the text)
f. or ff. = the following (page or pages) (used in the notes)
fr. = fragment
Ibid. = ibidem = in the same place
i.e. = id est = that is
interpr. = interpretive
introd. = introduction
Ital. = Italian
p. or pp. = page or pages
PS = practical syllogism
repr. = reprint
RP = rational plan (of life)
sc. = scilicet = that is to say, namely
s.v. = sub voce (under the item)
trans. = translation
suppl. = supplement
Univ. = University
viz. = videlicet = that is to say, namely
vs. = versus

Some journal titles are abbreviated in the bibliography:
Amer. Philos. Quart. = *American Philosophical Quarterly*
Arch. f. Gesch. d. Philos. = *Archiv für Geschichte der Philosophie*
Class. Journ. = *Classical Journal*
Classical Quart. = *Classical Quarterly*
Et. Philos. = *Etudes Philosophiques*
Intern. Philos. Quart. = *International Philosophical Quarterly*
Journ. Hell. Stud. = *Journal of Hellenic Studies*
Journ. Hist. Philos. = *Journal of the History of Philosophy*
Journ. of Hist. of Ideas = *Journal of the History of Ideas*
Journ. of Philos. = *Journal of Philosophy*
Midwest Stud. Philos. = *Midwest Studies in Philosophy*
Philos. Jahrbuch = *Philosophisches Jahrbuch*
Philos. Quart. = *Philosophical Quarterly*
Philos. Review = *Philosophical Review*
Proceed. Aristotelian Soc. = *Proceedings of the Aristotelian Society*
Rev. et. grecques = *Revue des études grecques*
Revue Philos. de Louvain = *Revue Philosophique de Louvain*
Trans. Amer. Philol. Assoc. = *Transactions of the American Philological Association*
Zeitschr. f. philos. Forschung = *Zeitschrift für philosophische Forschung*

CHAPTER 1

VIRTUE OR SCIENCE?

1. An *Ur-Ethik* in the *Topics?*

In 1927, in one of his most characteristic *Abhandlungen,* Hans von Arnim examined all the passages in the *Topics* that discussed ethical examples. He concluded that one could reconstruct the first phase in the evolution of Aristotle's ethical thought by reference to all these examples. For von Arnim the aim was to confute, by means of this reconstruction, the thesis of Werner Jaeger, who held that Aristotle, up to and including the writing of the *Eudemian Ethics,* had hung on to a Platonizing concept of practical knowledge (φρόνησις), identifying wisdom with an exact, precise and rigorous form of knowledge.[1] H. von Arnim intended to show that Aristotle had Platonically identified φρόνησις with an ἐπιστήμη, a rigorous type of scientific knowledge, only in the ethics of the *Topics,* but that later he had abandoned this identification. Von Arnim placed the change in perspective at the time of composition of what he considered Aristotle's first work on ethics, the *Magna Moralia.*[2]

H. von Arnim thus reconstructed, starting from the *Topics,* a theory of the various kinds of virtue, of the various πάθη, an examination of the nature of φιλία and many other discussions of ethical matters. But his reconstruction rests on unstable foundations. For he maintains (not entirely convincingly) that Aristotle, to illustrate more clearly the arguments and refutations that are the subject of the *Topics,* would have found it more convenient to refer to his own ethical thought, rather than to current ethical opinions or theories invented *ad hoc,* suitable for use as examples.[3] Later scholars have adopted a different slant and have usually found in the *Topics* evidence of the discussions that took place in the Academy. That is, in order to illustrate the various ways of arguing for and against a thesis, Aristotle is thought to have referred to the various discussions that actually took place in the Academy of his day.[4] We agree that this hypothesis appears to be the more reasonable one, and a comparison of the reconstruction of the concept of wisdom (φρόνησις) in the *Topics* made by von Arnim with the passages in which Aristotle speaks of φρόνησις in the text of the *Topics* seems to prove this.

We would like to claim that in the *Topics* various problems and aporias about the nature of φρόνησις can be traced, but that there is no unitary and satisfying doctrine. These problems and difficulties continue to be present in other texts by Aristotle, as for example in *EE* VIII 1, until they are finally solved, particularly in *EN*. It thus seems possible to examine the two opening chapters of *EN* VI against the backdrop of the aporias and problems discussed in the *Topics*. Von Arnim's reconstruction of Aristotle's *Ur-Ethik* will be used, in the first part of this discussion, as a sounding board or reference point that serves to clarify our position. In this way we shall be able to reconstruct the origin of Aristotle's concept of wisdom, or practical knowledge, starting from the Academic debates. Our reconstruction is systematic more than historical: rather than placing the origin of Aristotle's concept of φρόνησις in a precise historical moment, or in a particular stage of his intellectual development, we are interested in characterizing Aristotle's position within a philosophical debate that must have been very lively, as we can see from the few fragments of it that remain. We are especially concerned to define the features that make Aristotle's theory different from all others.

2. Φρόνησις in the *Topics*

H. von Arnim was convinced that in the *Topics* Aristotle still accepted a threefold conception of the soul, exactly like Plato's. Thus he maintained that Aristotle divided the soul into λογιστικόν, θυμοειδές and ἐπιθυμητικόν, assigning a virtue to each of these three parts of the soul: moderation to ἐπιθυμητικόν, courage to θυμοειδές and φρόνησις to λογιστικόν.[5] Indeed, in the *Topics* Aristotle often repeats that φρόνησις is the virtue of the rational part of the soul, or the virtue of the whole man, inasmuch as rationality is considered his most characteristic part (134a 33–36; 136b 10–14; 138b 1–5; 149a 29–30). Moreover, Aristotle says that the defining characteristic of man is to receive within himself ἐπιστήμη, and that ἐπιστήμη is found only in λογιστικόν (128b 35–38). On the basis of these assertions, von Arnim felt authorized to propose the following identifications: ἀρετή τοῦ λογιστικοῦ = ἐπιστήμη = φρόνησις.[6] Thus, in his opinion, Aristotle retained, in its main features, the Platonic conception of practical knowledge.

According to von Arnim, this φρόνησις in the *Topics* is both a theoretical and a practical science. As a matter of fact, in the *Topics* Aristotle does quote Xenocrates as saying that φρόνησις has the task of defining things, and in this sense he considers it a theoretical science. Elsewhere, however, Aristotle speaks of φρόνησις as a practical and political form of knowledge, typical of rulers and older people, in contrast to courage, which is typical of the young (117a 27–29; 141a 6–9). Here, if we accept the idea that Aristotle, in quoting Xenocrates, was taking up his position, the distinction between the virtue of θυμοειδές (courage) and the virtue of λογιστικόν (wisdom) seems clearly established, and the thesis of von Arnim would seem to be definitely confirmed.[7]

Yet things are not so simple. The identification proposed above (ἀρετὴ τοῦ λογιστικοῦ = ἐπιστήμη = φρόνησις) contains an identification of ἀρετή with ἐπιστήμη which, for Aristotle in the *Topics,* is not acceptable. Between ἀρετή and ἐπιστήμη there is a difference of genus; cf. 152a 39b 2: "and again [we must see] whether the genus of each is not the same, but one is good and the other is bad, or one is virtue and the other is science." In the *Topics* Aristotle had not yet formulated the concept of ἀρετὴ διανοητική, i.e. a virtue of the intellect, a concept applicable even to the most rigorous science, which was to be typical of the *Ethics*. In the *Topics* ἀρετή is a γένος, and is said to be so in only one way: it is virtue in the traditional sense of the term, i.e. an excellence of character, as are generosity, courage, moderation and self-control. It belongs to a different συστοιχία from that of ἐπιστήμη, as can be seen in the passage in which Aristotle compares ἐπιστήμη with one of the most important virtues, justice:

> if justice is knowledge, then injustice is ignorance; if 'justly' means 'scientifically' and is said of people of experience, then too 'unjustly' is said of 'ignorant people' or 'people without experience'. But these last two determinations do not belong together, nor do those belong together, on the basis of what has just been said. Indeed, 'unjustly' would seem to be applicable to 'experienced people' rather than to 'inexperienced people'. (114b 8–13)[8]

In this way, already in the *Topics* Aristotle criticizes the Socratic identification of error and ignorance, and the Platonic equation of virtue with knowledge.

This is true for ἀρετή in general. We must now see if, perhaps, φρόνησις is not an exception, and may not be both virtue and knowledge. There are texts in which this possibility, though mentioned, is not explicitly accepted, and others in which it is clearly affirmed. An example of the first type is in the *Topics* (*top.* III 6), which lists four possible ways of demolishing the thesis that only φρόνησις, *qua* virtue, is a science:

> this thesis can be demolished in four ways: [1] either by showing that every virtue is knowledge, [2] or that none is, [3] or that also some other virtue, such as justice, is knowledge, [4] or that φρόνησις itself is not knowledge. (120a 27–31)

An example of the second type is a rather obscure passage in *top.* IV 2, where it is explicitly stated that in the case of φρόνησις, and only in this case, the difference of genus between virtue and knowledge is overcome. Aristotle can reach this conclusion only at the cost of some disconcerting logical results, which, in our opinion, indicate that an unresolved difficulty still remains in his thinking. However that may be, in this passage, too, Aristotle repeats the general principle stated above, viz. that a virtue, such as justice, is not comprised in the genus of a science:

> As if, for example, one posited science as the genus of justice [and neither of the two genera includes the other]; so that science would not be the genus of justice, since, as it appears, when a species is contained in two genera, one of the two genera is included in the other. (121b 26–30)

But φρόνησις calls into question this general principle:

> in certain cases there is a difficulty in this respect: in fact, some think that φρόνησις is both virtue and knowledge, and that neither of the two genera is contained in the other. To tell the truth, not everyone admits that φρόνησις is an ἐπιστήμη. But if one admits that what has been said is true, it would seem necessary that the genera of it (φρόνησις) be both subordinated one to the other, or that both be subordinated to a third genus, and this is what happens in the case of ἀρετή and ἐπιστήμη, since both of them are contained in the genus, and each of them is a habitual state (ἕξις) and a disposition (διάθεσις). (121b 30–38)

The doctrine supported here seems scandalous for several reasons: it appears patently incompatible with Aristotle's usual doctrine, according to which one and the same species cannot partake of two co-ordinate genera except at the price of an equivocal predication.[9] And commentators have been at a loss when faced with this passage. Alexander of Aphrodisias[10] tries to solve the problems by saying that φρόνησις is a dianoetic virtue, but the solution is a weak one. Indeed, as we have said, the concept of dianoetic virtue is not present in any other passage of the *Topics;* moreover, Alexander finds a concept of ἀρετή that is applicable to "all" the sciences, to φρόνησις as well as σοφία and mathematics, while here Aristotle is talking about a meaning of ἀρετή and ἐπιστήμη that is applicable only to φρόνησις. It is thus a meaning of virtue that is still linked to the practical sphere, and is univocal, still comprising courage, justice, and generosity; it is not a "dianoetic" virtue, which may also be completely divorced from practical action and is the sheer excellence of the rational part of man. Modern commentators have preferred to regard this passage as a later addition, which contradicts what Aristotle explicitly says a few lines away. And as always in these cases, it is tacitly admitted that Aristotle, or whoever acted on his behalf, was so foolish as to add a text that contradicts other passages without bothering about whether it was compatible with its context.[11]

We prefer to regard this passage as a provisional answer to a problem that continues to occupy Aristotle's thoughts, and traces of which are to be found also in other passages of the *Topics*. The passage just read, as well as those to follow (taken both from the *Topics* and from the *Eudemian Ethics*) have one thing in common: they are all obscure and difficult texts, controversial even from the textual point of view, as if Aristotle were struggling with an unresolved difficulty in his thought. On the contrary, the passages in which, with the introduction of the concept of "dianoetic virtue," the problem of establishing how φρόνησις can be both knowledge and virtue is solved, are clear, unambiguous, plain and textually uncontroversial.

In fact, a passage that is no less difficult to interpret than *top.* IV 2 (quoted above) is *top.* V 7. Here Aristotle cites an example which assumes that φρόνησις has the defining characteristic of being the "science of good," and he sees some difficulties that derive from this. It is advisable to read the whole passage, which goes as follows:

> starting from 'what stands in the same relation', whoever wants to confute a thesis will observe if 'what stands in the same relation' is not proper to 'what [it] stands in the same relation [to]', since 'what stands in the same relation' is also not proper to 'what [it] stands in the same relation [to]'. But if 'what stands in the same relation' is proper to 'what [it] stands in the same relation [to]' this second thing will not be proper to the thing to which it is supposed to be proper.[12] For example: given that φρόνησις exists in the same way with respect to good and evil, in being ἐπιστήμη of each of them [and] it is not proper to φρόνησις to be the ἐπιστήμη of good, it will not be proper to it[13] to be the ἐπιστήμη of evil. But if it is proper to φρόνησις to be the ἐπιστήμη of good, it will not be proper to it to be the ἐπιστήμη of evil, since it is impossible for the same thing to be the defining property of more than one thing. For one who wants to defend a thesis this *topos* is not useful at all, since 'what exists in the same way' is one thing being compared with several things. (137a 8–20)

The *topos,* or dialectical argument, described here has given rise to many discussions,[14] even in recent times, but, seeing that it is useful only to one who wishes to demolish a thesis, it seems clear that it must be read as a refutation. If two notions, *a* and *b,* have the same relation, or behave in the same way, with respect to a third notion *c* (137a 18–20), one wishes to demonstrate that in no case can *a* and *b* be defining properties of *c*. In fact, there are two possibilities: (1) that *a* is not a defining property of *c*, or (2) that it is so. Now it is clear that (1.1), if *a* is not the defining property of *c*, then neither is *b*, since it behaves in the same way. But, Aristotle says (2.1), if *a* is the defining property of *c*, it *(a)* will not be the defining property of that of which it is posited as being the defining property. The only meaning, it seems, that can be given to this passage is that, if *a* is the defining property of *c*, *b* will not be, and hence *a* cannot be so either, since it behaves in the same way as *b*. But it is still not clear why, in case (2.1), *b* cannot be the defining property of *c*.

Things are clearer in the example: if φρόνησις behaves in the same way (it is science) with respect to good and evil, i.e. it has the role *c* with respect to *a* and *b* ('to be the science of good' and 'to be the science of evil'), these two identical ways of behaving that *c* has with respect to *a* and *b* cannot be defining properties. Indeed, if being the science of good is not the defining property of φρόνησις, neither is being the science of evil, following rule (1.1) given above. But if, on the contrary, being the science of good is the defining property of φρόνησις, being the science of evil cannot be. This follows from the definition of a *proprium*,[15] since being the science of evil is not predicated only of φρόνησις, nor is it predicated convertibly. If everything that is γραμματικός is man, not everything that is the science of evil is φρόνησις, as this property is predicated also of other forms of knowledge. Hence, given that it is impossible for the same thing to be the defining property of more than one thing (137a 17–18), *b* is not the defining property of *c* and hence, following rule (2.1), neither is *a*. It seems unnecessary to consider lines 17–18 as interpolations, as has been maintained even in recent years.[16]

The passage thus shows that being the science of good and evil cannot be the defining property, or principal characteristic, of φρόνησις in this sense it does not confirm von Arnim's thesis, as he believed.[17] Here we see an idea that reappears several times in the corpus of Aristotle's writings, i.e. the idea that a science, which has knowledge of good, also has knowledge of its contrary, as in the case of medicine, which can heal but can also, in a certain sense, kill.

This has some consequences: a science, unlike a virtue, can also produce evil, while a virtue is the cause of good actions only. It is with this second argument that Aristotle in the *EE* refutes those who affirm that φρόνησις is a science.

3. Virtue, Science and Φρόνησις in *EE* VIII 1

The problem posed by the particular nature of a science mentioned above, viz. that it can also be used to produce bad results, and the difficulties that derive from ascribing the status of ἐπιστήμη to φρόνησις, are discussed in *EE* VIII 1, a passage that presents enormous difficulties, both textually and from the standpoint of its interpretation. Here we shall not give a complete translation of it, but only a paraphrase, concentrating on the features that regard this study.

It appears that here Aristotle is continuing a discussion whose first part has been lost.[18] He (A) distinguishes various ways of using something: (A.1) for the purpose it was created for, or (A.2) for a different purpose. In the latter case, when something is used for a different purpose from the one it was created for, we can again distinguish between (A.2.1) a use of the thing as itself, and (A.2.2.) an accidental use of it.[19] From line 1246a 31 on, the argument is applied (B) to science: it too can be used (B.1) in a correct way (ὀρθῶς) or (B.2) incorrectly, as when one voluntarily errs[20] by, for example, writing erroneously. In this case one uses science as if it were ignorance (1246a 33). This principle is then (C) applied to the general problem of establishing (C.1) whether virtue is a science, or if (C.2) only φρόνησις is both virtue and science, or (C.3) no virtue is a science. The argument therefore proceeds in a similar way to that of *top.* IV 2, but it reaches the opposite conclusions, as we shall see. From line 1246a 35 on it is said that (C.1.1) it would be possible to make use of justice as if it were injustice, if all virtues were knowledge, and it would be possible to do an injustice starting from justice, as one makes an error starting from knowledge, voluntarily. But if this is impossible, it is clear that (C.3) virtues cannot be forms of knowledge[21] (1246a 38—b 1). As can be seen, Aristotle uses the argument of *top.* V 7, albeit in a slightly modified form, and says that it is not possible for ἀρετή to be a science, because if it were, it could also be used to do evil.

Later, from line 1246b 4 on, Aristotle speaks about φρόνησις, denying possibility (C.2), and saying that it is not ἐπιστήμη, but a different type of knowledge, a γένος ἄλλο γνώσ<εως> (1246b 36). The demonstration of this is complicated, and we shall try to indicate the clearest passages.

If we posit[22] (C.2) that φρόνησις is ἐπιστήμη and that it is something true, it (C.2.1) would behave just like other virtues: one could act foolishly on the basis of wisdom. The contradiction inherent in this idea is rendered by Aristotle by the use of terms which, when put together, give rise to an obvious absurdity: ἐνδέχοιτο γὰρ ἂν ἀφρόνως ἀπὸ φρονήσεως (b 6). In this way the Platonic position is quickly and decisively rejected (cf. also 1246b 33–35). And, Aristotle adds, if we deny principle (A)—which we started from—viz. that everything has a proper use and an accidental use, and we admit that for each thing there is one and only one use (ἁπλῆ . . . χρεία, b 7), the absurdities would be just as great. It would follow that a person, though behaving in that way (οὕτω = ἀφρόνως) would act as a wise man (φρονίμως).[23]

Further on Aristotle argues from the standpoint of Plato's followers, and he combats them with their own weapons;[24] again admitting (C.2) that φρόνησις is an ἐπιστήμη, and that (C.2.2) it can thus be used accidentally in a distorted way, one must ask (C.2.3) what could be the cause of this distortion (στροφή, b 9). The result Aristotle arrives at, after some logical acrobatics, is that (C.2.4) every possible statement about the cause of the distortion leads to absurd consequences (b 25–26) and that, therefore, if one denies (C.2.2.) and φρόνησις cannot be used in a distorted way by accident, one also denies (C.2), reaching the conclusion that φρόνησις is not a science, but a virtue (ἀρετὴ γάρ ἐστι καὶ οὐκ ἐπιστήμη, b 35–36).

Let us briefly summarize the points in Aristotle's refutation. First of all, φρόνησις cannot (C.2.4.1) be distorted by a superior science, as happens with other sciences,[25] because it is, from Plato's perspective, the supreme science and there is no science superior to it (b 8–10). But the cause of the distortion cannot be (C.2.4.2) an ethical virtue either, since it is the virtue of the dominant part, i.e. wisdom itself (τοῦ ἄρχοντος ἀρετή = ἀρετὴ τοῦ λογιστικοῦ = φρόνησις)[26] that uses the virtue of the dominated part (probably to be equated both with moderation, the virtue of ἐπιθυμητικόν, and with courage, the virtue of θυμοειδές), and not vice versa.

There is a third possibility (C.2.4.3), i.e. that φρόνησις, considered as an exact science, can be distorted by weakness of the will (ἀκρασία, b13). The refutation of this latter possibility is broken down further into a series of subrefutations of particular aspects of it. By means of this long discussion, Aristotle is able to establish some positive theories on the relation between φρόνησις and the virtues of character, this time in a fully Aristotelian sense. Let us briefly take a look at this discussion: first of all (C.2.4.3.1) Aristotle says that if weakness of the will (ἀκρασία) can distort the virtue of the rational part of the soul (ἄγνοια or ἄνοια, depending on the different readings),[27] or φρόνησις, then also the vice of the rational part of the soul can transform and distort the virtue of the irrational part.[28] We will therefore come to the same absurd conclusion as before, viz. that it is possible (C.1.1) to use justice unjustly[29] and (C.2.1) wisdom unwisely (φρονήσει ἀφρόνως b 18, the same expression as at b 6). The similarity in the conclusions shows the structure of Aristotle's refutation, which tends to reduce all the possible statements in favor of identifying φρόνησις and science to the same contradiction. Moreover, Aristotle says (C.2.3.2) that also the contrary cases hold true (b 18–19); if it is possible for φρόνησις to be distorted by the vice of the irrational part (μοχθηρία), it is absurd that the virtue of the irrational part[30] should not distort folly in the rational part, and act in such a way that folly judges rightly, just as a person should. Therefore right reasoning would be guaranteed by virtue of character. This situation is again discussed, and again denied, in *EE* II 11, for which see Chapter 2, Section 1. And again (πάλιν) (C.2.4.3.3): why, rather than it being weakness of the will that distorts φρόνησις, could it not be the latter that transforms ἀκρασία, making it act correctly (b 23–24)? In this passage the starting hypothesis is completely denied: in the sum of φρόνησις + ἀκρασία, why should the former, which dominates every other faculty (πασῶν κυρία), succumb to the latter?

Aristotle states that all these suppositions are absurd, and especially the statement that folly in the rational part can be transformed into its opposite by the virtue of the irrational part, given that a necessary additional element is missing (b 29). Indeed, it is capacity that harbors within itself incapacity, and not vice versa (b 30–32). In conclusion, in this passage it is maintained that in a φρόνιμος also the ἕξεις, the habitual states of the irrational part of the soul, must be good.[31] Therefore Socrates was right in saying that φρόνησις is the strongest thing (ἰσχυρότερον), but he was mistaken in affirming that it is a science: in actuality, it is a virtue, and is another kind of knowledge (b 32–36).[32]

Hence φρόνησις is not ἐπιστήμη, and is a virtue. This result has definitely been arrived at, and is no longer questioned. It still remains to be seen what kind of virtue it is, and what kind of knowledge, given that it is not a science. To say that φρόνησις is a virtue might also mean to make practical knowledge depend on a habitual, irrational state of the psyche, as in the archaic aristocratic tradition. We shall deal with these questions in the next section; now, by way of appendix, we would like to make some remarks about the *Magna Moralia*. This work presents the same doubts as the *Topics* regarding the epistemological status of φρόνησις, but only implicitly. The uncertainties can be observed by noting the contradictions in the text. In *MM* I 5 it is said that φρόνησις is not a virtue, where virtue is still identified with ethical virtue (courage, justice and so on) and is said to coincide with the field of ἐπαινετόν, that which is praiseworthy. Such an identification was already contained in the *Topics* and was to reappear later in the *Ethics,* though some scholars have denied that the sphere of virtues and that of praiseworthy behavior completely coincide.[33] Let us take a look at the text:

> The soul, as we have said, is divided into two parts, the rational part and the irrational. The part endowed with reason generates φρόνησις, perspicacity, [. . .] and the irrational part generates what are called virtues, such as common sense, justice, courage and all the character traits that seem praiseworthy. We are praised for these virtues, but no one is praised for the properties of the rational soul: indeed, no one is praised because he is wise, nor because he is φρόνιμος, nor, in general, for any of these things. (1185b 3 et seq.)

A little further on, however, it is said that φρόνησις is a virtue and not a science:

> It would seem that φρόνησις is an ἀρετή, and not a science, since the wise (φρόνιμοι) are praised, and virtue is what is praised; moreover, there is an ἀρετή for every science, but not of φρόνησις, since (it seems) it is itself a certain ἀρετή. (1197a 16–20)

In the *Magna Moralia,* as in the *Topics,* it is certain that a virtue cannot be science, but it is not certain what φρόνησις is; it is defined, first, as a science and not a virtue, and then as a virtue and not a science. In this case, too, von Arnim does not report the situation exactly, as he quotes only the passage in 1197a 16–20 to support the supposed agreement between the *Magna Moralia* and the *Eudemian Ethics,* forgetting the passage in 1185b 3 et seq., which states the opposite of what he says.[34] In our opinion, the *Magna Moralia* conserves traces of the difficulties discussed by Aristotle, but in a distorted and unclear way, as is appropriate for a text of dubious authenticity.

4. Φρόνησις as a Dianoetic Virtue

The solution given by Aristotle in *EE* II, and especially in *EN* I, is very well known, and it is sufficient to summarize it briefly here. Aristotle continues to identify virtue with the sphere of ἐπαινετόν (that which is praiseworthy) but, unlike what is said in the *Magna Moralia,* he includes also intellectual virtues among the capacities that are praised:

> There are two kinds of virtue, ethical and dianoetic, since we praise not only just people, but also intelligent and wise men; and it was admitted that the object of praise is a virtue or its actualization; (*EE* II 1, 1220a 5 et seq.)[35]

and further:

> also virtue is divided into two parts in accordance with this distinction, since we say that some [virtues] regard the intellect, and others the character [. . .] and we also praise the wise man for his habitual way of being (ἕξις), since we call virtues those habitual states that are praiseworthy. (*EN* I 13, 1103a 3 et seq.)

Up to this point, ἀρετή had been identified with the group of ethical virtues, the virtues of the irrational part of the soul, such as courage; virtue, therefore, was a γένος, a genus, and opposed to science as a different genus. Now, instead, virtue is understood as a broader genus, which we could also call ἀρετὴ ἁπλῶς, virtue without any specification (even if Aristotle does not do this), composed of two species, ἀρετή of the intellect or dianoetic virtue and ἀρετή of the character or ethical virtue. Virtue and science, therefore, are no longer two opposite and separate genera, but are two species of a wider genus, the excellence of the parts of the soul. For its part, φρόνησις is no longer a science, but another kind of knowledge. In *top.* III 6 Aristotle had distinguished four ways of denying the thesis that only φρόνησις is a science, and now he uses two of those four: (4) he no longer considers φρόνησις to be a science in the strict sense, and (1) he regards even the most rigorous sciences—indeed all the sciences—as being virtue, in a special sense.

Having solved this problem, one must still explain, as we said before, what φρόνησις is—an intellectual virtue like ἐπιστήμη, but not ἐπιστήμη. This is done in *EN* VI 2 (here we consider it to be composed of lines 1138b 35–1139b 13, according to the scansion provided by Bywater), which starts from a distinction between parts of the soul.[36] On the basis of this distinction, Aristotle also distinguishes the dianoetic virtues from one another, so as to make them correspond to the different parts of the rational soul:

> earlier we said that the soul has two parts, one rational and one irrational: now let us divide the rational part in the same way. Let it be posited that there are two parts endowed with reason, one whereby we consider entities whose principles cannot be otherwise, and the other whereby [we consider] entities that can vary. (1139a 3–8)[37]

In the vocabulary of this text commentators have frequently recognized reminiscences of Plato[38] and, indeed, the part of the soul whose proper virtue is φρόνησις is called, as in the *Topics,* λογιστικόν, 1139a 12. But just as φρόνησις undergoes an evolution in passing from the *Topics* to the *EN* and loses the nature of an exact and theoretical science that it had had in the earlier work, so also λογιστικόν is no longer the whole rational soul, but only that part that deals with practical choices and decisions, since:

> taking decisions and λογίζεσθαι are the same thing. (1139a 12–13)

As in the *Topics,* also in *EN* VI 2 the ethical virtues and sciences are ἕξεις in the *Topics,* as we have seen, the ἕξις, or habitual state, was the genus and ethical virtue and science were the species of it, and also in *EN* ἕξις comprises both ethical virtue and dianoetic virtue, both the virtue of character and that of the intellect. In the *Topics* and in the *Magna Moralia* the virtues correspond to ἕξις ἐπαινετή, a habitual state worthy of praise; here, on the other hand, in *EN* VI 2, Aristotle uses the expression ἡ βελτίστη ἕξις, which is basically equivalent to it. But not all the ἕξεις are virtues.

Thus every virtue is a ἕξις, but not every ἕξις is a virtue. In *EN* II 6 Aristotle had indicated what particular ἕξις the set of character virtues was:

> hence virtue is the habit of choosing (ἕξις προαιρετική) consisting in the mean with respect to us, and determined by a principle of reason (λόγῳ) which is similar to what the wise man (φρόνιμος) would establish. (1106b 36–1107a 2)

We shall come back to the problem of interpreting the term λόγῳ in this definition. *EN* VI 2, on the other hand, first of all establishes what ἕξις the set of intellectual virtues is; to do so, one must decide what is the ἔργον, i.e. the function of this part of the soul, since the best ἕξεις are those that make possible the carrying out of a proper function in the best way, because "virtue regards the specific function" (1139a 15–17). Now, the specific function of the entire rational soul is truth, or rather, the possession of truth:

> truth is the specific function (ἔργον) of both the rational parts, and the virtue of each of them is precisely that habitual state by which it attains the truth. (1139b 12–13)[39]

Just as the virtue of character is to find the mean, the virtue of intellect is to possess the truth or to be in it. It is important to underline this thesis of Aristotle's, whereby truth is an essential aspect of practical knowledge, as this fact is not always sufficiently acknowledged.[40]

This still does not tell us what kind of virtue φρόνησις is, since the definition we have obtained is too general, and must be further narrowed down, showing in just what way practical truth differs from theoretical truth. It clearly differs because it is not self-sufficient, but leads to the making of a choice or action. In this text Aristotle seems mainly concerned to point out those aspects of practical truth that are particularly linked to its necessary outcome in action, leaving the discussion of the other aspects of the question for the rest of Book VI. For Aristotle, since the characteristic of practical knowledge is to have action and good as its end, it is not sufficient for one who acts to know the principles, as instead happens in geometry, where whoever knows the principles is immediately a geometer.[41] In practical knowledge one is good only if one knows the principles and acts in accordance with them (cf. *EN* 1180b 7 et seq.): desire must therefore intervene, since for Aristotle desire is the only proximate cause of human action.

For this reason, because of its link with good action, from the *Topics* on we have seen that φρόνησις is not a real ἐπιστήμη, a type of knowledge that can also be used in an accidental or distorted way. Indeed, φρόνησις necessarily contains within itself an element of personal and emotional participation, of good desire; this makes it a different kind of knowledge from pure science. In order to define practical truth, the virtue of λογιστικόν, i.e. of the deliberative part of the soul, Aristotle is obliged to establish what is meant by "truth" or, better, "correctness" in speaking of desire. This may seem a strange question to us now, but Aristotle, also in the case of desire, regards a form of correspondence with its object as being truth. Just as in scientific knowledge truth is affirming or denying in conformity with the state of things, so too in desire truth is a movement tending toward the true good and away from the apparent good. In fact, Aristotle says:

> as in rationality there are affirming and denying, so in desire (ὄρεξις) there are pursuing and avoiding. (1139a 21–22)

It is thus characteristic of φρόνησις that it not only possesses practical truth, but also tends to put it into practice, harmonizing rationality and correct desire.[42] Thus, if one possesses φρόνησις, one's desire naturally tends toward the good and cannot be directed toward anything else, not even by accident, without causing φρόνησις itself to disappear. For this reason, of all the intellectual virtues it is the one closest to the ethical virtues, as we shall see more clearly in Chapter 2. We can now define the virtue of λογιστικόν as follows:

> and this is, therefore, practical rationality and truth: in fact, for theoretical, but not for practical or productive rationality, good and evil correspond to truth and error (since this is the entire function of the irrational part), but for the rational and practical part [good] is the truth that is in harmony with correct desire; (1139a26–31)[43]

and a little farther on:

> it therefore remains that it [φρόνησις] is a truthful habit, accompanied by practical reason, and concerned with the goods and evils peculiar to man. (1140b 4–6)

and also:

> so necessarily φρόνησις must be a truthful habit, accompanied by reason; it must regard human goods, and be practical. (1140b 20–21)

This definition is in sharp contrast with the kind of habitual state called science:

> and thus science is a habit of demonstrating, having all the other features we mentioned in the *Analytics:* since, when one is convinced in a certain way and is familiar with the first principles, then one has science [. . .] and, with regard to science, it should therefore be defined in this way. (1139 b 31–36)

Here we can clearly see that Aristotle emphasizes the fact that in the theoretical sciences it is sufficient to possess the principles and it is not necessary to act practically. In our opinion, therefore, the analysis of practical knowledge that Aristotle makes in *EN* VI 2 is neither strange nor accidental, as has sometimes been maintained. Rather, it answers a whole series of difficulties discussed in other works, both ethical and non-ethical, and keeps unchanged the position we have already seen in *EE* VIII 1. Φρόνησις is the strongest thing, because in it correctness of desire and true reasoning necessarily go hand in hand. But in

EE VIII 1 even more was asserted, viz. that in the φρόνιμος all the ἕξεις of character are good. Now, therefore, we have to deal with the more general relation between φρόνησις and ethical virtue. In this chapter, however, we shall restrict our attention to an examination of the first part of *EN* VI.

5. Φρόνησις and Ethical Virtue

The text we are about to examine does not talk about a problem that has been the subject of much critical discussion in this century, i.e. the problem whether φρόνησις has the end or the means as its object. (We shall return to this question in the next chapter.) Indeed, this same text contains passages that have been cited to support both positions, viz. that φρόνησις has knowledge of the end, and that it does nothing but find the means for the end. Before admitting that Aristotle is an author who can even contradict himself in the space of a few lines on such an important matter, it is advisable to look for some other solution.[44] In our opinion, in *EN* VI 2 Aristotle repeats with considerable emphasis what he had said in *EE* VIII 1, i.e. the idea that, in practical knowledge, the virtues of the intellect and of character necessarily go together.

So far we have proceeded as if ethical virtue and φρόνησις were two very different things, characterized by specific, particular differences that make them two species with nothing in common. The two specific differences are (1) being a habitual state that enables one to grasp the mean, and (2) being a habitual state that enables one to possess practical truth in accordance with correct desire. In reality, as is well known, for Aristotle the two states overlap, and cover the same practical area, that of choosing:

> therefore, since ethical virtue is a habitual state (ἕξις) regarding choice, and choice is a deliberative desire, for these reasons both the reasoning (λόγος) must be true and the desire must be correct, if the choice is to be good; moreover, the former must affirm and the latter must aim at the same things (τὰ αὐτὰ τὸν μὲν φάναι, τὴν δὲ διώκειν). (1139a 22–26)[45]

Here the λόγος ἀληθής, which acts in harmony with desire, is evidently the virtue of λογιστικόν, i.e. φρόνησις. Its object is a practical principle and this principle is also, at the same time, the object of desire, given that it must generate an action. Contemporary critics have sometimes given the impression that the distinction between λόγος and ὄρεξις is identical to that between ethical virtue and φρόνησις,[46] but this does not seem entirely correct. To be precise, both λόγος and ὄρεξις are components both of φρόνησις and of ethical virtue. Ethical virtue is a habitual state of choosing, determined by reasoning (ἕξις προαιρετική . . . ὡρισμένη λόγῳ), and practical intellectual virtue, φρόνησις, is truth in accordance with correct desire (ἀλήθεια ὁμολόγως ἔχουσα τῇ ὀρέξει τῇ ὀρθῇ). From the standpoint of practical choice the two elements can hardly be distinguished, and in *EN* VI 2 Aristotle does not yet clearly state what is the contribution of φρόνησις and what is that of ethical virtue. Those who think they find this distinction in lines 1139a 23–26 are then at a loss to explain lines 1139a 32–33 which, read on the basis of the distinction between ends and means, are difficult to reconcile with the previous passage.

Since it is composed of two elements, true reasoning and correct desire, the good practical choice is only one of many possibilities that can logically be distinguished. The general map of human behavior, based on Aristotle's theory of practical knowledge, can very simply be outlined in the following manner. There may be four cases:

1. true reasoning + correct desire: φρόνησις, good practical knowledge;
2. true reasoning + incorrect desire: ἀκρασία, weakness of will;
3. erroneous reasoning + correct desire: κακία, wickedness;
4. erroneous reasoning + incorrect desire: inability to act.

In this scheme we have assumed that the expression "correct desire" means, as in *EN* I 13, "desire that obeys the orders of the rational and practical part"; hence correct desire may also pursue a false good, if it obeys orders that come from mistaken reasoning. We do not interpret the expression "correct desire" in the more restricted sense of "desire that pursues a true good"; this happens only in case (1), for the man who knows how to live, that is, a wise man endowed with φρόνησις.

In these lines Aristotle seems mainly concerned with making a clear distinction between his concept of practical knowledge and that of Plato, by stressing its relation with non-rational factors:

> therefore, on the one hand choice is the starting point (ἀρχή) of practice, as that from which movement originates, and not as the end, and on the other hand the principles of choice are desire and reasoning that aims at something (λόγος ὁ ἕνεκά τινος); for this reason a choice is not made either without intellect and rationality (νοῦ καὶ διανοίας),or without a habit of character (ἠθικῆς. . . ἕξεως),[47] since acting well (εὐπραξία) and its contrary are not possible in practice without rationality (διάνοια) and without character (ἦθος). (1139a 31–35)

This "reasoning that aims at something (λόγος ὁ ἕνεκά τινος)" has been understood in two ways, mirrored in the current Italian translations: "ragionamento tendente ad uno scopo" (Plebe) ("reasoning tending to a purpose"), "calcolo dei mezzi per raggiungere un fine" (Mazzarelli) ("calculation of the means to reach an end") and "calcolo indirizzato ad un fine" (Zanatta) ("calculation directed at an end"). In our opinion, here Aristotle is speaking of λόγος ὁ ἕνεκά τινος to differentiate this λόγος from that of ἐπιστήμη, the science that possesses theoretical truth detached from desire and action, and not to tell us whether φρόνησις has the end or the means as its object.[48] Here Aristotle wants to typify this λόγος as practical reasoning, and the passage that comes right after it seems to confirm this interpretation:

> Rationality (διάνοια) by itself moves nothing, but (does so) inasmuch as it aims at something and is practical, since it also rules over production: for whoever produces something does so for a certain end and in an absolute way production is not an end, but is relative to something (else); [. . .] indeed, acting well (εὐπραξία) is an end, and desire is desire for this. (1139a 35—b 4)

Previously we put off the discussion of how to translate the term λόγος. Now it is time to say a few words about it.

6. Λόγος: Reason, Rule or Reasoning?

Early twentieth-century critics devoted much discussion to the question whether the term λόγος, which occurs in Aristotle's theory of ethical virtue, should be understood as being equivalent to "reason" (Cook Wilson) or to "rule" (Stocks, Burnet and, more recently, Gauthier).[49] Cook Wilson's interpretation is rejected mainly on grammatical grounds, since it would make λόγος be that which determines the mean; the dative form, λόγῳ, seems to indicate the "reasoning" or "rule" by which the mean between emotions and the actions deriving from them is established. However, the translation of λόγος as "rule" poses some problems, because this term may be interpreted as a command, i.e. a universal and necessary imperative, which determines good conduct in relation to a rational plan of life. Here, instead, Aristotle seems to be speaking of a more general practical "reasoning," as we shall see.

In the definitions of individual ethical virtues, this λόγος that determines the mean is apparently personified in expressions such as ὡς ὁ λόγος, or ὡς ὁ ὀρθὸς λόγος κελεύει,[50] in which λόγος is "reasoning," the act of φρόνησις, and not "rule"; this λόγος is determined by reference to a model of correct practical reasoning, rather than by reference to a universal rule. Let us take a look at the case of courage, in which λόγος determines the end and the mean in the following way:

> that which inspires fear is not the same for everybody, but we say that there is also something that is superior to human forces. This frightens everybody, at

> least those who have the use of reason (τῷ. . . νοῦν ἔχοντι);[51] instead, the things within man's scope differ in size and degree. This is true also of those things that inspire courage. A courageous man is as unafraid as a man should be, and therefore he will also be afraid of those things, but only as is right, and as λόγος dictates, having noble action (τοῦ καλοῦ ἕνεκα) as his aim, since this is the aim of virtue. (1115b 7–13)

In the case of temperance, the temperate man behaves as right reason commands (ὡς ὁ ὀρθὸς λόγος [κελεύει]) (1119a 20). The same is true of goodness, and the good-natured man

> wants to be unmoved, and not to be driven by passion, but to become irritated as reason (λόγος) would prescribe. (1125b 33–35)

EN VI 2 speaks of a λόγος that has the characteristic of being ἀληθής, and this λόγος is certainly a form of expression of rationality, i.e. an argument; in the case of praxis this λόγος is the act of φρόνησις, but it is not a rule.[52] The activity of this λόγος is, in general, expressed as a φάναι, a "declaring," which explicitly consists in "affirming and denying" (κατάφασις καὶ ἀπόφασις) and is directed toward something (ὁ ἕνεκά τινος). This λόγος is explicitly identified with διάνοια (1139a 33) or, rather, with one form of it. It seems to us that Aristotle did not mean to distinguish rigidly, within a concrete practical choice, between the type of practical rationality inherent in a wise and prudent man, and the objective rule of the mean, since for him the two things coincide (cf. also III 4, 1113a 15 et seq.).

In *EN* VI 1 Aristotle says he intends to deal with the λόγος that prescribes the mean; he states that this λόγος establishes the mean by aiming at a purpose (1139b 22–23), and that therefore the criterion, the measure of the mean between excess and defect, depends on the purpose. But since, in practical matters, this general and vague way of speaking, even if true, is not very useful (1138b 25- 32), then

> for this reason, with regard to the habitual states of the soul, not only must things be in truth precisely as we have said, but it is necessary to specify what right reasoning is as well as what its criterion (ὅρος) is. (1138b 32–34)

The program outlined here is carried out in the rest of *EN* VI. However, this book is not usually considered to be a well-organized text, from the standpoint of its stylistic composition and conceptual unity. Many scholars have maintained that it is a collection of passages without a well-defined structure and with a casual, disjointed development.[53] Any judgment about the book's structure depends on the judgment made about what its subject is; indeed, the compactness and coherence of a work is evaluated mainly in relation to its content. But critics are very uncertain as to what exactly the subject of *EN* VI is.

Two opposing views are in conflict, together with a whole series of intermediate shades of opinion and attempts at reconciliation.

One of the clearest positions is that of E. Zeller,[54] who, on the basis of the opening sentence of *EN* VI 1, maintains that Book VI is about practical knowledge, φρόνησις. Indeed Aristotle says that:

> Earlier we chanced to say that one must choose the mean, and neither excess nor defect, and since the mean is as correct λόγος dictates, we must now deal with this. (1138b 18–20)

The correct reasoning that determines a choice is obviously equivalent to φρόνησις.[55] Stewart,[56] instead, has maintained that the subject of Book VI is the set of dianoetic virtues, and not only φρόνησις, since they are an indispensable element in happiness, and one of them, σοφία, like θεωρία, is said in *EE* to be the ὅρος, the criterion used to find the mean. Stewart's position now seems very debatable (on the determination of happiness, see Chapter 4 below), but it appears to be supported at least by the beginning of *EN* VI 2:

> In dealing of the soul's virtues, we said that some of them are virtues of character and others are virtues of intellect. We have already dealt with the virtues of character; we shall thus speak of the others, starting first of all with the soul. (1138b 35–1139a 3)

Later interpreters occupy intermediate positions between these two extremes, although for the time being Zeller's position has become the prevalent one.[57] We would also tend to say that Zeller is right, but with this proviso: in *EN* VI Aristotle is dealing with all the dianoetic virtues, in a rather broad way; but he considers those aspects of them in particular that make them different from φρόνησις. The whole discussion appears aimed at giving a more precise definition of the nature of practical knowledge.

Although, in Stewart's view, *EN* VI 2 should deal with the dianoetic virtues in general, in reality it speaks almost exclusively about practical knowledge, and lines 1139a 27–29, which refer directly to theoretical knowledge, are obviously acting as a term of comparison, to clarify the peculiarity of the kind of λόγος Aristotle is dealing with here. Throughout *EN* VI φρόνησις is absolutely dominant, thus becoming the subject of the treatise; and this is true both of Chapter 2 and of the whole of Book VI. In this sense we can say that *EN* VI has a certain unity, given by its constant reference to the main problem: to determine the nature of practical knowledge, the virtue of λογιστικόν, and not ἐπιστήμη, as Plato had held.

The λόγος discussed here is the rationality implicit in practical reasoning, and coincides with the activity of φρόνησις. *EN* VI 2 mainly tries to answer the question, "What is λόγος?" and arrives at the results illustrated above. These results also provide some clarification regarding the problem of what the "criterion" (ὅρος) is, as we shall see later, in the discussion of Chapters *EN* VI 12–13 (see Chapter 2).

Aristotle has thus explained what is the virtue of λογιστικόν, which for him is the ability to make choices; this virtue, like every function (ἔργον) of the rational soul, consists in the possession of truth; but it is distinguished from the other dianoetic virtues by the fact that it is linked to correct desire and tends toward an end. The element Aristotle insists on is the mixture of reason and desire in the choice, which is several times called "deliberative desire" (ὄρεξις βουλευτική, 1139a 23), "desiring intellect" (ὀρεκτικὸς νοῦς, 1139b 4), and "rational desire" (ὄρεξις διανοητική, 1139b 5). He says:

> for this reason a choice is not made either without intellect and rationality, or without a habit of character, seeing that acting well and its opposite are not possible in the field of practical matter without rationality and without character. (1139a 33–35)

We have seen this before. There is a certain terminological nonchalance in this chapter: Aristotle interchanges terms that elsewhere he distinguishes with precision, such as νοῦς and διάνοια, φάναι and κατάφασις; he says that the union of intellect and desire is a choice, but also (more precisely) that the union of intellect and desire is the principle (ἀρχή) of a choice.

In this way Aristotle distinguishes between a form of practical, truthful rationality, which is naturally in harmony with desire, and a form of scientific, purely contemplative rationality. He assigns to the former the function of being the λόγος that guides one's choice of the mean.[58] To reach this conclusion it has been necessary to follow a rather tortuous path through Aristotle's discussions of φρόνησις. In the *Topics* and the *Protrepticus,* φρόνησις was both a virtue and a science, even though virtue and science were different genera. In both the *Eudemian* and *Nicomachean Ethics* it becomes clear that φρόνησις is not an ἐπιστήμη, and the whole distinction between science and the various forms of virtue is reformulated. In this way Aristotle intends to specify what form of knowledge is possessed by the man who acts, distinguishing it from the knowledge of the man who contemplates truth and who, if questioned, is able to tell the "why" of things. The other characteristics of φρόνησις are derived from this basic difference; they are described in Chapters VI 4–5 and 7–8. We shall give a brief summary of them in the next section, since this is one of Aristotle's best-known doctrines.

7. Wisdom According to Aristotle

In Chapters VI 3–4 Aristotle describes the features of two kinds of knowledge that are different from φρόνησις: science and technique (skill, or art). Then, in

Chapter 5, he describes wisdom by differentiating it from these two. "It is not possible for wisdom (φρόνησις) to be a science (ἐπιστήμη) or a technique (τέχνη); (it cannot be a) science because the object of conduct may also be otherwise (and it cannot be a) technique because the *genus* of conduct and that of production are different" (1140b 1–4).

Φρόνησις differs from production in that it tends toward an end in an absolute sense (ἁπλῶς, cf. 1097a 30 et seq.). This end is εὐπραξία, whereas the object of production is useful to someone or something (1139 b 1–4).

Aristotle describes the nature of φρόνησις by starting from current opinions or φαινόμενα.[59] One can decide what φρόνησις is by observing (θεωρήσαντες) one who is said to be φρόνιμος,[60] i.e.: (1) one who is able to make good decisions regarding his own good and benefit; (2) one who is able to decide not about particular ends (e.g., achieving a state of health), but about living well in general,[61] viz. about how to reach happiness (here we already find the identification εὐπραξία = εὖ ζῆν [= εὐδαιμονία] that we shall see in more detail in Chapter 4) (1140a 24–33). Some features of φρόνησις can be deduced from this: (3) its object is neither immutable things, as in the case of science,[62] nor the mutable things that do not depend on us; (4) it does not proceed by means of demonstrations, since, in its field of action, everything may also be otherwise; (5) it is therefore neither science nor technique (art). It is not a science for the reasons given in (3), and it is not technique, because φρόνησις and technique belong to different genera (on this point, see below, p.23 f.); (6) moreover, its end is not different from its activity, since it is εὐπραξία (1140a 33–b 7). This point should be understood correctly: for Aristotle it is not possible to carry out directly an act of pure and simple εὐπραξία, as εὐπραξία is always embodied in a particular act, in the exercise of this or that virtue πρὸς τὸ καλόν (acting nobly *per se,* and not in order to obtain some advantage), such as defending the city by performing this or that act of valour, or helping friends by performing this or that act of generosity, etc. It is not necessary to interpret the idea that the end of φρόνησις is εὐπραξία in the sense that "acting well" is a universal rule of life different from the whole set of individual good choices. As we shall see in Chapter 4, εὐπραξία, which is equivalent to εὐδαιμονία, is necessarily manifested in a set of individual good actions.

In support of this, Aristotle mentions the fact that statesmen such as Pericles[63] are considered φρόνιμοι, and that this type of knowledge is generally attributed to heads of families and heads of cities. Here Aristotle says that the end of φρόνησις is "what is good for ourselves and for men" (b 9); this distinction will reappear in Chapter VI 8, where the knowledge of the statesman is included in the general ambit of φρόνησις. We shall examine this passage below;

here, however, we may note that the expression in b 9, τὰ τοῖς ἀνθρώποις [ἀγαθά] indicates the knowledge of statesmen, and corresponds to what is meant by the expression "of that [φρόνησις] which regards the city" (τῆς. . . περὶ πόλιν, 1141b 24–25) in VI 8. By this expression Aristotle seems not to mean "human good" in an absolute sense, or in the abstract, but the "good of other men," of one's kinsfolk or fellow citizens, who are the concern of the οἰκονομικός and πολιτικός. This varies from one city to another, from one family to another, and in different historical circumstances. Only in the best city, or perfect community, will this good coincide with the "good of humanity" without any further specification, as we shall see in Chapter 4.

Lines 1140b 11–21 are dedicated to a new analysis of the relation between φρόνησις and the emotional part of the human soul. Unlike the other dianoetic virtues, φρόνησις is distorted by pleasure and pain, whereas such emotions have nothing to do with the axioms of geometry (b 11–16). The distortion brought about by the passions, already mentioned by Aristotle in EE VIII 1 (see p. 8 ff.), mainly affects the perception of ends: "Someone who is overwhelmed by pleasure or pain does not clearly perceive the principle, i.e. that one must, for it and because of it, choose and accomplish every thing" (b 17–19). Thus the problem of the relation between ends and means in φρόνησις begins to be posed. This very complicated and much discussed problem is the subject of the next chapter. For the time being, we may just point out that, as by definition φρόνησις is "a habit accompanied by reason, which is truthful, regards human good, and is practical" (1140b 20–21); it must pursue good ends. Therefore if, overcome by emotion, people do not follow good ends, of necessity they are not using φρόνησις in their choices, although this does not necessarily imply that practical principles as such are the object only of φρόνησις.

For the moment, let us leave aside lines b 21–25 which make a comparison with technique (art), as we shall return to this subject later on. Let us now look at the final part of Chapter VI 5. Aristotle says that φρόνησις is an "excellence" or virtue (ἀρετή) and that, since the parts of the soul endowed with reason are the seat of knowledge (ἐπιστημονικόν) and the seat of opinion (δοξαστικόν), "it will be the virtue of the other part, of the seat of opinion (τοῦ δοξαστικοῦ); indeed, opinion and φρόνησις regard what can be otherwise" (b 26–28). In the whole first part of *EN* VI Aristotle emphasizes, repeatedly and in a clearly anti-Platonic way, the distance and opposition between φρόνησις and science. Later, when talking about the practical syllogism, we shall see that this opposition does not prevent these two dianoetic virtues from having some features of rationality in common, and that between them there is not, for Aristotle, the distance that we suppose there to be, for example, between mathematics and aesthetic judgment. Here, instead, the distinction between science and φρόνησις is sharp, and clearly stated many times. The distinction between φρόνησις and technique (art) is much less clear.

In Chapter VI 7 Aristotle makes it quite clear that the archaic opinion, whereby the possession of σοφία, the highest form of theoretical activity, consisting in true knowledge of the first principles of reality and of what follows from them (1141a 17–18), necessarily implies also possession of φρόνησις and practical knowledge, is not acceptable. Indeed, it is well-known that many of the wise men of old were totally incapable of achieving their own good.

Lines 1141b 8–22 point out the differences between φρόνησις and wisdom (σοφία):[64] (1) φρόνησις deals with human affairs and the object of deliberation (and not of more divine things, as does σοφία, 1141a 34–b 2); (2) it deals with things that can be otherwise (and hence it varies, whereas there is only one σοφία, which is ἀκριβεστάτη, which means that it has an immutable object, 1141a 16–17 and 28–33); (3) it deals with things that have a τέλος, as the practical good of humanity has. This is the only passage in *EN* VI in which the overly general definition of the object of φρόνησις as "that which can also be otherwise" is specified to some extent, though not with the precision that we find in *EN* III 3: of all the things that can also be otherwise, φρόνησις regards those things that have an end, i.e. practical decisions;[65] (4) lastly, for φρόνησις it is more important to know the minor premise, regarding the particular situation, and to reach an individual decision here and now, rather than to know only the principles in a universal and abstract way. From this point of view, φρόνησις is the opposite of ἐπιστήμη and σοφία. We shall return to this point later on, in Chapter 3.

The opening lines of Chapter VI 8 (1141b 23–1142a 10) deal with an important problem, i.e. the relation between the knowledge of the statesman and the practical knowledge of a private individual. As, indeed, Aristotle remarks, wisdom (φρόνησις) almost by definition would seem to be the property of the private individual: "it appears that φρόνησις is mainly that which regards oneself and the individual" (1141b 29–30). On the other hand, the practical knowledge that regards the πόλις seems to be the most important kind (cf. also 1094b 7–10 and 1097b 6–11, for which see Chapter 4). And it is strange, for the Greek way of thinking, that the most important form does not give its name to all similar forms of knowledge. Aristotle thus finds that he has to discuss this ἔνδοξον, or current opinion, and to this end he draws up a complete map of the subspecies of φρόνησις:

> Politics [A] and φρόνησις [B] are the same habitual state (ἕξις), but they differ with regard to their being (τὸ . . . εἶναι).[66] As for that [A] which regards the city, the one [A.1] which is architectonic is legislative wisdom (φρόνησις), while the other, [A.2], which deals with individual cases,[67] has

> the name common to both, politics. This latter is both practical and deliberative; in fact, a decree (ψήφισμα) is practical in that [it is] an ultimatum.[68] For this reason it is said that only these latter govern the city, as they are the only ones who act, like manual labourers.[69] And it is also thought that [B] φρόνησις is mainly that which regards oneself and the individual; and this has the common name, 'wisdom' (φρόνησις); as for the others, one is [A.3] 'economics', another [A.1] 'legislation', another [A.2] 'politics', and, with regard to the last of these, one [A. 2. 1] is 'deliberative' and the other [A.2.2] is 'judicial'. (1141b 23–34)

As a systematic treatment of the types of φρόνησις this is rather complex, and badly organized:[70] "politics" in lines 1141b 24–26 is divided into "legislative" and "politics (making decrees)," while in lines b 32–33 "politics (making decrees)" is further subdivided into "deliberative" and "judicial"; these two types, and especially the latter, had never been mentioned before. Also "economics," which appears at the end of the passage, was absent at the beginning. In our opinion, here Aristotle wants to present a series of distinctions, typical of popular opinions,[71] reflecting the institutional and political structure of the Athenian society of his time; hence be briefly describes their different features and the aspects that may cause confusion. The best thing, as Aristotle says in the *Metaphysics,*[72] would be for every entity to have its own name, to distinguish it from others. Here, instead, there are nouns like φρόνησις and "politics" that designate both the genus and a particular species of it.

Moreover, Aristotle adds that it is thought (δοκεῖ) that only one who thinks of his own self-interest is wise, whereas politicians are "busybodies" (πολυπράγμονες, 1142a 2), and he quotes Euripides (fragments 787, 788 N.) to support the actual existence of this common opinion. Against this idea, Aristotle reaffirms some basic principles of his vision of practical knowledge (we shall talk about this in more detail in Chapter 4): Man is a political animal, and his self-sufficiency includes participation in social and political relations; for this reason politics is the highest and most noble form of wisdom:

> yet certainly it is not possible for people to pursue their own good without economics and without a political constitution. Moreover, how a person's affairs ought to be managed is still not clear, and ought to be investigated.[73] (1142a 9–11)

Therefore wisdom is not distinct from politics, as Euripides and various others had believed. It is, instead, different from τέχνη in many ways.

Technique (skill) differs from practical knowledge in the kind of end it aims at, viz. the production of objects and not the achievement of good behavior; however, it does not differ in the logical structure of its arguments, which is similar in the two cases, and can be described by using the same type of practical syllogism, as we shall see in Chapter 3. Both kinds of knowledge tend to generate an action (in the broad sense of the word, i.e. any movement of the human body aiming at an end), and they are both opposed to science, which is purely contemplative and does not generate meaningful movements leading to an end. Today, we are inclined to place praxis and production in two separate camps. This opposition between technique (art) and praxis has today become one of the strong points in the modern "rebirth" of Aristotle's practical philosophy.[74] However, it should be pointed out that the opposition in question occurs mainly between the modern conception of praxis and the modern conception of technique (art), while between the ancient conception of praxis and that of production the differences are not so sharp; indeed, Aristotle posits a relation of subordination and collaboration between them.

For Aristotle, productive knowledge and practical knowledge are two habitual states of the same part of the rational soul, which in *EN* VI is said to be "calculating" or "expressing opinions." It deals with things that do not always happen in the same way, but may vary, as we have said before (cf. 1139a 3–15; 1140a 1–5; b 25–30). Both are truthful ἕξεις, since one cannot have a τέχνη and at the same time express an incorrect judgment about how to make a product, just as it is not possible to have φρόνησις and be mistaken about how to achieve praiseworthy behavior (1139b 15, 1140a 10). Unlike theoretical rationality, practical and technical reason require that true judgment and correct desire should be made to agree; thus a desire must be transmitted from the ends to the means (1139a 27–31). But the two types of practical knowledge differ in *genus* (1140b 3–4), and neither of the two includes the other (1140a 5). In particular, φρόνησις is βελτίστη ἕξις, the best habitual state, while τέχνη is inferior to it. Indeed, φρόνησις is a type of knowledge that cannot be used to do evil, while a τέχνη can also be purposely distorted and used for a bad end (1140b 21–23). But since τέχνη is *per se* a truthful ἕξις, this statement may simply mean that, as in medicine, whoever knows how to cure also knows, by accident, how to do harm, as is said in *metaph.* VII 3. Therefore only φρόνησις, which can never be distorted, not even by accident, is the ἀρετή of the calculating part. Moreover, there are no degrees of φρόνησις,[75] precisely because it is an excellence, whereas there seem to be degrees of τέχνη, and one speaks of an excellence (ἀρετή) of τέχνη itself (1140b 21–22).

Thus the main difference between the two forms of practical knowledge lies in their different aims, and in the fact that τέχνη produces results that are not completely self-sufficient, but are tools for something else, i.e. for producing a good that may also be the object of praxis and wisdom. The end of τέχνη is, at times, a means for reaching the end of φρόνησις. Rather than the modern opposition between technique (art) and ethical/practical knowledge, here we seem to have the traditional Greek scorn of productive knowledge if compared with political praxis and, in general, "fine actions."[76] We shall return to this point later, to make a general evaluation of the two most important distinctions for Aristotle's theory of practical knowledge—viz., that between φρόνησις and τέχνη, and that between φρόνησις and ἐπιστήμη or σοφία. First, however, we must examine Aristotle's theory of the practical syllogism. Then we shall be able to discuss the matter not in general terms, or with rhetorical flourishes, as sometimes happens, but with greater precision, on the basis of a more detailed analysis of Aristotle's theory.

Let us summarize, then, Aristotle's description of φρόνησις as a kind of knowledge in general terms.

Aristotle picks up the traditional idea of a specific type of knowledge concerned with praxis, and in the opposition between Isocrates and Plato he tends to side with Isocrates on certain points: practical knowledge is not an exact science; it is valid "for the most part" and in most cases, and it is linked to the sphere of opinion. It bears a certain resemblance to physics, which is also valid in the main, but it has a different end, i.e. action, not knowledge. Hence in it, particular propositions, which tell us what to do in given situations, are more important than universal propositions, whereas the contrary is true in physics. But, in contrast with what was maintained in the archaic ethics, for Aristotle there is a certain consistency in human events, which are not completely unpredictable; it is possible to make inferences and generalizations about events and our practical behavior shows that we move in a world that is, in most cases, rather predictable.

Knowing what to do in any given situation means grasping the mean in the midst of many actions and many possible emotional states of equilibrium. The expression "right mean," which is one way of describing the end of practical knowledge, does not always indicate the same situation; hence the right mean cannot be found in a scientific way, but varies as the situation changes. Moreover, it is not absolutely indispensable to find exactly the best possible action; in every situation there is a certain range of feasible praiseworthy actions, and whoever chooses any of these is acting well, albeit not in the best way possible. There is, however, a certain limit to this oscillation around a given mean, viz. a point beyond which an action becomes bad; yet even this limit cannot be determined in a scientific way.

So far in Chapter 1 we have once again seen that one of the constant elements in Aristotle's theory is the opposition between practical knowledge and science. Practical knowledge, which from now on is almost always called φρόνησις, or wisdom, has features that make it the opposite of science; in many ways it is more similar to the virtues of character.

Φρόνησις is not a science, but a different type of knowledge. It is an intellectual virtue, belonging to that part of the intellect that deals with things that may also be otherwise, that depend on us, and in which there is an end to be reached. It thus belongs to the part of the soul which expresses opinions and calculates what to do. As an intellectual virtue, its distinctive function is to find the truth, and in this it does not differ from science. But inasmuch as its end is action and the good, it is very different from science. Indeed, in practice, a science (like medicine) or a technique (art) can also be used, accidentally, to do harm, but this is not true of φρόνησις. It is contradictory to think that wisdom can be used to act wickedly: the concept of wisdom contains, analytically, the concept of a good end.

From this standpoint wisdom is closer to virtue than to science, as not even the virtues of character can be used to cause wicked behavior. Furthermore, like virtue, φρόνησις is a habitual state, and hence cannot be forgotten. Like Pindar and Theognis, Aristotle thinks of practical knowledge as being something inherent in the nature of one who acts well, and not as a series of general prescriptions to be learned and memorized. Moreover, like virtue, and unlike science, wisdom can be overwhelmed by the emotions, by pleasure and pain, which make us lose sight of the good action to be performed. Finally, like virtue, and unlike science and technique (art), wisdom admits of no degrees, but is itself a state of excellence of the human intellect.

All these features, which make wisdom different from science, are due to the fact that wisdom, since it produces actions, is not only a habitual state of the intellect (or, better, of a part of the intellect), but is also linked to a habitual state of desire, i.e. to a balance between the two main drives of "pursuing" and "avoiding" which, in Aristotle's anthropology, are the only impulses that can move the human limbs. As it is not linked to any state of the emotions or of desire, science *per se* does not produce any actions, although anyone who acts may use scientific knowledge to achieve his ends. But in such a case, this knowledge is not used as part of the intellectual virtue called "science," whose pre-eminent function is to tell the truth about things; rather, it is used only as a tool. Since, however, wisdom tends, by its very nature, toward a good end, the desire that is part of it is good and correct, both because its object is the good, and because it obeys the instructions of the rational part of the soul. In wisdom, desire and reason agree to pursue the same end. This means that wisdom not only resembles the virtues of character, but is strictly linked to them, as we shall see more clearly in the next chapter.

From the standpoint of its object, wisdom deals specifically with particular situations, since the actions it gives rise to are always single events in definite situations. Therefore, for wisdom the most important thing is the "minor premise" of the practical syllogism, i.e. the one that deals with particular cases, as we shall see more clearly in Chapter 3. From the perspective of the end it tends toward, φρόνησις has, as its end, particular goods, which are the object of single types of human knowledge, such as victory in battle (object of the art of the strategist). The good of humanity in general is called by Aristotle "acting well" or "acting nobly," and coincides with happiness. But, since it is not possible to act well or nobly in the abstract, a fine and noble action is always a concrete action; it is the putting into practice, in a given situation, of one or more human virtues. Therefore, happiness, which is the end of wisdom, consists of a series of actions in which the best capacities and virtues of the individual are exhibited, as we shall see in Chapter 4.

From a more detailed standpoint, Aristotle makes it clear that φρόνησις takes many forms, such as politics or the administration of the home, and each of these forms is subdivided into other subspecies. Therefore, wisdom should not be identified with the shortsighted cultivation of one's own private interest, as some people might think. Here we can see Aristotle's idea that man is a "political" animal, whose nature leads him to live in a social community. We shall see below that even the notion of happiness involves a certain type of relation with the citizens of one's *polis*.

8. General Characteristics of Practical Knowledge According to Aristotle

In Aristotle the problem of the validity of practical knowledge, and the inevitable distance between knowledge, which necessarily consists of general propositions, and actions, which are individual acts that occur in constantly changing circumstances, takes on a more complex and theoretically more mature complexion. Aristotle discusses and clarifies, with profound methodological awareness, both the traditional teachings and the interpretation or transformation which Plato and his students had given to the idea of a type of knowledge especially oriented to practical matters.[77] This entire book is dedicated to illustrating Aristotle's ideas on this point, and the innovations he introduces regarding the ἔνδοξα that, for him, are important. These, as is well known, are not only the opinions of the philosophers, sages and experts, but also the opinions of hoi polloi (*top.* I 1, 100b 21–23).

In these few pages we shall outline some of the main features of Aristotle's ideas regarding practical knowledge, viz. those most similar to traditional ideas. We shall see that Aristotle in part holds fast to traditional opinions, and in part defends the changes and clarifications introduced by the Academy; by means of this synthesis, Aristotle then arrives at a profoundly innovative position, which cannot be confused with that of others. Thanks to this position, Aristotle abandons the legacy of "Platonism" (in the sense of a school that is faithful to the basic teachings of its founder) and initiates a new and different philosophical tradition. None of this is new or original, of course, and would not need to be mentioned here, were it not that recently this interpretation has been questioned by scholars of authority, who have adduced fairly weighty arguments.

In general, we may say that, in Aristotle, it is possible to distinguish practical knowledge (φρόνησις), which is dealt with in treatises such as the *Nicomachean Ethics* and the *Eudemian Ethics,* from the discourses (λόγοι or, as he says in *EN* 1094b 11, the μέθοδος) contained in these treatises. These discourses are not the result of practical knowledge, even if they have a certain practical aim. The practical purpose of Aristotle's *Ethics* is very clearly indicated in the *Eudemian Ethics:*

> Hence it is good to know (γνωρίζειν) each of the noble and fine things (καλῶν); yet, to tell the truth, as regards virtue, the most important thing is not to know it (εἰδέναι) but to know what it derives from. In actuality, we do not wish to know what courage is, but we wish to be courageous; nor do we wish to know what justice is, but we want to be just; likewise we wish to be healthy, rather than to know what it means 'to be healthy' and we wish to be in good physical shape rather than to know what it means 'to be in shape'. (1216b 19–25, cf. *EN* 1103b 26–31)

The discussion of virtue in the *Ethics* has a hortatory purpose; it is an invitation and exhortation (cf. *EN* 1179b 7), not unlike that of the *Protrepticus,* where the exposition of what philosophy is coincides with the exhortation to devote one's life to philosophy (fr. 2 Ross).[78] But it does not directly constitute a practical train of thought, like that set in motion by one who is deciding how to act.

The difference between the practical knowledge of a single individual and the treatment by the philosopher of other people's practical knowledge becomes clearer, when we consider the problem of the inevitable distance between general practical arguments and single, concrete actions. In the case of philosophical discussion, Aristotle, following Plato's lead (*leg.* XI 916E, 934B), feels it necessary above all to articulate his doctrine in detail, so as to bring it as close as possible to particular cases:

> one must not just state this [= that virtue is the mean] in general, but one must adapt it to particular cases. Indeed, in any talk about actions, universal principles are the emptiest,[79] whereas those that regard particular cases are the truest, since actions concern particular cases, and it is necessary to adapt our principles to them. (1107a 29–32)

This is repeated at the beginning of Book VI, which is specifically devoted to the description of the nature of practical knowledge:

> Earlier on we said that one must choose the mean, and neither too much nor too little [. . .] this is certainly true, but it is not at all clear [. . .] one who had in mind only this principle would not know anything more at all, just as if we were to say, [to one who asks] what care must be taken of the body, that [one must do] everything that medicine commands, in the proper ways. (1138b 18–32)

In this case, the relevant opposition is between "truth" and "clarity and obscurity." The explanations of the nature of practical knowledge given by the philosopher must be as detailed as possible, to be applicable to individual cases, just as the measures adopted by legislators must be. In both cases, the detailed measures, although they never reach down to actual cases, and never describe them perfectly, make it easier to choose correctly when decisions have to be taken.

In the case of the concrete practical knowledge of individuals who act, Aristotle states that the practical propositions and judgments that make up this knowledge, and which tend toward the direct accomplishment of an action by a person, are valid "on the whole" (ὡς ἐπὶ τὸ πολύ) and not by necessity. This holds true both for the knowledge of ends and for the knowledge of means:

> Noble and just things, which are dealt with by politics, involve many differences of opinion and many changing ideas, so that they seem to exist by convention and not by nature. Also the good things[80] exhibit similar fluctuations, since many people have encountered bad consequences coming from good things; indeed, it has happened that some people have been ruined by wealth, and some others have lost their lives by courage. We must be content if, in speaking of these subjects and starting from these premises, we indicate the truth in broad strokes, as in an outline (παχυλῶς καὶ τύπῳ); in speaking of objects that are "on the whole" (ὡς ἐπὶ τὸ πολύ) true and starting from such general premises, we also reach generally true conclusions; (1094b 14–22)

and later on:

> but we deliberate about the things that depend on us, and that do not happen always in the same way, as for example in those cases dealt with by medicine, or those considered by the art of making money [. . .] We deliberate in those cases that happen "by and large" (ὡς ἐπὶ τὸ πολύ), where it is not clear what the outcome will be, or where the outcome is indeterminate. (1112b 2–9)

Likewise in *EN* V 10 it is said that the laws of the city give prescriptions that are valid only ὡς ἐπὶ τὸ πολύ, with a clear reference to Plato's thesis. In reality, all laws are καθόλου (universal), yet they regard things of which it is improper to speak universally (1137b 13–14), since praxis can only regard single actions (1141b 16); hence they cover only most cases, ὡς ἐπὶ τὸ πολύ (1137b 15–16).

Contemporary criticism has found much to debate in this doctrine. The most relevant points are the attribution of a "general" (ὡς ἐπὶ τὸ πολύ) validity to the practical knowledge of an individual who acts, and the consequences that derive from this for the status of Aristotle's practical philosophy, as a philosophical discussion that has for its object the kind of knowledge possessed by an individual who acts.

Let us begin with the more general problem of the status of Aristotle's practical philosophy. The idea that practical knowledge is valid ὡς ἐπὶ τὸ πολύ has given rise to much discussion, especially among those critics who have believed it possible to extend the state of validity ὡς ἐπὶ τὸ πολύ of practical knowledge also to the treatise called *Nicomachean Ethics,* which deals with the method and principles of such practical knowledge. It is not entirely obvious, however, that in Aristotle things must always work this way: if it is not possible, at first sight, to distinguish between the physics or philosophy before Aristotle and the treatises entitled, respectively, *Physics* and *Metaphysics,* in other cases the situation is different. The *Analytica Priora* treat of scientific syllogisms in a true and complete way, but they are not written in syllogisms; and the *Rhetoric* describes how the various types of orations should be composed, but it is not an oration. With regard to rhetoric, the distinction between the two levels of discourse is very clearly drawn at the beginning of the treatise (1354a 1–11).

In the same way, it is not clear that the philosophical doctrines Aristotle expounds in his *Ethics* have, according to Aristotle himself, the limited conditions of validity that he establishes for the type of knowledge dealt with in the treatise. Indeed, in some cases the situation seems clearly to be just the opposite, while in others it is more doubtful. When Aristotle defines virtue as: "a habitual state regarding choice, consisting in the mean relative to us, determined by reasoning, such as a wise man would choose" (1106b 37–1107a 2) or practical knowledge (φρόνησις) as "a true habitual state, accompanied by reason, which is practical, and regards the goods and evils proper to man" (1140b 4–6), these definitions do not seem to be "more or less" true, but to have absolute validity. A habitual state of the human soul is ethical virtue or wisdom if and only if it has the essential characteristics given in these definitions. In other cases, however, when Aristotle's theses are, as we would say nowadays, more content oriented or "substantive," things seem rather dubious: it is, indeed, not clear that the philosophical life is absolutely and necessarily the happiest life, as Aristotle claims (to tell the truth, this claim does not even appear to be valid ὡς ἐπὶ τὸ πολύ). Even here, however, Aristotle could maintain that, even if it is not true that the contemplative life is in reality the aim of every individual life, nor can it or should it be the aim that every individual should set himself, yet it is true, in an absolute sense, that it is the best and freest form of life, and the one that corresponds most closely to the formal definition of happiness as "a complete life according to complete virtue." We shall deal at length with this subject in Chapter 4.

In the discussion of the methodological status of Aristotle's practical philosophy, then, which in recent decades has been carried on mainly by authors writing in German,[81] the differences of opinion regarding the logic of practical knowledge should be reconsidered in the light of the distinction between the treatise—the *Nicomachean* (or *Eudemian*) *Ethics*—and the subject of the treatise, φρόνησις. Indeed, the problem of the relation between dialectic and Aristotle's practical philosophy is posed differently, depending on whether we are dealing with the relation between opinions and φρόνησις or the relation between Aristotle's dialectic and the treatise known as *Nicomachean Ethics*.

The first of these questions requires a detailed examination of the nature of φρόνησις. The second question can be discussed briefly here. It seems to us that authors such as Burnet, Hennis, Cooper and Höffe are basically right when they indicate the dialectical nature of the *Nicomachean Ethics,* in which Aristotle starts from a discussion of opinions regarding the good, and comes to define the first principles of practical knowledge, i.e. a definition of "happiness." In Aristotle's system, it is dialectic that studies the ways of reasoning about the principles of a science (*top.* 101b 6), while the ability to judge whether a scientific discourse has been conducted well or not is the task of a sort of general culture (παιδεία). As we shall see in more detail in Chapter 4, the definition of happiness is arrived at by dialectical procedures, and actualizes the function of dialectic established in the *Topics:* to show the way (ὁδός) to grasp the principles, through the discussion of opinions and the clarification of their inconsistencies and partiality.[82] Dialectic is not just the discipline that deals with falsity and verisimilitude, as Greenwood, Gauthier and Kuhn believe; the use of dialectical techniques may result in true propositions. Aristotle's treatises frequently use dialectical procedures such as induction[83] or discussion starting from current opinions (such as: "for every thing that has a function, the good of that thing is to perform its function well"), which are explicitly presented by Aristotle as ἔνδοξα.

We are well aware that, in this way, the specific problem posed by the contemporary "rebirth of practical philosophy" is largely avoided, and to some extent emptied of content. In fact, this distinction between φρόνησις and the treatise called *Ethics* to some extent gets rid of the problem of the epistemological status of a practical philosophy that lies halfway between these two things, i.e. a type of philosophical knowledge aimed at praxis, which is distinguished from the particular practical reasoning of a man who acts, but does not try to set itself up as a scientific or sociological meditation on human action.[84]

This subject is certainly important, but we do not intend to deal with it here. After all, in Aristotle's writings there is not much about the status of a "practical philosophy" in the sense intended by some contemporary German philosophers. On the contrary, in his works there are many pages about the problem of the nature, function and status of individual practical knowledge; Aristotle's discussions of this topic are extremely interesting, both historically and theoretically, and even today constitute the basis of many studies of ethics and the theory of action.

But what is, according to Aristotle, the status of practical knowledge? The discussion so far outlined is not sufficient to establish this completely. Indeed, like practical knowledge, physics too is valid ὡς ἐπὶ τὸ πολύ (*phys.* II 5, 196 b 11, 20; II 8, 198b 36); physics too, like practical knowledge, requires much empirical knowledge, and hence cannot be grasped by young or inexpert people (*EN* 1142a 15–16 and 16–19). Aristotle uses similar arguments to uphold the superiority of first philosophy over both physics and practical knowledge: neither man nor natural substances in general are the best thing that exists in the universe, but there are better and nobler entities, and hence the science that deals with them will be the best (cf. *metaph.* VI 1, 1026b 27–30, and *EN* VI 7, 1141a 20–b 2).

Nevertheless, some have argued that, in reality, there is a great difference between natural events, which admit of exceptions, but by and large always occur in the same way and are the object of science and necessary demonstrations,[85] and human actions, which are much more variable and less regular.[86] This difficulty seems to have been grasped also by Alexander of Aphrodisias, who, in his *De fato* (VI 170, 15–171, 8) states that the character of a man is, in the soul, something like what natural dispositions are in the body. In this way Alexander tries to bring ethics closer to physics: an individual's actions would be ὡς ἐπὶ τὸ πολύ in accordance with the dispositions of his character. Thus, for Alexander it is very probable, and therefore true ὡς ἐπὶ τὸ πολύ, that a brave man will die a violent death, and a licentious man will wear out his days in pleasures.

From Aristotle's point of view, this solution appears unacceptable; for him, in no case is human behavior in the field of practical action due to nature, φύσει, but it always derives from ἐθίζεσθαι, from the assumption of stable habits, since φύσει, i.e. by nature, man is capable of behaving in contrary ways (*EN* 1103a 17–26; *EE* 1222b 15–1223a 15). Wrong, or morally unacceptable, behavior is thus more frequent than exceptions to the laws of nature, which are rare and monstrous (*de gen. an.* 770a 9–13). This seems to indicate that those who distinguish between types of "more or less" for physics and ethics are right. But on this point it is necessary to make two observations.

In the first place, it is not possible to compare physics and practical knowledge without considering the different τέλος of the two forms of knowledge. As we shall see in more detail in the following chapters, the practical end of φρόνησις inverts the degree of importance between particular and universal propositions. Given that the end is action, individual judgments are more important, since they show what is to be done in the present case,[87] than are universal judgments, which are valid ὡς ἐπὶ τὸ πολύ. This is made clear by Aristotle, who maintains that it is better to have both universal and particular practical knowledge, but that, rather than knowing only the end in general, it is better to have only detailed and concrete practical knowledge (*EN* 1141b 14–21). In biology it is enough to know that, normally, sheep have four legs (to use Barnes's example); in practical affairs, though, it does not suffice to know, in general and by and large, that (for example) tyrants kill their friends; rather, the problem is to know whether this particular tyrant will or will not try to poison us, who are his friends.

Secondly, it appears that Aristotle believes that, in practical choices, one can count on a relative consistency in human affairs. He states in the *Rhetoric* that in making decisions one can also make use of παραδείγματα, i.e. examples: "[they are] very useful for deciding on what happens through actions, since in most cases the future is similar (ὅμοιον) to the past" (1394a 6–8).

Practical actions do not happen of necessity (οὐδὲν ἐξ ἀνάγκης, 1357a 26–27); otherwise it would not be possible to make decisions regarding them. But it is still possible to reason (συλλογίζεσθαι, practically; cf. Chapter 4) starting from principles that are valid ὡς ἐπὶ τὸ πολύ, in cases that occur ὡς ἐπὶ τὸ πολύ (1357a 27–30). The relative consistency of human actions is the anthropological basis that enables Aristotle to maintain the traditional doctrine that the maxims and teachings of practical wisdom are valid ὡς ἐπὶ τὸ πολύ.

In the *Rhetoric* Aristotle states that it is possible to form general opinions about human events, using examples as the elements of an imperfect type of induction:

> [the enthymemes that are derived] by induction from similar cases,[88] whether one or more, when a person, after having grasped the universal, subsequently draws conclusions regarding a particular case, take place by example. (1402b 16–18)

A few pages earlier, he states:

> we have said that the example is induction, and with respect to which objects it is induction. It does not regard either the relation of the part to the whole, nor that of the whole to the part, nor that of the whole to the whole, but that of the part to the part, of like to like, when both parts belong to the same kind,

> but one is better known than another [. . . .] All these cases fall under the same universal (ὑπὸ τὸ αὐτὸ καθόλου). (1357b 26–35)

In the *Analytica Priora* (II 24) Aristotle describes this mechanism in detail, using an example that we can summarize as follows. Given four terms: *a* (evil), *b* (to make war on neighboring peoples), *c* (war of Athenians against Thebans, who are their neighbors), *d* (war of Thebans against Phocaeans, who are their neighbors), one can demonstrate that *a* is implied by *c*, and that therefore it is evil to make war on our neighbors the Thebans if, starting from the known fact that *a* is implied by *d* (let us suppose that everyone knows that the war against Phocaea was a disaster for the Thebans), and from other similar cases, one can infer a universal proposition, which says that *a* is implied by *b* in general, i.e. that in general it is evil to wage war on one's neighbors:

> the conviction (πίστις) of this comes from similar cases, for example the war of the Thebans against the Phocaeans [. . .] [one proceeds] in the same way even when the conviction that the middle term is implied by the extreme comes about by means of several examples (διὰ πλειόνων). (69a 4- 13)

In this way, according to Aristotle, who adopts a habit common among the Attic orators,[89] by means of examples it is possible to establish a series of prudential norms, which are the outcome of a sort of induction, but different from true induction.[90] An example of such general norms is a proposition like "Lean meat is more digestible" (*EN* 1141b 18), which is valid ὡς ἐπὶ τὸ πολύ and is indispensable for correct decision making. Experience of life and the fact of having seen many things make one ready for practical knowledge and capable of making decisions (*EN* 1095a 2–4; 1142a 11–15) precisely because they provide the individual with much knowledge of this type, which is generally valid. Without attaining the regularity of physical events, the field of human action is sufficiently consistent that one can form a type of knowledge concerning it that is "by and large" valid.

The Aristotelian conception of practical knowledge, starting from these passages, many seem rather static, and tied to a fixed framework of kinds of behavior that, despite the extreme variety of particulars, largely follow preestablished patterns. But this does not mean that it is a "conservative" position. For Aristotle, any single human action is not conceived of as a blind bet in an unknown environment, but as a behavior taking place in a largely predictable situation, so that one may be reasonably confident of being faced with the expected response. If, for example, we offer our hand to an acquaintance, in normal circumstances, we reasonably expect him to shake it and not, say, to burst out in tears, although one cannot absolutely exclude the possibility of that happening. This theory may seem less radical and fascinating than other, more modern theories, which stress the uncertainty and risk inherent in the human condition, wherein human action is seen as a gamble, but it has the merit of being closer to the real situations in which most of us decide what to do.

So far we have given a general description of Aristotle's idea of wisdom. Now we must start to analyze the procedures by which wisdom performs its operations and reaches its aim, since—as we have already said—it does not proceed on the basis of demonstrations like those used in mathematics. This analysis is the subject of the following chapters, which examine how φρόνησις arrives at an assessment of a situation and gives rise to concrete practical decisions. To clarify this process, Aristotle uses a distinction between the "end" and "what leads to the end" (which we generally call the distinction between "ends" and "means") and, at times, he resorts to the idea of a particular type of reasoning, ending in action, usually called the "practical syllogism." These are, respectively, the subjects of the next two chapters.

Appendix: The Right Mean

In the *Nicomachean Ethics* Aristotle says:

> by the mean of the thing itself, I mean what is equally distant from the extremes, which is one and the same for all, while the mean in relation to us, is what is neither in excess nor in defect, and this is not one single thing, nor the same for all. For example, if ten is too great an amount and two is too little, then six is the mean with respect to the thing, since it exceeds and is exceeded to the same extent, i.e. it is the average according to the mathematical proportion (κατὰ τὴν ἀριθμητικὴν ἀναλογίαν). But with regard to us things must not be considered in this way, since it is not true that, if eating ten minas is too much and two minas is too small an amount, a trainer will prescribe six minas, as perhaps also this amount is too much or too little for a person who has to follow the diet: for a Milo it will be too little, but for one who is just starting to do physical exercise it will be too much. (1106a 29—b 4)

According to the *Metaphysics* (1056a 6–18), "equal" is contrasted with "excess and defect" not as an opposite (since a thing cannot have two opposites, nor can what is equal be, *per se,* more opposite to excess than to defect) but as a privation (or, better, a negation that takes away).[91] What is "equal" is "good and the mean"; it is thus not a synthesis of values, as Hartmann thought, and as it is in Plato's *Euthydemus* (306A), since the extremes it is contrasted with are not values, but excesses, and it is defined inductively, starting from the excesses themselves.[92]

This doctrine, which may seem ethically scandalous, must be understood from the standpoint of how to find the right reaction in actual cases. It is immediately clear when one overreacts, i.e. when an emotional reaction is too strong or too weak; it is more difficult to decide when the emotional reaction is right. Therefore, to determine the mean starting from excesses means to try to find the clearest one for oneself starting from the clearest one for us (cf. *EN* 1095b 2–3, in a different context).

With respect to the distinctions made in the *Metaphysics,* in the *Ethics* the language is less precise. Aristotle here uses the concept of comparative opposites ("more opposite than"), and this differentiates the use in the *Ethics* from that of the *Metaphysics,* in which being opposite is the maximum difference, and thus admits of no degrees (1055a 6–10). In this imprecise use he can even take entities such as good and evil as opposites, though they belong to different genera (cf. below, Chapter 2). At one time he maintains that the mean is more opposite with respect to the extremes, because it is good and they are bad (*EE* 1234a 34); at another he holds that the extremes, inasmuch as they are opposite behaviors in one single type of situation (e.g., recklessness/cowardice), are more opposite to each other than to the mean (*EN* 1108b 26–28). The first definition is more axiological, while the second is more descriptive, but Aristotle's wavering from one to the other shows that he has moved away from the rigid ontological structure of the Academy.

Aristotle clearly accepts Plato's position that the mean is one of the possible choices along a continuum of possible behaviors, but he suggests ways of identifying this medium that are different from Plato's and closer to those of the tradition. He insists that it is difficult to find the mean:

> we have explained sufficiently that ethical virtue is a mean, and in what way it is so, viz. that it is a mean between two evils, one of excess and the other of defect, and that it is such a mean because it aims to attain the golden mean both in feelings and in actions. And this is why it is difficult (ἔργον ἐστί) to be a man of worth, since it is difficult to find the mean on every occasion, just as not everyone can find the center of a circle, but only an expert (εἰδότος) can. (1109a 20–26)

He feels it necessary to give practical advice on how to reach it:

i. it is necessary to stay farther away from the more opposite excess. Not all excesses are opposites in the same way with respect to the mean, since it does not lie exactly in the middle, and even if one exceeds a little in the other sense, one will not be very wrong; hence it is preferable to behave so as to appear a little reckless, rather than to seem somewhat cowardly;

ii. one must try to react to one's natural inclinations, which always drive us toward one of the extremes;

iii. one must not give in to the pleasurable (this is a repetition of point [ii]).

By so doing we will be very likely to grasp the mean (1109b 18–20). This advice presupposes that the right answer varies with the situation, and that it is impossible to determine it exactly. But this is not all: for Aristotle the mean is not conceived of as a point, but as a segment. This is clear from point (i). One's behavior may be praiseworthy not only if one grasps exactly the right amount of emotion between excess and defect, but also if one comes close to it. We may show this graphically:

A ____________ B ________ C______________________ D

Here, if A stands for recklessness and D is cowardice, the segment from B to C indicates a series of behaviors that are brave enough to be acceptable.[93] This is said in Chapter 2 9:

> One who strays from the good by just a little is not to be blamed, neither if he tends to excess, nor if he tends to defect, but those who move farther away are blameworthy, as they do not pass unobserved. It is not easy to decide by reasoning up to what point and to what extent one may stray from the mean without incurring blame, just as it is difficult to decide regarding every perception; things of this sort concern individual cases, and judgment is left to perception.[94] (1109b 18–23)

In Aristotle the theory of the mean is mainly a method used by the philosopher to describe what conditions of character and the emotional part of the soul best stimulate virtuous behavior and lead to a happy life. It is not, generally, a method used by men who act in order to decide on what to do, as it is in Pindar and the tragic poets.[95] As we shall see in Chapter 3, the "mean" is an end of one's actions, and as such it determines one's practical choices, but it is not itself an object of choice.

Aristotle believes that, to be effective, practical knowledge requires harmony between the intellectual and emotional parts of the soul (cf. *EN* I 13, for which see above, pp. 10–16). The emotional part of the soul must be in a state (ἕξις) of habit that encourages good behavior. Since the basic drives of desire are the tendency to pursue and the tendency to flee (*de an.* III 7 and 10), there must be agreement between what reason finds to be good and what desire pursues. As we have seen, this principle was already present in traditional ethics, but Aristotle developed it further in his ethical philosophy.

Below, we shall examine in detail the various aspects of this idea; for the time being, we may point out that Aristotle does not consider that a man is good and virtuous if he manages to dominate his instincts, and, by controlling himself, to act well; rather, a good man acts well without effort, because he has educated his emotions to desire good actions and to shun bad ones (*EN* I 13; VII 1–2). Aristotelian virtue cannot be compared to virtue in the modern sense, whereby a virtuous person does good with no thought of any reward, punishment or form of pleasure connected with it.[96] Rather, it is the expression of a balanced and harmonious character and, as such, is part of a complete and happy life.

CHAPTER 2

ENDS AND MEANS

1. The Ends Are Provided by Virtue, the Means by Reason

Aristotle devotes one of the most difficult chapters of the *Eudemian Ethics* (II 11) to various matters that are important for his ethics: the relation between λόγος and virtue in making practical choices, the function of λόγος in the correct identification of the means for obtaining a virtuous end, and the relation between the theory of the mean and the distinction between ends and means. The text is concise and at times doubtful, but in recent years considerable progress has been made in the direction of a correct interpretation of it.[1]

At the end of Chapter 10, Aristotle affirms that he has shown that virtue is the habitual state (ἕξις) of character that chooses the mean with respect to us as regards pleasure and pain (1227b 8–9). The following chapter, which is the one we are interested in, opens with a discussion of another aporia regarding ethical virtue:

> after having made these distinctions, let us say whether virtue makes the choice free of errors and the end correct, so that one chooses what is proper, or, as some people think, [virtue makes] the reasoning [correct].[2] (1227b 12–15)

Aristotle here discusses the possibility of making ἀρετή the cause, not only of right actions, but also of correct reasoning in general, as is the case in Homer, for whom the ability to argue well in assembly is one of the virtues of a warrior.[3] If this were true, the consequences for Aristotle's ethical theory would be quite considerable, since it would be sufficient to be of good character and virtuous in order not to be mistaken in one's arguments.[4] But this opinion is untenable;

moreover, in Aristotle's opinion the second thesis, supported by "some" people, has been caused by a confusion between virtue and ἐγκράτεια (continence, in the sense of self-control). The position thus refuted is re-examined in *EE* VIII 1, 1246b 21–29, a text most likely referred to in this chapter, in lines 1227b 16–17. There Aristotle says that some people might think that virtue in the irrational part of the soul is the cause of correct reasoning in the rational part, but this is not possible, since virtue lacks a necessary additional element.[5] The opinion confuted seems to be one of those maintained in the debates of the Academy, and in this chapter we shall see some other places where Aristotle refers to contemporary debates.

Therefore virtue is not the cause of the correctness of λόγος and of all that depends on λόγος only the first possibility remains, i.e. that ethical virtue is the cause of correct behavior. In lines b 12–14, Aristotle said that one of the two possibilities is that virtue makes the choice and the end of the choice correct, so that a virtuous person chooses in view of the end that befits him. The expression ὥστε οὗ ἕνεκα δεῖ προαιρεῖσθαι (b 13–14) already expresses the idea that, when one makes a choice, one does so in view of an end that differs from the immediate act being performed.[6] Since the first alternative given is, in reality, composed of two elements, the end and what is chosen for its attainment, it must be seen whether the correctness of both actually depends only on ἀρετή. Aristotle states that in order to determine this it is necessary to discuss another problem:

> it is possible that the aim is correct and one is mistaken about what should be done to reach the aim, or it is possible to be mistaken regarding the aim, but to take the right steps to reach it, or it may be that neither of the two [is right]. (b 19–22)

There is also another possibility, viz. that the aim may be reached by inappropriate means: Aristotle does not mention it here, but refers to it in *EN* VI 9, 1142b 17–26. The above-quoted passage is paralleled by another passage in the *Politics,* which amplifies on and clarifies a concept that is already quite clear.[7] Here the distinction between the "choice" and the "end of the choice," discussed in the previous lines, is replaced by that between two objects of choice, the "end" and "what leads to the end," τὰ πρὸς τὸν σκοπόν or, more commonly, τὰ πρὸς τὸ τέλος, an expression that nowadays we translate, rather imperfectly, as "the means."[8] The topic of choice will be dealt with again only later, from line b 28 on, after having made the distinctions required to solve the following problem:

> does virtue make the aim[9] or what is done in view of the aim [correct]? (b 22–23)

The answer has left Aristotle's critics speechless:

> we establish that it is the aim, because for this there is neither syllogism nor reasoning (οὐκ ἔστι συλλογισμὸς οὐδὲ λόγος). (b 23–25)[10]

From the formal point of view Aristotle's reply is impeccable[11]; indeed, the correctness of the end or aim of one's actions must depend on virtue, if:

1. the only sources of correctness are ἀρετή or λόγος (b 34);

2. the objects whose correctness depends on one of the two sources have no relation with the other. Thus virtue is not the source of the correctness of what depends on λόγος (b 15–19), nor is λόγος the source of correctness for that which depends on virtue;

3. the aim is not the result of λόγος thus its correctness must depend on virtue.

There is a certain discrepancy between the beginning of the chapter, where Aristotle envisaged the possibility that ἀρετή could also be a source of the correctness of λόγος, and this part, in which λόγος is an autonomous source of correctness, but there is no real contradiction between the two passages: if virtue is not the source of the correctness of λόγος, then λόγος and all that depends on it are by themselves the cause of their own correctness.

But, from the standpoint of its content, Aristotle's doctrine seems, at first sight, amazing. He says that, in order to posit a correct end, one must have ethical virtue,[12] which appears to be not only a necessary, but also a sufficient condition for possessing the right aim. And the lines that follow confirm and clarify this position:

> let us therefore take this as a principle; for indeed a doctor does not ask whether [a patient] must get well or not, but whether he should take walks or not; nor does a teacher of gymnastics ask whether [an athlete] must have a good physical constitution or not, but whether he should take exercise or not. In the same way no other science worries about the end. And, just as the theoretical sciences have hypotheses as starting points, so for the productive sciences the end is both starting point and hypothesis. (b 25–30)

Modern commentators have accused Aristotle of making an inappropriate comparison, since he uses examples drawn from technical activities such as those of doctors and trainers to clarify the nature of ethical choices. They maintain that doctors and trainers, in their capacity as such, do not try to determine the aim of their activity, but merely carry out their functions in the best possible way. This is not true, they say, for moral choices. One should, however, keep in mind that all the Greek thinkers of the fourth century B.C., such as Gorgias,

Plato, Isocrates, Aristotle, and many others, used the examples of medicine and gymnastics to clarify the nature of ethical-practical thought. They all use such a comparison at crucial points in their arguments,[13] so it is not strange that Aristotle should resort to it, too, to clarify his ideas on the correctness of moral choices. He means to say, in the clearest possible way, that the object of λόγος is the ways of achieving one's end, i.e. the "means," and he repeats this shortly afterward:

> therefore, the end is the starting point of reasoning,[14] and the conclusion of reasoning is the starting point of action. And if it is true that the cause of every right choice is either λόγος or ἀρετή, and it is not λόγος, then ἀρετή must be the cause of the rightness of the end, though not of what leads to the end. (b 32–36)

It is reasoning that deals with what-leads-to-the-end, i.e. the means, and the correct choice of means depends on reasoning, even if we consider the term "means" in the wide sense used here. Reasoning takes the ends as given and devotes itself to investigating the ways of achieving them. The theoretical sciences operate in a similar way with respect to their principles:

> since such-and-such a person must get well, there must be so-and-so, if there is to be that, just as in the other sciences, if a triangle has two right angles, then such-and-such things follow. (b 30–32)

Aristotle uses the same word, ἀνάγκη, to indicate two different kinds of necessity. In the second case it is a logical and analytical necessity, whereas in the first case it is a practical and teleological necessity, related to a given situation; to cross a river without a boat or a bridge, one has to know how to swim (*phys.* II 9).

Having established this, let us return to the subject of choice, προαίρεσις. Every choice is an individual act, which is exerted on a certain object or situation, and sets itself a certain goal (b 36–37). The end is determined by ἀρετή which, in *EE* II 10, is defined as the capacity (δύναμις) that determines the mean; thus it is natural to identify the end with the right mean. Indeed, Aristotle does make this identification in the following passage, whose interpretation is quite difficult and controversial: it is the only passage in Aristotle's *Ethics* where we find together two subjects that are usually kept quite separate in Aristotle's thought, i.e. the distinction between ends and means and the theory of the mean:[15]

> the what-for is the end; indeed, every choice is a choice of something and for something; [therefore] the mean is the what-for, the cause of which is virtue, the choosing of the what-for.[16] However, the choice is not of this, but *of what leads to* this. (b 36–39, our italics)

The proper sphere of practical reasoning is limited by two things that are not reasoning, as Ross has said:[17] the end, given by ethical virtue, and the action or concrete situation, which close the syllogistic chain of reasoning. For Aristotle, nevertheless, "to make a good choice" does not mean to find the technically most effective means for the realization of just any end; rather, it means to find the effective means for achieving a good end.[18] We shall see below that the distinctive character of φρόνησις is to be able to reach good ends effectively. In conclusion, Aristotle reaffirms, virtue is the cause of the correctness of the end and another faculty (ἄλλη δύναμις) is the cause of grasping what must be done in order to reach the end (b 39–1228a 2).

At this point we encounter, in an apparently paradoxical way, the subject of the ethical evaluation of choices. Aristotle says that one does not choose the ends, but the means-toward-the-end, and it is for this reason that we judge people by the choices they make. This has surprised modern critics, who instead find it natural to judge people by the ends they set themselves. But the paradox is only apparent, since Aristotle says:

> one does not choose the end, but what leads to the end. Therefore it is the property of another faculty to grasp what must be done to reach the end, while virtue is the cause of the correctness of the end chosen; and this is why we judge the quality of a person by the choice made, i.e. by that-for-which he acts, and not by what he does; (1227b 38–1228a 4)

and later he adds:

> furthermore, we all assign praise or blame by looking more at the choices than at the deeds [. . .] since it is not easy to see what the choice is, this explains why we are compelled to judge the quality of a person on the basis of what he does. (a 11–17)

The expression ἐκ τῆς προαιρέσεως κρίνομεν ποῖός τις· τοῦτο δ' ἐστὶ τὸ τίνος ἕνεκα πράττει (a 2–3) clearly means that a person is not judged merely on his ability to reach any end whatever, just as one is not judged either for the ends one sets oneself with an ineffectual desire.[19] What we see are only the actions of individuals, which are normally directed toward some end; and one and the same physical act may be performed for different aims. This explains why Aristotle, like Plato in the *Gorgias,* insists that what is done for an end must be judged on the basis of the end itself. If we can determine precisely the action of a certain individual as the choice of something for a certain end, we can praise or blame him without fail (1228a 5–11).

It seems strange to hear that ends are not set by reason, λόγος, but by ethical virtue;[20] yet Aristotle repeats this concept too often for us to be able to doubt that, for him, this is the reality of things.[21] Therefore, rather than trying to change the obvious sense of his words, it is useful to try to understand the intention and meaning of his position.

We believe that, by this thesis, Aristotle wants to show that the practical premise, which is the result of a ἕξις, a habitual state of the character, is not restricted to reason alone, but is also proper to desire. This is strictly necessary if any action is to take place, since for Aristotle ὄρεξις, desire, or one of its parts, is the only motive force for movements of the human body; an end that is only asserted cannot give rise to an action.[22] This is stated also at the end of *EN* 1179a 33–1180a 5.[23] Like the sophists and poets before him, Aristotle affirms that one must possess a good nature in order to learn how to be a good citizen.[24] Teaching may be sufficient only for those whose souls are properly disposed, so that they experience pleasure in doing good and pain in doing ill (cf. also 1179b 23–31). In special situations—when, for example, we are, as Socrates was, in prison awaiting death, unjustly condemned—the choice of the good and right action does not depend, in Aristotle's opinion, on an act of practical reasoning to which the emotions have to conform. Rather, it is our ἀρετή and the kind of men we are (*EN* 1113a 25 et seq.) that make us choose good or evil; thus, in order to bear witness to the coherence of our life as philosophers, we shall choose to remain in prison and face death, or we shall flee in order to survive.

In our opinion,[25] this doctrine of Aristotle's shows that, no matter what meaning we assign to the expression "naturalist fallacy," Aristotle's position avoids such a charge, as he refuses to deduce a behavior from an assertion and makes the end an object of virtue, i.e., at least, of desire. All this has a decidedly anti-Platonic air,[26] and detaches practical knowledge from theoretical philosophy: indeed, the conclusions of theoretical reasoning cannot be taken immediately as practical premises since, as Aristotle says in *EE* II 11, the practical premises are not the outcome of συλλογισμός or λόγος, but are given by virtue and hence are the object of desire. Theoretical philosophy can be the principle of practical thought as being the content of the βίος θεωρητικός, hence as an end; but this is another matter, as we shall see in Chapter 4.

One important problem to be dealt with here, though, is whether the ends are the object "only" of desire, and not of reasoning also. If they are only the object of desire, Aristotle's departure from Plato runs the risk of becoming very "costly," as the ends of human action would become completely irrational.[27] Now, in this connection, we should observe that here, in *EE* II 11, as in other similar texts, Aristotle contrasts virtue with reasoning (ἀρετή vs. λόγος) and not desire with reasoning (ὄρεξις vs. λόγος), and the two oppositions are not equivalent.[28] Moreover, the conclusion of *EN* quoted above seems to suggest that, in order to become good, one needs virtue and rational teaching, and not only good habits.

Both virtue of character and practical knowledge are each compounds of ὄρεξις and λόγος, desire and reasoning, although in different forms and mixtures. In the following sections we shall see how these elements are found both in the choice of means and in the determination of the end.

2. The Means Are the Object of Reason and Desire

In general Plato connects the distinction between end and means with the concept of ultimate end, and makes all choices depend on the correct determination of the ultimate end, as happens in *Lysis* (218D–219D). Instead, Aristotle tackles the question of ends and means without referring to the problem of whether the end in question is the ultimate end or an intermediate end, and in his discussion of this subject he never mentions the concept of "ultimate end." In general, an end—any end—is not an object of deliberation; therefore recent attempts to maintain that, in the final analysis, all ends except happiness are the object of deliberation[29] (since all particular ends are means for the ultimate end, i.e. happiness) are not very convincing. Even if this interpretation were to be accepted, in any case all other ends would be the object of deliberation as means and not as ends.[30] This would therefore confirm Aristotle's thesis, viz. that ends are not the object of deliberation.

In *EE,* as well as in *EN,* Aristotle limits the field of choice and deliberation to the choice of means for an already given end. Indeed, he says that one does not choose an end, e.g. to be happy; rather, one chooses an action that leads to an end (1111b 16–30); and if the end is acting well or right action (τὸ καλόν, ἡ εὐπραξία) not intended as a means for anything else, also in this case no one would choose to "do a good action" in the abstract, but in every case this good action is embodied in a particular choice. This point must be clarified, and some light may be thrown on it by looking at Aristotle's analysis of deliberation.

In *EN* III 3 Aristotle illustrates the nature of deliberation: first of all, he indicates its object, which is the field of ethics and politics and, more specifically, those actions which, in these fields, depend on us (1112a 21–31) and are not determinable precisely, on the basis of an ἐπιστήμη, but fall within the province of things that happen "for the most part" (1112a 34–b 11).[31] These statements clearly show that Aristotle intends to analyze not only technical, but also ethical deliberation, even if (as we shall see) he uses technical examples, as he had done in *EE* II 11. There is no reason to suppose that these comparisons are inappropriate for explaining the object of this chapter.

As we shall see in the next chapter, deliberation is not a syllogism, nor does it take place by means of various syllogisms: rather, it is the search (ζήτησις) for the middle term of a practical syllogism. In our opinion, this is the meaning of the following statement by Aristotle:

> no one [. . .] deliberates about the end, but, given the end, they investigate how and by what things it can be achieved. (1112b 14–16)

As a research activity, deliberation is a stochastic and conjectural type of knowledge.[32]

In our opinion, deliberation cannot be identified with the "justification" of actions discussed by contemporary moral philosophy. This is so for two reasons: first of all, because Aristotle always speaks of deliberation as a way of determining an action that is still to be performed; and secondly, because the logical structure of an investigation aiming at the justification of an action that has been carried out is, at least in part, different from the deliberation of an action that is still to be performed. This can be shown by the example of a teleological syllogism described by Aristotle in *Analytica Posteriora* II 11, 94b 8–26. In the next chapter, dedicated to the practical syllogism, we shall make an attempt at a comprehensive interpretation of this difficult passage. Now we shall use it only to point out the difference between the search for a theoretical justification of an action that has been carried out, and the search for the means to be used to achieve a purpose.

In our interpretation, the text (which we shall transcribe below, at pp. 82–83) poses the following problem: given an action and a final cause that justifies it, find a middle term that links the other terms. Aristotle says: "Why take a walk [after a meal]?[33] To stay healthy." We therefore have two elements: a general end and a single action carried out in a given situation:

C to take a walk after a meal
B *x*
A to stay healthy.

We need the middle term *x* to link the other two terms. The ζήτησις in this case will be the search for an explanatory middle term. When we know this middle term, we will actually have a justification. In the above passage, Aristotle supposes that the middle term is "to digest, not to leave undigested food at the pit of the stomach." Thus we shall have this scheme:

C to take a walk after a meal
B to digest one's food
A to stay healthy.

Here the term (B) is the final cause, in that it is the definition and specification of term (A), staying healthy, in a particular situation (καιρός), after a meal (this statement is very debatable; for the time being, we merely assert this point, referring once again, for a more complete justification of our position, to Chapter 3, p. 82 et seq.) Stated in another way, we have a chain of final causality of the following sort:

C "to take a walk after a meal" has as its final cause
B "to digest," which is a partial definition of
A "to stay healthy," which is the ultimate end.

Hence, after a meal one takes a walk in order to digest one's food, which is a particular way of staying healthy in that situation.

In deliberation, the situation is different. As Aristotle says, in deliberation, too, at the beginning two elements are present:

> it therefore appears, as has been said, that man is the origin (ἀρχή) of his actions, and deliberation is about the actions that he can carry out; such actions aim at something besides themselves. Indeed, one does not deliberate about the end, but about what leads to the end; likewise, one does not deliberate about particular circumstances, as for example whether this is bread or whether it is baked well, as this derives from sensation, and if one deliberated all the time the process would go on to infinity. (1112b 31–1113a 2)

Returning to the example of *a. po.* II 11, we could say that, at the beginning of deliberation, we have an end (A), "to feeling well," and a given situation (C") "after a meal," but we are lacking the action (C) that is to be performed in the given situation. We therefore do not have the third term (C), but only, so to speak, the conditions for it. We could summarize the situation schematically as follows:

A to feeling well
B *x*
C to do *y* after a meal.

The task of deliberation is more difficult than that of justification. It is not just a question of finding the middle term; we must also find term (C'), which is an action (cf. Chapter 3, section 5), the "doing *y*" that produces the effect of "feeling well after a meal," and that results from the application of the end to the given situation, by specifying it. In this way the end, which is still universal, is determined by the means.[34] We must therefore start from the end and specify it analytically, deciding what, concretely, is meant by "feeling well after a meal." We shall find that it is "digesting"; then we shall, if it is necessary or proper, look for some middle terms that particularize this end further, until we arrive at a concrete action (C') that is *y*, the still unknown part of (C), which tells us what to do. Let us say that this action is "to take a walk." At this point deliberation stops, as Aristotle says:

> but, given the end, they investigate how and by means of what it is to be achieved; and if it appears that it can be achieved in many ways, they try to find out how to achieve it in the quickest and best way; if, instead, it can be achieved in only one way, they try to find out how to achieve it in this way, and that by means of what else, until they reach the first cause, which is the last to be discovered. (1112b 15–20)

If, in the *Analytica Posteriora* there is need of a λόγος, a definition that specifies the end, in *EN* there is need of an action, and not only a λόγος, because both the middle term (B) and the extreme (C) have to be found. Once the action has been identified, it is immediately carried out, as Aristotle says, and thus one has, as in the *Analytics,* the sequence "to take a walk—to digest—to feel well." The deliberation is successful if it arrives at a feasible action:

> and if they run up against something impossible they stop, as for example, if money is needed and it cannot be procured; if, instead, the action appears to be possible they prepare to act. (1112b23–27)

The success of deliberation does not depend entirely on the person who performs it; human actions depend to a large extent on chance and luck.[35] If an effective action is possible, it must be taken as an object, not only by λόγος, but also by desire, in order for the action to be performed. Λόγος and διάνοια serve to determine the effective choice, but this choice, inasmuch as it is a means for a desired end, becomes the object of desire, which obeys reason (cf. p. 106):

> everyone stops inquiring how to act, once he has brought back the principle (of action) to himself, and to the dominant part of himself, since this is the part that makes decisions [. . .] the object of choice being something which is deliberated on and desired from among the things that depend on us, also choice will be a deliberate desire of something that depends on us. (1113a 5–11)

In reality, if προαίρεσις has as its object the ways of achieving an aim, and if the object of προαίρεσις is that which is both deliberated on and desired, then the means in practical action are not only the object of analysis and rational choice, but they are also the object of desire. But it is a desire that follows analysis and does not determine it:

> in fact, judging on the basis of deliberation, we feel desire in accordance with (κατά) deliberation. (1113a 11–12)

We decide to take a walk, here and now, in order to be in good health, and we therefore wish to take a walk only because we perceive[36] that this fosters the good that we really desire, viz. "being in good health."

With respect to what we saw in *EE* II 11, here Aristotle sheds further light on the subject. If, indeed, it is true that the correctness of the λόγος in deliberative analysis is responsible for the choice of the appropriate means, it is also true that the means are not only the object of λόγος, even though they do not depend on ethical virtue. The choice involves the arousal of desire, and is "desiring intellect" (1139b 4), "rational desire" (1139b 5) or, as here, "deliberative desire" (1113a 11, cf. 1139a 23).

We must now demonstrate the second part of our thesis, i.e. that the ends, though an object of virtue, are not for that reason given by pure desire and the emotions. The text we have to refer to in this connection consists of the last two chapters of *EN* VI; this passage has often been tortured by Aristotle's critics, who have frequently seen in it more than Aristotle actually says. We suggest a unified interpretation, starting from the hypothesis that there are no contradictions in what Aristotle affirms.

3. The Ends Are the Object of Desire and Reason

In *EN* VI 12 and 13 Aristotle discusses only one problem.

> It could be doubted, with regard to these [virtues of the intellect], what is the use of them? Theoretical wisdom (σοφία) does not deal at all with what makes a man happy, because it does not deal with anything that comes into being; practical wisdom (φρόνησις), instead, does have this object, but for what purpose should it exist? (1143b 18–21)

The solution of this difficulty makes it possible to clarify the relation between φρόνησις and ethical ἀρετή, against the objections of those who believe that φρόνησις and σοφία are useless for man (we do not know whether such adversaries really existed or whether these are fictitious objections, given here for the sake of argument). In short, the objection is that ethical virtue suffices for action, and there is no need at all for a virtue of the intellect whose object is human praxis; moreover, if φρόνησις is useful to one who wants to become an honest man, and not to one who is already honest, then it will be useless to one who already knows how to live. Lastly, although perhaps φρόνησις is indispensable, maybe it is sufficient to obey one who possesses it, as one does in the case of medical science, without acquiring it personally (b 21–35). From line 35 on Aristotle gives his answer, treating of three subjects: the usefulness of φρόνησις with respect to praxis, the usefulness of σοφία for happiness, and the mutual relation between φρόνησις and σοφία. Here we shall deal only with the first point, reserving the others for Chapter 4.

Aristotle's answer to the first point is divided into various stages. A first, general answer is given in lines 1144a 6–11; a second answer goes from 1144a 11 to b 1; this second answer in turn requires clarification of the nature of ethical virtue, which goes from 1144b 1 to 1145a 6; this latter is the part that most interests us. In our opinion, however, it is useful to summarize briefly Aristotle's whole argument, so as to understand better the final part.

3.1. The First Answer: Aristotle Restates the Position of the *Eudemian Ethics*

To show the usefulness of φρόνησις, first of all Aristotle assigns it the task that in *EE* he had given to λόγος in general, viz. that of finding the means for achieving an end:

> the characteristic activity (ἔργον) [of man] is carried out in accordance with (κατά) φρόνησις and the virtue of character, since virtue makes the purpose correct and φρόνησις makes right that which leads to the end. (1144a 6–9)

On the basis of what we have said so far, we can suggest an interpretation of this passage. Although it is not sufficiently supported by the lines just quoted, in our opinion it is able to account for the entire argument contained in chapters 12 and 13. If this opinion of ours proves to be true, then the present interpretation of this passage will have been sufficiently confirmed. It seems to us that here Aristotle means that, in order for there to be a virtuous action, it is necessary that there should be both an immediate response of desire and of the sphere of the passions, and an analysis of the situation made by practical λόγος. The role of desire is that of indicating the direction in which one must move, through a reaction of pleasure and pain; the role of λόγος is that of determining exactly what the result is that is to be reached, and how to arrive at it. The former by itself could only provide a confused and ineffectual reaction; the latter by itself would not lead to action, as it consists only in a κρίσις, a judgment concerning the facts relating to action. The two elements are on the same plane and help one another: this very fact distinguishes the determination of ends from the choice of means; on the contrary, in the choice of means, desire follows the dictates of reason.[37]

3.2. The Second Answer: Φρόνησις Is a Type of Practical Knowledge That Requires the Presence of Virtue

In this answer Aristotle touches on two points: first of all, he points out that the task of φρόνησις, as we have said above, is to find the means needed to achieve an aim; thus he is able to state that φρόνησις makes us more capable of acting (πρακτικώτεροι, 1143b 24, 1144a 11–12). Secondly, he distinguishes φρόνησις, wisdom or a knowledge of how to live, from ability in general or δεινότης (1144a 20–28). Indeed it is absurd to say that one acts badly on the basis of wisdom, as it, *qua* wisdom, can have only good ends (*top.* 137a 8–20; *EE* 1246b 4–6 and 33–35). Φρόνησις is thus linked to the virtue of character, and it is impossible to be φρόνιμος without being good (1144a 29–b 1). In other words, "possession of φρόνησις" analytically contains "possession of ethical virtue." The problem we are now concerned with is determining whether this implies that φρόνησις also establishes the ends, and not just the means.

Also in this section, Aristotle repeats that the correctness of the end depends on virtue, and the correctness of the means for the end depends on φρόνησις. In making a correct choice, then, there must be both, as he says in the following passage:

> therefore virtue makes the choice correct, but that which is to be done to implement the choice does not pertain to virtue, but to another faculty.[38] (1144a 20–22)

The other faculty he is referring to is φρόνησις, which is not self-sufficient, as it is not the capacity to achieve just any end, but only a good end, one provided by virtue.[39] It is thus distinguished from mere ability, δεινότης, which, as a rational faculty, can be used for contrary extremes, just as medical knowledge can be used to heal, but also to harm.[40] But, in the case of medical knowledge, the harmful use is, so to speak, secondary or accidental, whereas δεινότης as a faculty is value neutral[41] and provides us with the means for the end, whatever it may be:

> this [faculty] is one that enables us to carry out the actions required for the purpose we have set ourselves and thus reach it. (1144a 24–26)

Depending on the end it is addressed to, this "ability" may become wisdom, φρόνησις, or wiliness, πανουργία. Therefore both the wise and the wily are said to be "able."[42] Φρόνησις, as the ability to find the means for a good end, is not ability, but it does not exist without that type of ability (a 28–29). Here, it seems to us, the task of φρόνησις is once again that of determining the means for a good end provided by virtue, and this is the way we should interpret what Aristotle says in the following passage:

> this habit [φρόνησις] does not arise in that eye of the soul without virtue, as we have said before and as is quite clear: in fact practical syllogisms that have a starting point sound like this: 'since the end and the best thing are of this kind . . .', whatever it may be (let us say it is anything, for the sake of our argument); now, this does not seem clear to one who is not good, since wickedness corrupts (διαστρέφει) and leads us astray regarding practical principles, so that it is clear that it is not possible to be φρόνιμος without being good. (a 29–b 1)

As in *EE* II 11, here too virtue is the cause of the correctness of the end; in *EE* VIII 1, 1246a 33–34, Aristotle said that sciences can be distorted (μεταστρέφειν) in their use, but not φρόνησις, which is knowing how to live in a praiseworthy manner. One cannot simultaneously be wicked, i.e. pursue wicked ends, and reach them with φρόνησις.

The "eye" of the soul that Aristotle speaks of is not the ability to see the ends.[43] Aristotle himself argues against this thesis, in a previous passage.[44] Rather, it is the ability to see concrete situations, as he says in *EN* VI 11:

> one must heed the unproved sayings and opinions of the experienced, the elderly and the φρόνιμοι, no less than demonstrations: for, as they have an "eye" that comes from experience, they see correctly (1143b 11–14).

In the previous section we saw that the end, which is universal, is particularized in relation to a concrete situation, and that this procedure is already part of the investigation (ζήτησις) that concerns τὰ πρὸς τὸ τέλος, the ways to reach a good end. Therefore, as we shall see more clearly in Chapter 3, the eye of the soul sees the means and the minor premise. With respect to the first answer and also with respect to *EE* II 11, it has been made clear that λόγος (= φρόνησις) and ἀρετή are not two juxtaposed faculties, but are intimately connected, since φρόνησις necessarily requires the presence of virtue of character to be itself and not δεινότης. As for the object of φρόνησις, it is the set of means for the end, and not the end in itself, detached from the means. The end appears to one who is good because he is good.

3.3 The Third Answer: Virtue Without Φρόνησις Is Blind

In this section Aristotle repeats that the object of φρόνησις is the means for reaching one's aim, but he also explains that, just as φρόνησις is not itself without virtue, so too virtue is not itself without φρόνησις. This time he starts from the nature of virtue to show that it is necessarily linked to φρόνησις, proceeding in an inverse way with respect to the previous lines. This time, too, Aristotle wonders what one of the pair of terms, ἀρετή-φρόνησις, would be without the other, but he asks it of ἀρετή:

> and in fact virtue has the same relation that φρόνησις has with δεινότης [ability]: it is not the same thing, but it is similar; so too is natural virtue related to virtue in the strong sense (κυρία). (1144b 1–4)

Here Aristotle uses the expression "natural virtue" to indicate a spontaneous and generic tendency to do good, without knowing how to achieve it in practice.[45] Natural virtue by itself does not enable one to act; the views of those Aristotle is trying to confute maintain just the opposite. Their point of view is expressed in the following lines:

> since it appears that everyone is somehow endowed by nature with each type of character, and ever since birth we have been just and temperate and brave, and we have had the other qualities; but all the same we are seeking for something else: good in the strong sense (κυρίως) and being endowed with those virtues in another way. (b 4–8)

No one likes to have virtuous tendencies and not know how to put them into practice, thus being ineffectual and useless, like children or handicapped people:

> though even children and animals are endowed with natural habits, yet without νοῦς such habits seem to be harmful. Besides this, we apparently observe that, just as a strong but sightless body, when it moves, may perhaps fall headlong, because it cannot see, so it may happen in this case, too. But if a person acquires νοῦς, the difference is seen in action, and though the habit is the same as it was before,[46] now there is virtue in the strong sense (b 8–14).

Sight in a strong body corresponds to φρόνησις in the soul. Its object is the data of experience, and it tells how to give concrete actualization to one's natural tendencies. Here, too, the object of φρόνησις is the means and not the ends,[47] and what is said here makes a perfect counterpart to what was said in 1144a 30, where the eye of the soul was said to be the seat of φρόνησις. Aristotle says that the possession of φρόνησις produces a difference ἐν τῷ πράττειν (b 13); in our opinion, this may be interpreted only in the sense that the possession of φρόνησις makes those who already possess natural virtue able to find the means and ways needed to actualize their good tendencies. In this way the parallelism with the previous chapter is perfect: there it was said that whoever has δεινότης knows how to find the means and that when he has ethical virtue, he has the right ends, and therefore his δεινότης is φρόνησις. Here it is said that whoever has natural virtue tends toward a good end (and if things were not like this, one would not even be able to speak of virtue, since it is the task of virtue to make the end good), and when he has φρόνησις, he is able to find out how to act in practice, and thus his ἀρετή is κυρία. Moreover, the νοῦς spoken of in line b 12 is, in our opinion, the practical νοῦς spoken of also in chapter 11, 1143a 35–b 2: the νοῦς that grasps the minor premise of the syllogism and the data of experience (cf. 74 below):

> and νοῦς deals with the extremes on both sides, and indeed regarding both the first terms and the last there is νοῦς and not λόγος and the one (νοῦς), with regard to demonstrations, deals with the first and unchanging terms, while the other, with regard to the practical premises, deals with the last extreme, and with what can be otherwise, and the minor premise. (1143a35–b 2)

Aristotle's good man is not a well-meaning but harmful bumbler; he is one who possesses the end and knows how to achieve it, one who knows how to behave and has praiseworthy ends. Aristotle posits ability and natural virtue as two extremes, and ἀρετὴ κυρία, which is not ἄνευ φρονήσεως (1144b 17), as the mean, according to the following scheme:

ἀρετὴ κυρία
δεινότης ———————— with ———————— ἀρετὴ φυσική.
φρόνησις

So far φρόνησις has had the task of finding the ways of achieving the end, which is given by virtue. And now we know also that the virtue which determines the end cannot be itself without φρόνησις. The respective functions of ἀρετή and φρόνησις, moreover, cannot be performed independently of one another, and at different times. This will be seen in the next section, where Aristotle illustrates the ways and forms of the relation between φρόνησις and virtue.

4. Virtue and Wisdom

In the lines that we shall examine now, Aristotle is no longer discussing the opinion of those who deny any necessary relation between φρόνησις and virtue, and therefore consider φρόνησις useless. He has shown that virtue is not itself without φρόνησις, and now he must discuss the positions of those who admit a necessary relation between these two faculties, but understand it wrongly. This discussion will shed further light on the reciprocal role of intellect and desire, on the one hand, and of virtue and wisdom on the other, in the determination of the end.

The first adversary to be confuted is Socrates, who lies at the extreme opposite of those who deny any relation between ἀρετή and φρόνησις. Indeed, he identifies the two things, and even identifies φρόνησις with ἐπιστήμη, science (b 29). Therefore for Socrates virtue is knowledge: this is the "Socratic paradox." Aristotle finds something right, but also something wrong, in this position:

> for this reason some people say that the virtues are forms of φρόνησις, and on the one hand Socrates was right in his investigation, while on the other he was mistaken: he was wrong in thinking that the virtues were forms of φρόνησις, but he spoke well when he maintained that they could not exist without φρόνησις. (1144b 17–21)[48]

For Aristotle (*top.* 152a 35–b 2) the equation ἀρετή = φρόνησις = ἐπιστήμη is impossible, because there is a difference in genus between ἀρετή and ἐπιστήμη, as we have seen in Chapter 1.

The other contemporaries of Aristotle, indicated by the expression νῦν πάντες, and who are probably the Academics,[49] made a lesser error. They maintained that virtue is acting in conformity (κατά) with φρόνησις they thus posited a lower level of integration between ἀρετή and φρόνησις than that maintained by Socrates, if, as we think, this κατά is to be understood like that of *EN* 1113a 11–12 (cf. p. 48). Aristotle holds that there is a greater degree of integration between virtue and φρόνησις than they think:

proof [of this] is that even today, when they define virtue, first of all they posit that it is a habitual state, and then what things it is concerned with—this habitual state that is in accordance with (κατά) right reason (ὀρθὸς λόγος), as the λόγος that is in accordance with φρόνησις is right; it seems that they all have some sort of vague idea that such a habit, which accords with φρόνησις, is virtue (1144b 21–25).[50]

The position of the Academics can be outlined as follows:

A virtue is the ἕξις that is in accordance with (κατά) correct λόγος (b 22–23),
B the λόγος that is in accordance with (κατά) φρόνησις is correct (b 23–24);

C virtue is the ἕξις that is in accordance with φρόνησις (b 25).

The text actually says, "the ἕξις that is in accordance with φρόνησις is virtue," but the two formulations are substantially equivalent. Aristotle does not say whether these "moderns" identified φρόνησις and ἐπιστήμη, as Socrates did, but from his presentation it is clear that they made φρόνησις the element that determines ethical virtue, i.e. that in compliance with which virtue is virtue.

Aristotle intends to forge a closer link between φρόνησις and ἀρετή, and render the two elements equal, as he says in *EN* X:

[the two] are joined, both φρόνησις with virtue of character, and virtue with φρόνησις, for the principles of φρόνησις are in accordance with (κατά) the ethical virtues, and the right [reasoning] of ethical virtues is in accordance with (κατά) φρόνησις (1178a 16–19).

In this passage virtue and φρόνησις are determined by one another,[51] and neither prevails. There is no vicious circle, as many nineteenth-century critics believed,[52] since the two elements, φρόνησις and virtue, belong to two different parts of the soul, and their collaboration poses no logical problems. Instead, Aristotle's intention of not subordinating either of the two parts of practical knowledge to the other is very clear. The same concept is expressed in *EN* VI 13, the chapter we are examining, in a different way, through the suggestion of a small change in the position of the Academics:

but it is necessary to make a small change. Virtue is not simply (οὐ μόνον) a habitual state that is in accordance with (κατά) right reason, but rather (ἀλλά) one which is accompanied by (μετά) right reason, and right reason in these things is φρόνησις. Socrates therefore thought that all virtues were λόγος[. . .], but we say that they are accompanied by (μετά) λόγος.[53] (1144b 25–30)

This "small change" is of decisive importance, as all have observed; it means placing a very close implication between ἕξις and λόγος, habit and reasoning.

Aristotle's position, too, is expressed almost in the form of a syllogism: if we start, as Aristotle does, from line b 25, where the term ἕξις is the subject, we obtain the following scheme:

A an ἕξις accompanied by correct λόγος is virtue (b 26–27);
B correct λόγος in this case is φρόνησις (b 27–28);

C [an ἕξις accompanied by φρόνησις is virtue]
(not said explicitly).

Here Aristotle does not say that correct λόγος is accompanied by φρόνησις he directly identifies ὀρθὸς λόγος with φρόνησις.

4.1. Virtue and Wisdom. Corollaries

From all this Aristotle draws some conclusions: first of all, since Socrates identified ἀρετή with φρόνησις and the latter with ἐπιστήμη, for him the virtues could easily be linked to one another. There are passages, like *pol.* 1260a 20–31, where Aristotle seems to prefer the position of Gorgias, who listed a mutually differing "swarm of virtues"; here, instead, Aristotle too wants to show that it is possible to defend the basic unity of virtues, even starting from his position. Apparently this serves to rebut a possible objection (b 32–35). It appears to be possible to be better endowed with one virtue than with another, if one refers to natural virtues, but this seems impossible when speaking of virtue accompanied by φρόνησις:

> this can happen with regard to natural virtue, but it cannot happen with regard to the virtues for which a man is called absolutely good, since if φρόνησις, which is one, belongs to a man, all the virtues will belong to him. (1144b 35–1145a 2)

In this way Aristotle comes very close to the Socratic position, since, although he denies the equation:

φρόνησις = ἀρετή (b 19–20),

he admits the equation:

to possess φρόνησις = to possess every ἀρετή (a 1–2):

Secondly, Aristotle closes the discussion about the usefulness of φρόνησις by summarizing the main arguments put forward in the course of the discussion. He says:

> it is therefore clear that, even if it were not practical, one would need it [φρόνησις] because it is the virtue of a part,[54] and it is clear that there can be

> no correct choice without φρόνησις and without ethical virtue, inasmuch as the one, in practice, posits the end, and the other the means for the end (1145a 2–6).[55]

Thus, Aristotle's position in *EN* VI 12–13 can be summarized as follows:

1. to make a virtuous choice, both ἀρετή and φρόνησις are necessary;
2. it is not possible to have one of the two elements in one of the two parts of the soul to which they belong, without having also the other element in the other part of the soul; i.e. no one can be φρόνιμος unless the soul's passions are in equilibrium, nor can one's passions be in equilibrium unless one has φρόνησις;
3. both ἀρετή and φρόνησις involve a relation of harmony and collaboration between reason and desire; nonetheless, this relation of collaboration is different in the two cases of determining the end and determining the means to be used to reach the end.

In the determination of the means, as we have seen in section 2, rational deliberation establishes which means are effective for reaching a given end; that is, it connects the end to be reached with the actions that it is up to us to perform (*EE* 1227a 15–18). The desire to perform these actions, and the bodily movements generated by desire, which is the efficient cause (*EN* 1139a 31, *de motu an.* 701a 35), arise only after reason has determined the necessary link between this means in this situation and the desired end. Thus desire, as regards the means, is kindled in conformity with (κατά, 1113a 12) reason. The passage from desire for the end to desire for the means is mediated by a rational analysis that Aristotle calls the ζήτησις of a middle term.

5. End and Mean

We have seen that various commentators suppose that the relation between reason and desire is identical also in the case of ends; in our opinion, in Aristotle things are not like that. The determination of the end is a matter that regards virtue (one who has good ends is virtuous, not skilful or prudent or wise), and in it desire and reason work together, i.e. they determine each other (*EN* 1144b 27, 1178a 16–19), as components of virtue in the strong sense.[56] Desire manifests itself in "pursuit" and "flight" (δίωξις καὶ φυγή, 1139a 22), since a virtuous man finds pleasure in doing good and pain in doing evil. This reaction is measured and determined by reason (*EN* II 3), which establishes the exact measure of the passions and emotional reactions in relation to the time, the situation, the ends and the correct means (*EN* 1106b 21–23).

We see this relation of desire and reason in Books III and IV of *EN*, books in which Aristotle examines the individual virtues. For virtue to exist, there must be a correct relation between habitual desire and λόγος as Aristotle says in *EN* VI 2, the former must desire what the latter affirms, and the right mean of the emotional part of the soul is determined by right reason, in relation to the given circumstances, and the appropriate object, quantity, duration and moment.[57] Λόγος determines the right mean in relation to the end, since the correct determination of the μέσον depends on the end one tends toward; only if the end is virtuous is the μέσον determined correctly. As we know, the end of virtuous action is acting well (εὐπραξία, 1139b 3) and not, as in the case of the productive arts, an external good. In Books III and IV the same concept is expressed by the term καλόν: to act well is to perform fine and praiseworthy actions (τοῦ καλοῦ ενεκα· τοῦτο γὰρ τέλος τῆς ἀρετῆς, 1115b 12–13).[58] It is thus wisdom that determines the right mean of emotions in relation to the end, i.e. to εὐπραξία and καλόν.[59] This formulation is not in conflict with Aristotle's theory, often repeated in the *Ethics,* that the end of human action is happiness, since, as we shall see in detail in Chapter 4, happiness is a whole series of virtuous actions, of εὐπραξίαι thus to pursue εὐπραξία in any individual case is precisely to achieve, in the present instance, one's happiness. There is no opposition between a single act of εὐπραξία and happiness; rather, the relation is one of part to whole.

As we saw in Chapter 1, in virtue reason and desire join forces and become one, like water and wine; they do not merely mix, like water and oil. But they do so in proportions that vary with the situation. This can be seen if we ask which of the two faculties, in the various virtues, causes error by its malfunctioning. In all virtues error consists in an improper reaction of desire, which wins over λόγος but there are virtues such as courage and, in part, temperance, in which it is due mainly to the force of the passions (1115b 26, 1119a 3 and b 5–10). In other cases, instead, there is a deficiency of λόγος (1115b 12–13, 1119a 20, 1126a 1), which does not manage to dominate desire and gives rise to foolish behavior.[60]

Aristotle's theory aims to rule out the possibility of deliberating passionlessly about the end to be pursued, in the way a mathematician analyzes a problem. The orientation to good action depends on φρόνησις, which takes its ends from virtue, which is determined by a λόγος which is, in its turn, φρόνησις. To many, especially in the nineteenth century, this has seemed to be a vicious circle.

Let us collect our ideas. In many passages Aristotle clearly shows that he understands the structure of practical reasoning as being similar to that of theoretical reasoning: both start from first principles that are not the result of reasoning or syllogisms, but are given, and then draw conclusions from them.[61] In the case of theoretical reasoning, the principles are universal judgments about reality; in the case of practical thinking, they are general practical ends of such a nature that, as we shall see in Chapter 3, they are able to generate action programs which the individual agent can then implement.

Aristotle does not explicitly or extensively deal with the origin of the practical principle, though the question is very important for contemporary critics, and has been much discussed. He repeats several times that virtue provides the ends and wisdom finds the means; his interest is decidedly focused on the ways in which practical choices and concrete actions are determined. We may, however, make an attempt at explanation, starting from some hints contained in his works, and basing our hypothesis largely on the analogy with theoretical thought.

In theoretical reflection, a special cognitive faculty of the rational soul, called νοῦς, takes a certain propositional content as the beginning of the deductive process. According to some authors, in practical thinking the same role is played by another type of practical νοῦς, having as its object the ends of human action. As we shall show in more detail in Chapter 3, we do not believe this is the case. The passage (1143a 35–b 2) in which Aristotle is supposed to have talked about this practical νοῦς, assigning it as its object the principles of ethical action, is rather obscure, and can be more convincingly interpreted if we exclude this hypothesis. We shall see that Aristotle does, indeed, admit the existence of a practical νοῦς, but he does not consider the first principles of action to be its object.

On the other hand, there are many passages (very clear ones, too) where Aristotle says that virtue provides the end of human action, and in our opinion these passages are to be taken seriously. They adequately describe the way in which the ends are assumed, not by a transcendental agent, but by noble and respectable individuals who really existed, like Pericles or Ischomachos, the "perfect gentleman" Xenophon speaks of.

But what is meant by saying that the virtue of character, which is a state of excellence of the emotional part of the soul, provides the practical principles? Some have maintained that this is tantamount to giving the emotions and desires a cognitive function, and at a very high level. This opinion does not seem acceptable either; it seems to be, in a way, the extreme opposite of the abovementioned interpretation, which made practical principles into an object of noetic intuition.

The fact that practical reasoning is based on the assumption of a principle that is neither demonstrated nor the result of λόγος does not, in our opinion, mean that a person undertaking practical reflection starts from a state of mental void, as is implied in Aristotle's description of induction, and of the grasping of the principles by theoretical νοῦς (*De anima* 430a 1), and that he then fills this void with a practical principle, given by some psychic faculty designed to do this. It means, rather, that a given propositional content, already present in the mind of the individual as a simple opinion or notion, at a certain point is assumed as a practical principle, and receives the status of an end. The sources of this propositional content may be personal experience, education, or the laws of the city. From these sources one draws the opinion that certain kinds of behavior are good, and acceptable to the members of the community. For its part, the community tends to support this idea by a complicated mechanism of praise and blame, punishments and rewards. This is the way in which a predisposition to assume practical ends correctly is created in the agent's psyche.

Our hypothesis, then, is that, according to Aristotle, virtue in general can, in a given situation, take some non-practical, pre-existing δόξα as a practical principle, making it into the object of desire, and therefore turning it into an end (cf. p. 69).

It seems to us that this hypothesis is suggested also by one of the crucial passages of *EN,* chapter VII 3, which we shall discuss in the Appendix to Chapter 3. Even the passage of *metaph.* 1072a 26 used by Loening to confirm his interpretation does not contradict what is affirmed here. Virtue, as Aristotle says in *EE* VIII 1, cannot suggest the contents for φρόνησις, as it lacks a necessary additional element, and it is the excellence of the emotional part of the soul; but it could transform a notion or a mere theoretical judgment into a practical principle, assigning it the role of an end, and making it the object of βούλησις (rational desire).

From the point of view of their relation with desire, the two functions of φρόνησις can easily be distinguished. As part of ethical virtue, φρόνησις is on the same plane as desire and what is known as "natural virtue"; indeed, only if one is well brought up and takes pleasure in performing good actions will desire take as its end the content of a correct judgment regarding human good (*EN* II 1–3). But as the faculty that deliberates and finds the means, φρόνησις governs over desire. In this case desire depends on wisdom, and must take as its object what φρόνησις has shown to be an effective means for attaining the proposed end. In the choice of the action to be performed, there is a moment when reason has priority, and desire adapts itself to it. This occurs in the analysis of a given situation that is known as "deliberation"; substantially, it consists in finding one or more chains of efficient and final causes that connect the end we set ourselves to the situation in which we find ourselves. We thus have two fixed terms *e* (the end) and *s* (the situation), and we must find a series of intermediate terms *m1, m2, m3,. . . , mn* (the means) that can connect *e* to *s* in such a way that *e* is achieved. This activity is similar to the search for the middle terms of a theoretical syllogism; hence it is a stochastic and conjectural procedure. It is carried out, as we shall see more clearly in the next chapter, through a series of ever more detailed redefinitions of the end in relation to the concrete situation, specifying what the general aim we have set ourselves means here and now. The process ends when one finds an action that can be put into practice immediately and that serves to achieve the proposed end. The two functions of φρόνησις are not too dissimilar, since in both cases φρόνησις details and specifies the practical contents, which are otherwise too general to give rise to an action.

Deliberation thus takes the form of a plan, i.e. an anticipation, inside the mind, of a series of steps, consisting of actions aimed at achieving a desired state of affairs. This planning is based on a series of reasonable expectations regarding the results of each single behavior; it is based on a series of notions that are "by and large" valid, which tell us what doing one thing or another is useful for, and what are the good or bad results of undertaking a certain course of action. Even though they are not as stable as natural events, human behaviors must be rather constant; otherwise, action and interaction would become impossible. This explains why, in Aristotle's philosophy, a relative stability in the world of human action is an indispensable condition for action to be possible; otherwise, it would become merely a series of irrational body movements. This is also why Aristotle insists so much on experience, i.e. on the observation of certain regularities connecting action and response, as a necessary condition for acting in a morally assessable way, as well as for practicing wisdom.

It should be noted that an action performed may very well not be anything external or purely instrumental to the end to be achieved; it may be a partial or particular actualization of the end. If, after a meal, one takes a walk in order to keep fit, taking a walk is not, at first sight, part of keeping fit, but rather a means or a therapy for reaching the end. But if one goes to the library to read the latest book published on Aristotle's ethics, this act is both a means and a part of that examination of the authoritative opinions of ancient wise men, which in its turn is a moment in the dialectic and philosophical discussion that constitutes happiness. Therefore, going to the library and reading the latest book published on Aristotle's ethics is one of the possible ways of being happy.

CHAPTER 3

THE PRACTICAL SYLLOGISM

1. Perhaps It Doesn't Exist. No One Knows What It Is About

Few subjects have aroused as much controversy among Aristotle's interpreters as the practical syllogism (hereafter: PS). On this topic extremely different positions have been taken by scholars of considerable stature; the PS has been called both "one of Aristotle's best discoveries" and "one of Aristotle's less happy inventions."[1]

Uncertainty surrounds both the function and even the existence of the PS. While in the traditional exegesis it was viewed as the very form of practical reasoning, in 1968 W. F. R. Hardie dedicated an entire chapter of his book *Aristotle's Ethical Theory* to showing that, in the general economy of Aristotle's ethics, the role of the PS is rather limited. Interpreting the PS as the application of a rule to a specific case in view of an end, Hardie maintains that this cannot be the general form of every practical reasoning.[2] For his part, Kenny has held that the expression "PS" is particularly unhappy, if it is used to indicate the form of practical reasoning according to Aristotle: "'Practical syllogisms'," he maintains, "are not, and most of them do not even look like, syllogisms."[3]

There are some arguments to support those who want to eliminate the expression "PS" from Aristotle's ethical vocabulary. The term as such never appears in Aristotle's writings, and in the treatises of the *Organon* there is no mention of this kind of syllogism. Aristotle lists apodeictic, dialectical and rhetorical syllogisms (*a. pr.*, 68b 10–11); he even calls eristic arguments "syllogisms," though properly speaking they are not syllogisms, since they seem to conclude but do not. But he makes no mention of the PS. In the *Topics,* to tell the truth, Aristotle distinguishes three types of premises and problems: ethical, physical and dialectical (105b 19–25). As an example of an ethical premise he gives the following: "whether one must obey one's parents rather than the laws." But, clearly, this is a distinction of the subjects to be discussed in dialectical meetings; it has no direct relation with actual conduct, like that which should be achieved in the PS. On the other hand, in the *Analytica Priora* Aristotle states that the ὁδός, i.e. the way or method he describes, is identical for every subject, both for those connected with love of knowledge (περὶ φιλοσοφίαν) and those connected with any τέχνη or discipline (μάθημα) (46a 3–4). And in the *Sophistici elenchi* (*Sophistical Refutations*), Aristotle admits that there are false syllogisms both in the theoretical sciences, such as geometry, and in the practical sciences, such as medicine (170a 30–34). Does this perhaps mean that practical reasonings, or at least some of them—the ones carried out μετὰ τέχνης (*EE* II 10 1227a 6–13)—proceed according to the syllogistic model?

Aristotle uses the term συλλογισμός to indicate practical reasoning: in *EE* he says that there is neither συλλογισμός nor λόγος for the end. This would seem to imply that there are both for what-leads-to-the-end, i.e. the "means" (1227b 24–25). In *EN* it is said that one can reach the good also by means of a συλλογισμὸς ψευδής (1142b 22), which says what is to be done, but not how to do it. Further on, in 1144a 31–34, he speaks of συλλογισμοὶ τῶν πρακτῶν, i.e. the reasonings, or syllogisms, that regard actions. In *de an.* 434a 7, Aristotle states that the deliberative imagination (φαντασία βουλευτική), which is part of the process that generates action, is proper to man and not to the other animals. Men possess it, and this kind of φαντασία is a δόξα. In the treatise *On the Movement of Animals,* the term συλλογίζεσθαι is used to refer both to theoretical study and to practical reasoning, since the two have a similar structure (701a 7–13). In *EN* 1149a 33 it is even said that when θυμός (impetuous desire) gives rise to an action, it does so ὥσπερ συλλογισάμενος, in a fashion similar to that of (practical) reasoning; the same idea is expressed, in different words, in *de motu an.* 701a 29–33. This comparison of a non-rational motion of the soul to a reasoning process is not a peculiarity of *EN;* also in the treatise called *De memoria et reminiscentia* it is stated that remembering is οἷον συλλογισμός τις, like a kind of reasoning (453a 10 et seq.). We shall return to this passage later.

In the above-mentioned texts we have translated the term συλλογισμός as "reasoning" rather that as "syllogism." It seems that Aristotle uses the term συλλογισμός in the field of theory to mean what, according to the definition of *a. pr.* 24b 18–20, is a deduction in general, rather than a "syllogism" in the strict sense: "συλλογισμός is a reasoning process in which, given certain things, because they are as they are, something different necessarily follows." However, he tries to demonstrate (I 23) that all deductions made according to the definition just quoted must take the form of one of the three types of syllogisms (*a. pr.*

41b 1–3, cf. 44b 7–8).[4] Therefore, even if the meaning of the term συλλογισμός in Aristotle is wider than that of the modern term "syllogism," it is nonetheless true that he believes it can be shown that every deduction is made in accordance with one of the three types of syllogism, and that the "syllogism," as we understand the term, is the basic structure of συλλογισμός.[5]

But can it be maintained that also the practical συλλογισμός follows these rules, and that the three types of syllogisms dealt with in the *Analytica Priora* are the rigorous expression also of practical reasoning? That is, is it possible to trace the lineage of the reasoning that gives rise to action back to one of the types described in the *Analytica*? The discussion has mainly developed around *de motu an.*, in which we find examples like:

I need an overcoat
a greatcoat is an overcoat

I need a greatcoat (701a 17–18).

Many have denied that this example can be reduced to a valid syllogism; even those who have held that such a reduction is possible have had to introduce a series of important changes in the examples given by Aristotle.[6] It thus remains to be asked if modern exegetes, when they speak of the "PS," are not making an unwarranted translation of the Greek word συλλογισμός, which should be interpreted here as a generic "reasoning process." We would thus have a practical "reasoning process," whose rules would bear no relation to the rules of scientific deduction as described in the *Analytica Priora*.

This seems a bit excessive. On several occasions Aristotle compares scientific and practical reasoning, thus implying that there are important analogies between the two. Moreover, in many cases he uses technical terms taken from the vocabulary of logic to describe the phases and elements of practical reasoning.[7] Aristotle states that a PS is composed of δύο τρόποι τῶν προτάσεων, two types of premises, one that is καθόλου, universal, and one that is κατὰ μέρος or καθ' ἕκαστα, particular. Such premises are also called, more generally, two ὑπολήψεις, assumptions, and it is repeated twice that the particular one (καθ' ἕκαστα) regards τὰ πρακτά, the different actions.[8] In *de motu an.* a further distinction is made: this treatise, too, speaks of two premises, which are, however, subdivided into διά τε τοῦ ἀγαθοῦ and διὰ τοῦ δυνατοῦ, regarding the good and regarding what is possible, respectively.[9]

Aristotle says that the major premise is an ἀρχή, a principle (*EE* 1227b 8; *EN* 1144a 32), consisting of a λόγος ἐν τῇ ψυχῇ, a reasoning inside the soul (*metaph.* 1032b 5; *de an.* 434a 16). This λόγος is defined in various ways, some of which are general, while others are more specific: it is a διανοητόν, an object of reflection (*de motu an.* 700b 24), a θέσις, thesis (*EN* 1112b 15: θέμενοι) and, more precisely, a ὑπόθεσις, a position or hypothesis (*EN* 1144a 33–36; *EE* 1227b 25 and 29–30). Aristotle repeatedly compares this kind of ὑπόθεσις to that of the theoretical sciences, and he explicitly states that the term should be understood in the same sense as it has been in the *Analytica* (*EE* 1227a 8–11, cf. b 29–30). That is: "A hypothesis is a kind of thesis that assumes one or the other side of a contradiction, as for example when I say that something is or is not, while a definition is a thesis that does without this" (*a.po.* 72a 18–21).

In its turn the minor premise is an ἔσχατος ὅρος, an ultimate term (*EN* 1142a 26), a λογιζόμενον, or object of rational calculation (*EE* 1226a 33–b 2; *de an.* 434a 7–10; *de motu an.* 701a 26–28); it is the object of σκέψις, research, investigation (*EE* 1226b 28; 1227a 10–12; b 13–18) and of νόησις, intellectual reflection in general (*metaph.* 1032b 17). It derives from αἴσθησις, sensation, or rather from a particular form of it (*EN* 1142a 27; 1143b 5).

The middle term is the object of ζήτησις and ἀνάλυσις, research, analysis (*EN* 1112b 20, 22, 23–24, 28–29, 1113a 5, VI 9 in general); it is ἀφωρισμένον and κριθέν, the object of delimitation and judgment (*EN* 1113a 3–4).

The conclusion is called συμπέρασμα, i.e. conclusion (*EN* 1147a 27; *de motu an.* 701a 11–12, 20, 23), and when this term is used, it is specified that the συμπέρασμα is a πρᾶξις, an action. It συμβαίνει, i.e. it is derived from the principles (*EN* 1147a 35).

It therefore becomes difficult to maintain the above-mentioned thesis. The use of technical terminology suggests that Aristotle is thinking of the PS as being something structurally similar to the type of reasoning described in the *Analytica Priora*. Nonetheless, even if at this point it seems quite justified to speak of the PS in the context of Aristotle's ethics, there are still strong doubts regarding the opinion, held also by some contemporary exegetes,[10] that the PS is the "form" of practical reasoning in general and of deliberation in particular. This thesis can be formulated in various ways but, at least in some commentators, it means that, when faced with a practical problem, an agent should—at least in theory—deduce, starting from the supreme principles of human action, the good deed appropriate for the case at hand, proceeding systematically in accordance with the rules of the theoretical syllogism.[11] We have already mentioned the position of Hardie, who on the contrary states that the PS is not even part of deliberation;[12] more recently, Cooper has proposed an alternative model, in which the PS chronologically follows deliberation and consists in applying the outcome of it (the choice of a certain "type" of action, according to Cooper) to an individual case.[13] This model has not met with great success, but the idea that the PS is a way of formally representing the reasoning that leads to a specific actual act, whether it be human or—in a derived form—animal, has been given great consideration, and has even been accepted by several scholars. It has therefore been held that the PS is useful for giving a theoretical model of human action.[14] As we shall see later, this approach to the PS seems plausible and useful also to us; but it also seems too limited to the data that can be derived from *de motu an.* Moreover, it hardly seems plausible to us to completely separate the PS from deliberation. Indeed, in various places Aristotle connects the two topics (*EE* 1227b 24–25; *EN* 1142b 22, 1144b 31–34; *de an.* 434a 10–12). There is also a text (albeit not often quoted) in which he states that deliberating is a συλλογισμός τις (*de mem.* 453a 7–14), an expression which we take to mean "a sort of syllogism" and not a full-fledged syllogism. In this passage deliberating is compared to remembering, which was spoken about earlier, inasmuch as both are forms of ζήτησις. As we shall see in more detail later on, the point of similarity between deliberation and remembering seems here to be the fact that in both psychic events a particular experience is viewed in the light of something else.

Aristotle says several times that deliberation is a ζήτησις in our opinion, this enables us to hold on to the idea that the PS is a formal representation of the psychic process that generates action, while including deliberation in this process. As we said in the previous chapter, deliberation is the "search" for the middle terms (*a. po.* II 2).[15] This search does not necessarily have to be carried out in syllogistic form, but it coincides with the stochastic and conjectural phase of practical knowledge which Aristotle so insists on.

This interpretation must now be defended. It is therefore necessary to examine the PS, distinguishing the nature and function of the two premises that compose it, the link that unites them and that binds them to the conclusion, and the nature of the conclusion itself. An Appendix (p. 100 et seq.) will compare the results of this analysis with Aristotle's theory of the weakness of the will (*EN* VII 3).

2. The Major Premise

2.1. Analysis of *EE* II 10

EE II 10 contains a lengthy discussion of deliberated choice (προαίρεσις). Unlike the parallel passage in *EN* (III 3), this text fortunately gives some information about the nature of the major premise of the PS. We shall therefore begin our discussion with it.

Both in *EE* and in *EN,* Aristotle denies that προαίρεσις, choice, can be identified with δόξα, opinion. But in *EN* III 2, 1112a 11 et seq., he refuses to deal with the problem of whether δόξα can precede choice, while in *EE* he tackles this question as well.[16] Among the various arguments used to exclude an identification of προαίρεσις with δόξα, there is one we are interested in:

> and δόξα and βούλησις (opinion and rational desire) have this[17] in common: no one ever makes an end the object of choice, but rather what leads to the end. What I mean is that, for example, no one chooses to be healthy, but rather to take a walk, or to sit down, in order to be healthy [. . .] and in general anyone who makes a choice always makes it clear what (τί) and for the sake of what (τίνος ἕνεκα) he chooses.[18] The 'for what' is that for which one chooses something else; the 'what' is what one chooses for something else. One desires mainly[19] the end [= the 'for what'] and believes that one must be healthy and happy [. . .]. Desire in accordance with reason (βούλεσθαι) and opinion (δόξα) are mainly concerned with the end, not the choice (1226a 7–17).

Since choosing is choosing something for something else, Aristotle admits that there is a ὑπόληψις τοῦ διὰ τί, an assumption regarding the reason (1226b 23), which in this context is an assumption of the final cause. This assumption of the end occurs in the deliberative part of the soul, not in the scientific and contemplative part, as is said in the following passage:

> in fact, the part of the soul that keeps its eyes on a certain cause (τὸ θεωρητικὸν αἰτίας τινός) is deliberative (βουλευτικόν)[20] (1226b 25–26).

Possession of the final cause is a necessary condition for deliberation to take place. The thing-for-which is such a cause:

> for example, the transport of goods is a cause of walking, if one walks for this purpose. Therefore those who have no aim in mind do not deliberate (1226b 28–30).

Since it is a cause and that-for-which something is done, the end is ἀρχή and ὑπόθεσις, principle and hypothesis, or else it is derived from an ἀρχή and from a ὑπόθεσις.[21] This is stated in the following passage:

> Indeed, whoever deliberates, always deliberates for the sake of something, and whoever deliberates always has a purpose, in relation to which he examines what is useful; by contrast, there is no deliberation about the end, which is both starting point and hypothesis (ἀρχὴ καὶ ὑπόθεσις), just like the hypotheses of the theoretical sciences. We have briefly spoken of this at the beginning of the treatise[22] and, with exactness, in the *Analytica*. On the contrary, everyone carries out an investigation (σκέψις) regarding what leads to the end, whether he follows the dictates of some skill (τέχνη), or whether he does without it, as for example when one deliberates about whether to make war or not. (1227a 6–13)

One may therefore draw, from this chapter of *EE* II 10, the well-founded opinion that for Aristotle the end of action is the object of ὑπόληψις, a consistent assumption in the association between a δόξα and one of the forms of desire.[23]

This in part confirms the conclusions of Chapter 2, as we shall see in more detail later on. The seat of this δόξα is the part of the soul called in *EN* VI τὸ λογιστικόν or τὸ δοξαστικόν, the calculating part or the opinion-forming part (1139a 12 and 14, 1140b 26, 1144b 14). By means of this ὑπόληψις it is posited that a certain state of affairs, or behavior, is good or bad, and this position is associated with an act of desire. This ὑπόθεσις is a δόξα, and not an ἐπιστήμη, i.e. the result of an opinion and not of a science, since even an apparent good can be taken as an end.[24] In our opinion, the assumption of the end in the forms indicated here is the major premise of the PS.

To state that an end is composed of δόξα + ὄρεξις (opinion + desire) is tantamount to saying that it, as such, usually is not able to generate an action immediately (cf. *EE* 1227a 18 et seq.).[25] Although it concerns a practical good, the major premise, in most cases, is not practical, in the sense that it does not immediately give rise to an action. Only deliberation and φρόνησις, practical knowledge, can transform this δόξα into a principle of action. Deliberation and ὑπόληψις of the end differ precisely because, though ὑπόληψις may remain a mere statement, φάσις (1142b 13–14), deliberation is a search for the middle term to which desire is to be directed, in view of a concrete action.

2.2. The Two Forms of the Major Premise

The search for the middle term from which an action is derived is necessarily connected with the nature and form of the major premise. The various examples that Aristotle gives of this major premise can be grouped into two different types. There are, first, premises that assume, in general, that

(A) δεῖ τὸν τοιοῦτον τὸ τοιόνδε πράττειν

(= "it is fitting for such a person to do such a thing," *de an.* 434a 16–18).

This formulation of the major premise, in the case of a correct practical reasoning, expresses the virtuous action related to the person that acts, and the mean determined by ὀρθὸς λόγος, correct reasoning.[26] In the example given in *EN* II 8, the expression δεῖ τὸν τοιοῦτον τὸ τοιόνδε πράττειν corresponds to statements to the effect that, in any given particular situation, one must find the mean between δίωξις and φυγή, the desire to pursue and the desire to escape:

> for example, in feeling fear and courage, in desiring, getting angry, feeling pity and in general feeling pleasure and pain, there is an excess and a defect, neither of which is good. Instead, doing so when one should, for the right reason and towards the right people and for the right ends and in the way one should, this is the mean and the best thing, which is a property of virtue. (1106b 18–23)

Formulation (A), which in a more or less complete form is found in various works, contains the word δεῖ, which has been interpreted[27] as an absolute ethical imperative, but which more probably merely indicates the behavior that befits a certain moral or social category of people.[28] This δεῖ can easily be replaced by the statement that doing a certain thing is ἀγαθόν, or καλόν, or by the verbal suffix -τέον, or other similar forms.[29] Sometimes the formula is expressed in an abbreviated and incomplete form,[30] i.e. in such a way as to indicate the τοιόνδε ("such a thing") and not the τοιοῦτον ("such a person"). In these cases it is understood that the kind of person who is assigned a certain end is clear from the context, or else that a certain end is good for everybody (*EN* 1147a 29–32; 1149a 33–34). In *de motu an.* 701a 16–18, Aristotle seems to describe, as in the examples already given, two major premises, in which it is said that a τοιόνδε must be fulfilled, or that it is right that it should be fulfilled, μοί, by me. Here there is no indication of the kind of agent that a certain end befits; it is at once assumed that the individual in question should have just that kind of end. These premises are clearly incomplete and would need to be clarified with the addition of other premises and further information.[31]

In *EN* VI 12, 1144a 31–32, on the other hand, the major premise is formulated differently:

> indeed, syllogisms[32] which concern actions, having a principle (ἀρχή), sound like this: 'given that (ἐπειδή) the end and the best thing are of this kind (τοιόνδε) . . .' whatever they may be (let us suppose they are anything at all, for our argument's sake).

In this passage the expression τὸ ἄριστον appears, and here again some scholars[33] have understood this in an ethical and normative sense, supposing that by this expression Aristotle meant to point out the end of human existence; but it is not necessary to interpret the passage in this way. Indeed, Aristotle says that the τέλος to be assumed may very well be anything; he indicates this by the words ὁτιδήποτε and τὸ τυχόν, "what one wants," and "what happens." What is called τὸ ἄριστον, the best thing, is not the best thing in an absolute sense, the ultimate end of human life; or, at least, though the expression may also indicate this end, it does not necessarily indicate only this ultimate end. The expression indicates the end of practical reasoning in general, οὗ ἕνεκα (that-for-which): as a τέλος in itself and not in relation to anything else, it is always an ἄριστον (*EN* 1106b 22; *EE* 1218b 10), even if it is not the best end of all.[34]

The formulation in VI 12 tends to emphasize the necessary connection with the minor premise, as can be seen if it is compared with a series of other passages. In general, therefore, the major premise can be expressed also in the following form:

> (B) ἐπειδὴ τοιόνδε τὸ τέλος [ἀνάγκη τάδε γένεσθαι καὶ ὑπάρχειν](= "since the end is of such a type [it is necessary that these things be generated and present]")

The major premise is not found in these exact terms in the *corpus,* but many passages express it by means of examples, usually that of "health," as in *EE* I 8, 1218b 19–20 ("since being healthy is this thing [τοδί], it is necessary [ἀνάγκη] that this [other] thing [τόδε] be useful for it"), cf. 11, 1227b 30–31 ("since one must heal this person, it is necessary that there be this [τοδὶ ὑπάρξαι] if that is to exist"); *metaph.* VII 7, 1032b 6–7 ("since this [τοδί] is health, it is necessary, if one is to be healthy, that there should be this [τοδὶ ὑπάρξαι]"); *phys.* II 9, 200b 2–3 ("since this is health, this other thing must needs be generated and exist").

If we compare formulations (A) and (B), we note that both of them contain the specification of an end (τοιόνδε) and join another element to it. In formulation (A) there is an indication of the kind of person who should manifest a certain type of behavior. For example, it is proper for a brave warrior to fight off the enemy. Formulation (B), instead, indicates the definition of the end, on the basis of which one can identify the "necessary" conditions for its realization (cf. p. 90). For example, since fighting off the enemy means not to let them over the walls, such-and-such defensive measures are necessary. Formulation (A) tends to emphasize the role of the agent; it is therefore somewhat more "prescriptive" than formulation (B), which is slightly more technical. This explains why there is some justification for the opinion of those who wonder whether formulation (B) contains only the major premise.[35]

There are, however, some Aristotelian texts, such as *EE* I 8, 1218b 17 et seq., quoted in part above, and *de motu an.* 701a 21 ("if there is to be a cloak, first there must be this") where formulation (B) is clearly treated as the major premise of the PS. In our opinion, formulations (A) and (B) are not incompatible.

But this point is disputed. Grant[36] also noticed that there are two forms of the major premise of the PS. He stated that the major premise can express either a general rule or an end. But, he added, in reality the two forms coincide, since the expression of a principle, as for example "abstention from swallowing heavy foods is a good" may be considered both a rule and an end. On the other hand, in a well-known article Allan objected that "following a rule" is not the same as "pursuing an end," except in a very special sense—if, that is, one takes it as being equivalent to "having as an end obedience to the rule." Moreover, according to Allan, the contrary is not true, and the end is never a universal and a rule.[37] Allan therefore held that in the *Nicomachean Ethics* there is a progressive movement in the discussion, like that in Plato's dialogues. In his opinion, Aristotle considers the formulation given in *EN* III 3—which corresponds roughly to (B)—as only a first step in the explanation of the PS, which was later to be replaced, in *EN* VI, by a more complete formulation, similar to (A). Allan's reconstruction is not supported by the text (in fact, the most general example of formulation (B) is found in *EN* VI) and has been much criticized.[38] Today it is no longer commonly accepted.

Also Gauthier and Jolif, in their commentaries, pointed out the existence of two different formulations. However, they deny that one can speak of an evolution in Aristotle's thinking from type (B) to type (A), since the two formulas are present both in *EN* and in *de motu an.*, as well as in *de anima.* Gauthier thinks that the two formulations correspond to two different forms of causality: the efficient cause (type B) and the final cause (type A). So much for Gauthier.[39]

In our opinion the two formulations are not incompatible, because—Allan's statements notwithstanding—the identification of an end in formulation (B) is, in a certain sense, the indication of a universal, of which the so-called "means" are particular realizations. And, vice versa, in formulation (A) the identification of a particular case of the end (τοιόνδε) is tantamount to finding a way of realizing the end, expressed in the major premise in universal form by means of δόξα + ὄρεξις, with respect to a single case. To support this thesis, however, we need a more precise idea of the nature of the minor premise. We shall therefore come back to this later.

If this position can provisionally be accepted as true, it follows that Aristotle can legitimately use either formulation (A) or formulation (B) of the major premise, according to the aspect of the PS that, in each case, he wishes to emphasize. Formulation (A) is used when he wants to express the "necessity"[40] or, rather, the inevitability that, given certain premises, a certain type of action derives from them; this form appears in the physical-psychological explanations of movement and human action, and when the subject of the weakness of the will is discussed. Despite its outer form (ἐπειδὴ . . . ἀνάγκη) linked to the concept of "necessity" (cf. pp. 70 and 90) understood in a broad sense, formulation (B) is more concerned with determination of the "means," and sums up the results of the ζήτησις of the middle term. This formulation is used as a point of departure when useful examples are given to describe deliberation, choice, and in general the functions of φρόνησις. It is also present in those passages that focus mainly on technical action, as in the case of sciences that have no particular ἀκρίβεια and leave room for deliberation. We shall come back to this distinction later. But there is no reason to reduce the premises formulated under (B) to nothing but the premises of technical and productive reasoning in the strict sense.

2.3 The Origin of the Major Premise

In *EE* I 8, 1218b 13, it is said that the τέλος, or end, which is the object of the major premise is the principle of the supreme science (κυρία πασῶν), i.e. of "politics, or economics, or φρόνησις." On this occasion Aristotle defers discussion of the differences between these disciplines. We have already mentioned (pp. 69–70) the fact that, since the end and the best thing are principles of practical reasoning, some scholars have held that these principles could be acquired in the same way one acquires the first principles of the theoretical sciences, that is, by noetic intuition. In this respect Ando has compared Aristotle to Kant. Cooper has picked up an old argument of Burnet's, and has stated; (1) that the major premises of the syllogism derive from noetic intuition, and (2) that this intuition is a result of the dialectical discussions typical of the schools of philosophy; these discussions lead one to grasp the principles, and enable one to justify them. Even more recently it has been maintained that, although Aristotle states that the source of the principles of practical knowledge is ἐθισμός, "getting used to" something, i.e. an event that also involves the emotional part of the human psyche, this "acquiring of habits" is a form of intuition.[41]

Kenny is one of those who maintain that there is noetic intuition of the practical first principles. He has attempted to base his interpretation on one of the most difficult passages of *EN* VI. The relevant text for this issue is in Chapter 11:

> νοῦς deals with the extremes on both sides, and indeed, there is νοῦς and not λόγος both of the first ὅροι[42] and of the last; the one, with regard to demonstrations, deals with the first and immutable ὅροι, while the other[43] with regard to the practical [premises][44] deals with the last extreme, and what can be otherwise, and the other premise.[45] Indeed, these are first principles of the end, since what is universal derives from single cases, and of such cases one must have αἴσθησις, an αἴσθησις that is νοῦς. (1143a 35—b 5)

Kenny maintains that here νοῦς has to do with the "major premise" (p. 171), which contains a reference to the end, and that this "having to do with" corresponds to the intuition of axioms in the speculative sciences, such as mathematics; moreover, he takes the expression τῆς ἑτέρας προτάσεως to mean "the other premise," i.e. the other major premise (the practical one), as opposed to the theoretical major premise.

Actually, the text should be interpreted both in reference to the subject of the chapter where it occurs (VI 11), and by comparison with the other occurrences of the term νοῦς in *EN* VI. As for the first point, it is well-known that the expression νοῦν ἔχειν ("to have sense") is frequently used by Attic authors to mean "to behave sensibly." This can also be expressed by: εὖ φρονεῖν or σωφρονεῖν, i.e. to be φρόνιμος, as opposed to acting strangely, indecently or in a self-destructive way. This latter behavior can easily be labeled as παράνοια, μανία, i.e. madness, foolishness and so on. "To have judgment" is opposed to the state of madness, in the weak sense that this pejorative term has in expressions such as "Are you mad?"[46] In such fixed expressions the term νοῦς does not indicate the faculty that grasps theoretical principles; it takes on a meaning close to that of terms like γνώμη and σύνεσις (cf. *EN* 1112a 21). In the chapter that we are examining Aristotle clearly wants to fit this expression (νοῦν ἔχειν) into his conceptual scheme; this can be clearly seen in lines 1143a 25–28: "All (these) habitual states are addressed, as is logical, to the same thing. In fact we ascribe to the same people γνώμη, and σύνεσις, and φρόνησις, and νοῦς, saying that they have understanding and sense (γνώμην ἔχειν καὶ νοῦν) and are wise and perspicacious (φρονίμους καὶ συνετούς)."

Therefore, in these expressions the term νοῦς has a different meaning from the one it has in the rest of *EN* VI, for example in 1139a 14–17. There it is said that νοῦς is one of the five ways of grasping the truth by means of affirming and denying. In other passages it is said that νοῦς, in particular, has as its object the ἀρχαί of the theoretical sciences (VI 4) and that, added to ἐπιστήμη, it gives σοφία (1141a 19). The differences between the two senses of the term νοῦς can easily be recognized if one considers (1) that, understood in the sense of Chapter VI 3–8, νοῦς is opposed to φρόνησις, and (2) that in the sense found in Chapter VI 11, it corresponds to φρόνησις.

Aristotle states that νοῦς is opposed to φρόνησις in VI 8, 1142a 25–30. After having stated that φρόνησις is not ἐπιστήμη, since it deals with the practical extreme (ἔσχατον) and not the universal (1142a 23–25), he maintains that φρόνησις is opposed (ἀντίκειται) to νοῦς, which deals with the ὅροι that cannot be deduced by λόγος. Therefore, φρόνησις deals with the other extremes, particular and practical, for which there is αἴσθησις and not (theoretical) νοῦς. Such αἴσθησις, in our opinion, must be regarded as something different from mere sense perception.[47] We shall return to this point later. Now we wish to point out that it is not possible to ascribe all three of the following theses to Aristotle:

1. φρόνησις corresponds to αἴσθησις,
2. φρόνησις is opposed to νοῦς,
3. αἴσθησις corresponds to νοῦς

unless the term νοῦς is given two different meanings in (2) and (3).

The νοῦς Aristotle is talking about here is the capacity to grasp the particular meanings of practical situations; for this reason it is attributed to the same people who have γνώμη, σύνεσις and φρόνησις (1143a 26–28). The object of all these faculties is individual, practical cases (τὰ καθ' ἕκαστα, τὰ πρακτά, 1143a 33–35), i.e. the object of voluntary behavior (cf. 1110b 6–7).[48] The type of (practical) νοῦς we are talking about here is acquired by experience (1143b 6–9), whereas science is acquired by means of διδασκαλία and in similar ways. This type of practical νοῦς is not an immediate knowledge of the ultimate ends and first principles of human action, but is like a general knowledge of the facts of life.[49] It is defined as a sort of αἴσθησις, and it seems to us very much like that practical ἐμπειρία described, with the usual medical example, at the beginning of the *Metaphysics:*

> to formulate the judgment (τὸ ἔχειν ὑπόλεψιν) that this particular thing (τοδί) benefited Callias, who had this particular disease (τηνδί), as well as Socrates and each of many men, is ἐμπειρία. (981a 8–12)

Therefore, in our opinion the passage of *EN* VI 11 discussed here does not regard the major premises of the PS, but rather indicates a kind of knowledge like that of φρόνησις, whose object is particular cases and the minor premise. The expression ἑτέρα πρότασις, found in this passage (1143b 3), is to be interpreted in the simplest way possible, as "minor premise."

On the contrary, the acquisition of practical principles, according to Aristotle, takes place by ἐθισμός (1098b 4). This term indicates the process of social transmission of models of behavior, through a series of rewards and punishments. The combination of δόξα + ὄρεξις, which constitutes the practical principle, whereby virtuous people act in a praiseworthy way, and find pleasure in doing so (1104b 3 et seq.), is transmitted, as we said in Chapter 2, through a series of teachings and pressures. Legislators should pay close attention to this point (1103b 2 et seq.) and accustom citizens to living well.

Therefore, the process of internalizing practical principles, which is what being good substantially consists of,[50] does not take place by a form of noetic intuition, helped along by the reading of *EN* or by attending the lessons of the philosophers. It is rather an acquisition of habits, a stage in the character formation of a good citizen.[51] Although Aristotle emphasizes the practical nature of his treatise (see also, in the passage we are summarizing, lines 1179a 33–b 4), he admits as well that any man who is not a philosopher or a disciple of philosophers, but who has carefully observed what happens, case by case, by means of ἐμπειρία (1180b 17–18), can reach equally good results and behave as a morally upright man. This is why Aristotle says that his λόγοι do not suffice to make men good (1179b 4). The purpose of the treatise is προτρέψασθαι (b 7): to invite and encourage citizens who already have a good character to live a virtuous life. In practical life, teaching (διδαχή) is effective only with personalities that are already oriented rightly (b 23–26).

On the other hand, the work of legislators is also insufficient. They give only general rules, while the character formation of each good citizen must be personalized, and adapted to his character and habits (1180b 13 et seq.). Here, as in *EN* VI 7 and in *metaph.* I 1, we find the idea that in practical affairs there is the following ranking in terms of worth and efficacy:

1. those who possess knowledge of the universal and are experts on individual cases;

2. those who have experience of individual cases but do not possess scientific knowledge of the universal;

3. those who possess the universal in theory and in the abstract, but are not able to relate it to individual cases.

In conclusion, the acquisition of knowledge of practical principles is similar to the process whereby one starts from the experience of particular cases and, by means of an inductive procedure which Aristotle expounds in a rather obscure way,[52] one finally manages to formulate the principles of a science. According to Aristotle, the practical principles are largely already "given"; they are established in a city's laws, in customs, in the teachings of the family and group; they survive as opinions, which must become also the opinions of the agent, both rationally and emotionally, if they are to be actually operative practical principles.

3. The Minor Premise

3.1 Sometimes It Is Not Necessary

In studying the minor premise, it seems useful to examine first of all three cases in which this premise does not appear. For, once we identify their features, we can more easily understand the precise function of the missing premise.

At first sight, these cases seem very different from one another. They are (A) actions governed by certain particular sciences that possess ἀκρίβεια, (B) actions deriving from a particular form of weakness of the will, (C) cases in which the minor premise is only too obvious.[53]

In our opinion (cf. Chapter 2) case (A) falls into the category studied here, since in it there is no deliberation (1112b 1) and, in our interpretation, deliberation is the search for a middle term. Therefore, in such cases we have only the end, and the action that is useful for reaching it. How this happens is explained both in *EN* and in *EE:*

> and with regard to the exact and autonomous sciences, there is no deliberation, as for example, with regard to spelling. In fact, we are in no doubt about how to write [words];[54] (*EN* 1112a 34–b 2)

> what is deliberated on and done is part of 'what depends on us'; for this reason,

> a person might even wonder why doctors deliberate about things they have knowledge of, whereas grammarians do not. The cause is this: error occurs in two ways; either they make a mistake in reasoning, or a mistake in perception, when they do something. Now, in medicine both types of mistakes are possible, whereas in grammar, one can [only] make errors of perception or execution. The discussion could go on indefinitely if one wished to investigate also about these things. (1226a 33–b 2)

Some commentators have confused the error described here with the one Aristotle discusses in *EE* II 11 and in *pol.* VII 13 (see Chapter 2). In those passages Aristotle distinguishes the error that consists in establishing the end incorrectly, from the error that consists in incorrectly determining the means of reaching it; such an error can be committed only in those sciences that require deliberation, and therefore make use of the minor premise. On the contrary, here Aristotle is distinguishing sciences such as medicine, which must deliberate on how to reach the end, since the middle term is not obvious, from sciences such as grammar, which have rigid and precisely determined rules that can be immediately applied to individual cases. For example, if one has to write the name Θεαίτητος, grammar tells us what letters to use—in this case a Θ and not a T. There can be only an error of perception or execution, as when one performs badly what the rule prescribes. A person may think he or she has written a V, when really he/she has written a U (little children often do this).[55] The general rule that establishes the combinations of letters to be used in writing words is valid for every case, and has only to be put into practice.

The same could be said for all the rules that govern ritualized human behaviors, such as ceremonies and the like, as well as for instructions that have to be carried out to the letter, such as directions for using equipment or manuals and military codes of conduct.

Case (B) deals with a special form of ἀκρασία, or "lack of willpower," as we would say today. This occurs when ἀκρασία is the result of impetuosity and not of unreasonable desire (of θυμός and not ἐπιθυμία). In this case, too, one passes directly from the perception of a particular situation to action, without stopping to deliberate and without a minor premise:

> we shall see that ἀκρασία deriving from impetuosity (θυμός) is less shameful than that deriving from desires (ἐπιθυμιῶν). It would, in fact, seem that impetuosity does somehow listen to λόγος, but misunderstands it,[56] like hasty servants, who run away before they have heard the whole order, and then mistakenly carry out what they were told to do; or like dogs who, before knowing whether or not it is a friend at the door, bark as soon as they hear knocking. In the same way, on account of the heat and rapidity of its nature, impetuosity does listen, but not to the order it is given, and runs off to take its revenge. That is, if λόγος or φαντασία should make it clear that he has been

> the object of insolence or scorn, the impetuous man immediately becomes enraged, as if he reasoned (συλλογισάμενος) that 'one must fight against such a thing.' (1149a 24–34)

It is clear that here there is no real practical reasoning, but that θυμός acts in a way that resembles how one acts when carrying out a practical argument. If reason or the imagination says: "There has been an insult," θυμός, as if applying a practical major premise, immediately becomes furious, and does not wait to deliberate or consider what are the best ways of reacting to an insult. It seems to us that what Aristotle says in lines 1149a 33–34 is a major premise;[57] in form it is very similar to that of the practical major premise given in *de an.* 434a 18 (δεῖ τῷ τοιούτῳ πολεμεῖν, cf. δεῖ τὸν τοιοῦτον τὸ τοιόνδε πράττειν). We therefore seem to have here a case in which θυμός acts like one who applies to a given situation a practical major premise that is sufficient to give rise to a course of action. Also in this second case the major premise needs no further specification to give rise to an action.

Case (C) is described in *de motu an.* 701a 26–33. In it the minor premise is so obvious it need not be formulated:

> as some dialecticians do, so also διάνοια does not stop to examine the minor premise at all, as it is obvious. For example, if walking is good for a man, one does not waste time thinking: "I am a man." This is why we do quickly also what we do without reasoning [practically]. In fact, when one uses, at present, sensation, imagination and intellect (αἴσθησις, φαντασία, νοῦς) regarding the end, one does at once what one desires. For it is the activity of desire that is generated, not that of investigation or reflection. "I must drink,"[58] says desire. "This is a drink," says sensation, imagination or intellect, and forthwith one drinks.

Here Aristotle presents two different cases in which action is the immediate result of the application of a general end ("walking is good for a man") or of a particular impulse ("I must drink") to the analysis of a given situation.[59] The second case is the clearer of the two; if we admit that the indeterminate impulse "I must drink" is correct and appropriate to the situation (e.g. if one is lost in a desert), there is no deliberation, but only immediate action. The only error possible lies in the act of perception, as when one says, "This is a drink," when in fact it is a mirage.

In sum, Aristotle seems to be saying that the minor premise is unnecessary when the major premise is applied directly to the facts of a situation, and when the combination of the end (established in the major premise) and the perception of sense data causes a bodily movement (or abstention from all movement) on the part of the agent.

From this starting point we can easily reach the conclusion that the function of the minor premise is that of connecting the major premise to the concrete situation when, from the immediate juxtaposition of the two elements, it is not clear what kind of behavior should be adopted, and when, before acting, and in order to be able to act, it is necessary to search for the middle term. This search is what Aristotle calls "deliberation." To use Aristotle's example, a man who asserts: "I must become king of the entire human race" (*EE* 1225b 33–34) may or may not need the minor premise. If he is Alexander the Great's most powerful general and is behind the king's back, with a dagger in his hand, in a safe and solitary place, he may not need anything else. In this case, on Aristotle's theory—and against that of von Wright—if he really desires the end, he will strike.[60] But in all other cases it appears that our ambitious fellow will need a certain number of minor premises and a good deal of deliberation.

3.2. The Role and Function of the Minor Premise

In Section 3.1 we saw that the role of the minor premise is to express an element called καθ' ἕκαστα and δυνατόν. This is the πρῶτον αἴτιον (1112b 18–20), the immediate cause, which is the first to be put into practice, and is the efficient cause with respect to the end (*EE* 1218b 19–21). This is true in the simplest model of PS, in which there is only one intermediate premise; but, as in the theoretical syllogism (*a. pr.* I 25), so too in the PS the conclusion can be reached by means of several contiguous middle terms (42b 5 et seq.).[61] Each of these terms is a "practical good," i.e. the end of action for the following term, but it is so only in an indirect way, as being useful (συμφέρον) for the ultimate end. Therefore, each of them is δυνατόν to a greater extent than the one that precedes it.[62] This point is illustrated in three passages in Aristotle's works. These texts come not only from the *Ethics,* but also from other works, especially the *Analytica Posteriora* and the *Metaphysics*. Let us take a look at them one by one.

In *EE* I 8, 1218b 16–20 Aristotle states that διδασκαλία (which, as is well known, is carried out by means of syllogisms) clearly shows (δηλοῖ) that the end is the starting point for that which depends on it. The procedure for obtaining this result is outlined by Aristotle in the following way:

> having defined the end (ὁρισάμενοι γὰρ τὸ τέλος), they demonstrate regarding the other things, that each of them is a [practical] good, since the starting point is the objective. For example, since 'staying healthy' is such-and-such a thing [e.g., 'digesting well after dinner'], then necessarily this other thing [e.g., taking a walk] will be what is useful for it. (1218b 17–20)

The words in square brackets are our explanatory additions; their function will be clarified below. In our case we have to show that, for example, "staying healthy" is the starting point for "taking a walk," as it is the objective (τὸ οὗ ἕνεκα) of taking a walk. In other words, the purpose of the syllogism is to demonstrate, by means of a final cause, that in actuality it is possible to find a way of reaching the end, i.e. "staying healthy," in the given situation. Here we have an end (A), a definition of the end (B) and an efficient cause (C) (cf. 1218b 20–21: αἴτιον ὡς κινῆσαν) called τὸ συμφέρον, i.e. that which is useful for the end. We already know that, for Aristotle, the specification of the end (τοιόνδε) given in the major premise is necessary for determining how the end is to be reached, whenever the definition does not immediately give rise to an action. This is further clarified in the other two passages we still have to examine.

In *metaph.* VII 7, 1032b 6–29 we can find other hints that help us understand this question. Here Aristotle is distinguishing between what is generated naturally and what is generated by τέχνη with regard to the latter type of generation, he separates the role of thought from actual production. His attention is here entirely focused on the function of the formal cause, and the determination of the middle terms takes, generally, the form of a progressively more precise specification of the end. Let us look at the text:

> a 'healthy person' is produced by reasoning as follows: since 'health' is such-and-such a thing, then of necessity, if a person is healthy, there must be something, e.g. 'equilibrium' and (for this to exist there must be) something else, e.g. 'warmth'; and one continues reasoning in this way, until one comes at last to a thing that one is able to produce. [. . .] Of the elements of generation and movement, one is called reflection (νόησις), and the other is called production (ποίησις); the one that starts from the first principle and the form is reflection, while the one that starts from the conclusion of reflection is production. And each of the other intermediate terms is generated in the same way: I mean, for example, that if one has to get well, one has to regain the harmony [of heat and cold].[63] What therefore does it mean to 'regain harmony'? It is like this. And this will happen if a person is warmed up. And what is this other thing? Another thing still. But this other thing is [already] present (ὑπάρχηει) potentially; in fact it already depends [on the subject who acts]. Hence the efficient cause and the starting point for the movement of getting well, if it is the result of τέχνη, is the form present in the soul. [. . . .] In getting well, the starting point is to get warm, and the agent produces this effect by rubbing. Hence the heat that is in the body is either a constituent part of health, or is the source from which something that is a part of health is derived, either immediately or through several middle terms. And this extreme is what produces a part of health, and is itself a part of it, as e.g. stones are part of a house, and so also in other cases.[64]

In this dense and complex[65] passage, some points need to be clarified: (1) in line 1032b 6 et seq. the expression ἐπειδὴ τοδὶ ὑγίεια . . . indicates a definition of health, and the first step in deliberation is to establish this definition; (2) as Jaeger points out, in line 1032b 9 (and line b 27), the term ἔσχατον indicates the last element that is reached in deliberation, defined in *EN* 1112b 23 as "the last in analysis and the first in genesis"; (3) the term μέρος, line b 28, indicates a constituent part of the end, as e.g. "heat" or "cold" are constituent parts of "health." The greatest problems of interpretation are found in the second part of the passage, viz.: (4) Aristotle says that the extreme of determination is part of health, or produces part of it. The manuscripts give two different texts, which go like this: "and this extreme is what produces part of health, and it is itself part, as for example stones are of a house, and in the other cases" (Jaeger's text), or: "and this is the extreme, that which produces part of health and also of the house (such as stones) and so in the other cases" (Ross's text). It is therefore not clear whether Aristotle means that what produces part of the end is, in this way (οὕτως, b 29 in Jaeger's text), a constituent part of it or merely a part or whether he intends to maintain the distinction between being "part of the end" and being "what produces part of the end."

In this passage Aristotle posits a chain of terms of this type: "get well"—"regain equilibrium"—"get warm"—"rub." In this chain the deliberative analysis starts from an as yet undetermined form present in the mind of the one who acts, and gradually specifies it in relation (1) to the given situation, and (2) to a series of technical and practical notions, such as "rubbing produces heat." In this way the end is defined ever more closely; starting from these definitions, the means for reaching it are identified. Aristotle here makes it clear that the deliberative process can even go on at length, but it always proceeds in the same way. At every stage it is possible to redefine the means found, considering it as the end of a still more specific means. Thus the end/means distinction is relative. We shall return to this point later; see *EN* 1097a 25–28. This deliberative process continues until an immediately feasible means is found.

In the *Metaphysics* Aristotle insists (perhaps excessively) on the idea that the realization of the means is, in some way, "part" of realizing the end; but, obviously, not all means can be considered a part of the end. Of itself, deliberation may lead to an immediately practicable act, which is either "part" of the end, or merely an "external means" for reaching it (Greenwood). Instead, it appears that Aristotle almost always considers the search for the means as an analysis of the end. This is clear, for example, in *EE* II 11, 1227b 30–32, previously quoted (cf. Chapter 2). It is for this reason that Aristotle likes to compare a man who deliberates to a man who undertakes a geometrical analysis.[66]

In this connection, it might seem strange that Aristotle places at the heart of his practical reasoning a notion such as that of "analysis," which might seem more typical of theoretical knowledge. But we must keep in mind the differences and modifications he makes to this concept when it is applied to deliberation. Aristotle often compares the procedures of theoretical and practical knowledge, showing the similarities between the two, but also the profound differences, due to the different aims pursued by the two types of reasoning. The passage in *EN* II 7, 1107a 29–32 is exemplary; it expounds the different roles of καθόλου and ἐπὶ μέρους in practical knowledge as compared to theoretical knowledge. Sometimes one has the impression that Aristotle wants to say that the whole difference between practical and theoretical reasoning lies in the typical inversion of procedures and values that takes place as one passes from one kind of reasoning to the other, and that is again justified by the different aims that the two types of reasoning pursue (knowledge vs. action). In the case of analysis-deliberation-ζήτησις, this point should be particularly stressed.

When Aristotle speaks of analysis and deliberation, here in *EE* II 11, as also in *EN* III 3, he does not mean to envisage a procedure consisting in positing that a given good is an end, and then analyzing the posited term by moving back to its antecedents, until a clear starting point is found, or a superior end whose goodness is already known, according to the method of mathematical analysis illustrated by Pappus. Aristotle's procedure consists rather in positing that a certain activity, or state of affairs, e.g. "contemplation," is a good and a practical end, and then, starting from that, searching for a particular specification of it, one whose feasibility is either already known or immediately evident. In other words, the analysis of the end seems not to be directed at establishing its goodness, but rather at demonstrating its practicability, on the basis of the consequences that derive from it; the analysis therefore proceeds, not toward first principles and basic supreme ends, but rather toward particular premises and practical actualizations. In fact, as Aristotle says, "the last term in the procedure of analysis [seems] to be the first in generation" (1112b 23–24).

Moreover, in Aristotle there are also examples where the specification of the end enables us to point out a means, i.e. a way of reaching it, which cannot be properly said to be a constituent part of the end, or a *component means,* as Greenwood would say, but is actually an external means. One clear example seems to be this passage from *a. po.* II 11, 94b 8 et seq. , already partially discussed in the previous chapter (p. 46 et seq.). Let us now return to it. The text goes as follows:

> for the cases in which the cause is the end of something: for example, why is he taking a walk? to stay healthy, or, why is there a house? to protect the property. The one has the aim of staying healthy, the other has the aim of protecting. Why one has to take a walk after dinner, and for what purpose one has to do it, are the same thing. Taking a walk is (C), not leaving one's food undigested is (B), being in good health is (A). Let us assume that taking a walk after dinner implies not leaving one's food undigested at the pit of the stomach, and that this is good for one's health. In fact, it appears that (B), not leaving one's food undigested, belongs to (C), taking a walk, and (A), good health, belongs

> to (B). What then is the cause of (A)'s belonging to (C) as a final cause? It is (B), not leaving one's food undigested; this is, in a way, its definition, given that (A) is so explained. And for what reason is (B) [the final cause] of (C) ? Because this is staying healthy, being in this condition. And the λόγοι must be transposed, so that everything may be clearer. (b 8–23)

The purpose of this passage is to show that the middle term may also express a final causality. The syllogism described in it, then, is a theoretical syllogism, not a practical one, but it is a syllogism of a special type, since it does not express the formal cause, and its subject is practical behavior. By this type of syllogism Aristotle expresses a middle term that is the cause of the greater extreme's belonging to the lesser extreme. If we take the more elaborate of the two examples that Aristotle gives here, we have:

one who digests well stays healthy
one who takes a walk digests well

---

one who takes a walk stays healthy.

For the purposes of our discussion, it is important that the middle term, "digesting," i.e. "not leaving one's food undigested at the pit of the stomach" is given by Aristotle as the definition and specification of the general end of "staying healthy," regarding a particular καιρός, "after dinner" (94b 11, 19–20). Starting from this definition of the end, the minor premise identifies the way of achieving the end ("to digest after dinner it is useful to take a walk"). Therefore, as is stated in *EE* 1218b 20–22, the third term is the efficient cause of the realization of the first, and the first is the cause of the third term's being a practical good.[67] "Taking a walk" is not a practical good or an end in itself, but it is a good inasmuch as it produces "staying healthy," which is the ultimate aim. Nonetheless, the link between "taking a walk" and "staying healthy" is not immediately obvious, but it becomes clear if "staying healthy" is defined as "digesting." Thus, "digesting," being a specification of the end, is the final cause of taking a walk.[68]

In this sense, and in opposition to Allan's interpretation, we may say that the ultimate end is in some way a wider and more indeterminate universal than the middle term, and that deliberation consists of the search for one or more intermediate terms that specify the end so as to make it immediately practicable. Already in the nineteenth century Hegel seems to have understood the PS in this way, since he sees in the means a particularization of the universal end.[69]

We can therefore understand why Aristotle describes the minor premise as one that is κατὰ μέρος or καθ' ἕκαστα or even διὰ τοῦ δυνατοῦ.[70] He does not insist on identifying the kind of person to whom a given end belongs. This part of the minor premise, which Aristotle sometimes mentions (cf. *EN* 1147a 6 etc.), is generally clear, and needs neither ζήτησις nor ἀνάλυσις. One who deliberates about how to act usually already has a clear idea about his proper end, just as every doctor knows that his task is to make people well. As is said in *de motu an.* 701a 25, no one wastes time considering this part of the premise.

There is, however, a different interpretation of the minor premise, according to which Aristotle's expressions κατὰ μέρος and διὰ τοῦ δυνατοῦ may even be incompatible. This interpretation must be discussed, but not before we have examined the origin of the minor premise. This investigation will provide us with useful clues for solving the problem we have just posed.

3.3. The Origin of the Minor Premise

As far as we know, all commentators agree that the source of our knowledge of the intermediate terms between the end and practical action is φρόνησις. Its task is to "see," in a metaphorical sense,[71] what is to be done, and what immediately feasible practical good connects the end to the data of the situation. Φρόνησις supplies the minor premise, drawn from deliberation:

> φρόνησις regards human affairs and that about which one deliberates; indeed, we say that above all else the function of the φρόνιμος is to deliberate well. (1141b 8–10)

The object of deliberation is a practical good, which is what is sought in deliberation, and is done with something else in mind (b 12). Deliberation consists of a στοχάζεσθαι κατὰ τὸν λογισμόν, a searching based on practical calculation.[72] Deliberation and the search for the means also involve the knowledge of certain general rules, as the following passage shows:

> moreover, an error in deliberation may regard either the universal or the particular: either [in thinking] that all heavy waters are noxious, or that this particular water is heavy. (1142a 20–23)

The error described here is different from that described in *EE* II 11 and in *pol.* VII 13. Here it is not a question of distinguishing between an error in determining the σκοπός and an error in determining τὰ πρὸς τὸν σκοπόν, i.e. that which leads to it. Here the error regards only deliberation and the search for the middle terms, which involve also general knowledge of various sorts. Aristotle insists that this knowledge is proper to men with experience of life (1142a 11, b 16–22). One who deliberates should therefore know what means are universally useful (e.g., "light meat is good for one's health"), but especially, he must seek out the most practical means ("chicken meat is light and thus good for my health"). Of these two types of knowledge of the means, it is better if the more general sort is lacking, rather than the specific knowledge, given that the aim is practical (cf. p. 75).[73]

When one reaches the last intermediate term in the series, one "sees," in a sense, what to do. Aristotle expresses this "seeing" in a passage whose interpretation is controversial:

> it is clear that φρόνησις is not ἐπιστήμη. In fact, it is concerned with the ultimate,[74] as we have said, since this is the object of conduct.[75] And it is opposed[76] to νοῦς, since νοῦς is concerned with first principles (ὅροι), for which there is no λόγος. It (φρόνησις), instead, is concerned with the extreme, for which there is no science, but αἴσθησις. Not [1] αἴσθησις of sense-data proper,[77] but [2] that by which in mathematics[78] we perceive that the extreme is a triangle. In fact, there too one will stop, but this [2] is more αἴσθησις than φρόνησις[79] is; the genus [of these two] is, however, different from that [1]. (1142a 23–30)

We have already seen (cf. p. 74) that here Aristotle means by νοῦς theoretical νοῦς, that which grasps the true first principles. Φρόνησις is contrasted with νοῦς in this sense, and is compared to αἴσθησις, as in *EN* 1109b 23. Φρόνησις supplies the minor premise, perceiving the state of things in the light of the principle, and not simply assuming the sense-data.[80] Φρόνησις is not αἴσθησις, but is compared to αἴσθησις, inasmuch as it is linked to the particular fact. Its distinctive feature is to see this particular fact in the light of an end, and hence to give it a positive or negative emotional value.

In *De anima* this seeing a particular fact in the light of an end is called φαντασία βουλευτική (434a 5–12), an expression that recalls the analogous expression βουλευτικὴ ὄρεξις in *EN* 1113a 11, and implies it. In fact, we desire a certain kind of behavior because we see it as appropriate for reaching the end that we set ourselves.[81] In the same way, in the *De anima*, the minor premise is presented as follows:

> (C) ἡ δὲ ὅτι τόδε τοίνυν τοιόνδε, κἀγὼ δὲ τοιόσδε (434a 18–19) (= "the other instead [says] that this, therefore, is [a thing] of such a kind, and I am [a man] of such a kind").

The minor premise is thus supplied by a faculty that sees particular facts as cases, parts or ways of realizing an end and not as mere sense data. In our opinion, the much-discussed passage in *EN* 1143a 31–33 could be interpreted in the same way:

> if, therefore, good deliberating is peculiar to the φρόνιμος, good deliberation will turn out to be that which regards what is useful for the end, which φρόνησις understands correctly.

Here Aristotle says that φρόνησις makes the ἀνάλυσις of the end taken as a principle and hypothesis, in such a way as to show how it can be realized in practice, and how it can be made concrete and specified step by step;

φρόνησις finds the συμφέρον that, in the light of the end, is ἀγαθόν (*EE* 1218b 20).

Some other passages, such as *EN* 1147a 7, 26, 29 and 33 must also be understood in this sense. They present minor premises such as: εἰ τόδε τοιόνδε, "if this is a thing of such a kind" ; τουτὶ δὲ γλυκύ, "this thing is sweet." In our opinion, these premises do not just express the data of sense perception, but rather an assessment of experience in view of an end.

We shall return to these passages of *EN* later (see Appendix). Now, instead, we wish to go back to the interpretation of the minor premise at the point where we broke off the discussion (p. 84). According to this interpretation, the minor premise supplies only factual information. This makes it necessary to discuss some examples of minor premises given by Aristotle in *de motu an.* 7, viz.: οἰκία δ' ἀγαθόν; ἱμάτιον δὲ σκέπασμὰ; ἱματίου δέομαι ("a house is a good thing"; "a mantle is an overcoat"; "I need a mantle," 701a 17, 18, 19). In our view, contrary to what other commentators have thought, all these premises do not express merely a fact, but rather a judgment concerning a fact. This is very clear in the example found in 701a 17: a house is "a good thing" in a particular context, and "a very bad thing" in another context, given that the "being good" of a house is not the fruit of experience, as is the "being white" of snow. In the same way, the example in 701a 18 takes a particular thing, a mantle, as the specification of the end which, in this syllogism, the acting subject has to obtain, i.e. a coat to cover himself with. Lastly, the example in 701a 19 takes a specific thing, a mantle, as something which the acting subject needs. Hence it is once again an assessment of the result of experience in view of an end—in this case, producing what one needs. And, again, this being-what-I-need is not a "given" supplied by experience in the same way as the being-white of snow.

If the minor premise furnished only sense data, it would be impossible to explain the example given in lines 701a 32–33 quoted in section 3.1. In that passage the expression τοδὶ δὲ ποτόν (= "this is a drink," 701a 32) may actually be a fact of experience; indeed, it is supplied not only by νοῦς, but also by φαντασία and by αἴσθησις. But, Aristotle says, it is just in this example that the minor premise is lacking (701a 25–26).[82] In our opinion, the information "this is a drink" in this example does not function as a minor premise; it is not the result of research and deliberation, but is rather a piece of information about the situation, like that indicated in *EN* 1113a 1 ("for example, if this is bread, or if it has been well cooked"). This information is not supplied by φρόνησις, but by another faculty, such as sensation, imagination or thought. It regards "givens" of the situation, elements that are not the object of deliberation, but things that must be taken into consideration by anyone who deliberates. We can thus understand how Aristotle can say that in this example there is no minor premise;

indeed, there is no premise that assesses the situation in such a way as to find a specification of the practical end that makes it actually realizable.

4. The Link Between the Two Types of Premise

If it is true that Aristotle formulates the theory of the PS in order to give a formal representation of the thought process that is inherent in action and determines it, the two premises of this syllogism must be the cause of the action that results from them. It must therefore be possible to identify, between the premises of the PS and the action, a special link[83] that connects the "practical premises" to a physical movement. As we shall see below, for Aristotle the conclusion of the PS is an action (cf. section 5), and it is by virtue of such a link that it can result from the premises. But since, for Aristotle, the only motive force of action is desire (cf. *de an.* III 10, 433a 21) and the faculty related to it, the link in question will inevitably consist in a transmission of desire.

The object of desire is, in the first instance, the practical good indicated in the major premise as an end, e.g. "to stay healthy"; and, in an indirect way, the objects of desire are the ways of achieving the end, e.g. "to take a walk," about which we spoke above. These goods are not desired for their own sake, but for the sake of the good effects that they produce. This is made clear by Aristotle in *EN* III 3:

> as the object of choice is what is deliberated and desired from among the things that depend on us, also choice will be a deliberate desire of something that depends on us; in fact, if we judge on the basis of deliberation, we feel desire in accordance with the deliberation.[84] (1113a 9–12)

Now, that which is desired on the basis of deliberation is what is intermediate between the ultimate end and the action. This relation is analyzed by Aristotle in the *Metaphysics:*

> [a cause is defined], moreover, as an end: this is the thing-for-which, as, for example, health with respect to taking a walk. Why do we take a walk? We say: To stay healthy, and in so saying we think we have adduced the cause. And so too those things that, when another thing moves, are intermediate between it and the end, as for example, with regard to health, losing weight, cleaning the bowels, and the instruments. [. . .] In fact, all these lead to the end, but they differ from one another in that some are instruments, while others are actions.[85] (1013a 33–b 4)

In the above passage the sentence "And so too those things . . . instruments" has no verb and must be completed. But it can be interpreted very differently, depending on how the missing verb is supplied. Starting from Alexander of

Aphrodisias,[86] it has been thought that "losing weight," "cleaning the bowels" and so on were all efficient causes of the ultimate end, health. On the basis of this supposition, the passage is completed with expressions such as "are all causes of health" (Reale). But recently Kirwan[87] has observed that the passage could be understood in another way; that is, it could be said that "losing weight," "cleaning one's bowels" and so on are the final causes of the efficient cause hinted at in line a 36 (κινήσαντος ἄλλου, "when another moves"). On this interpretation, the passage should be completed with something like "are the end of it." In fact, the intermediate terms can be viewed both as that of which the ultimate end is the final cause, and as final causes of the action. Desire is transmitted from one to the other of them, until an immediately practicable term is reached.

Nonetheless, desire is not transmitted at random. The problem is to make clear by what kinds of "logical" link desire passes from the term enunciated in the major premise to the concrete action. As we saw in Chapters 1 and 2, desire follows the results of deliberation in accordance with practical reasoning, and desires as good what reasoning shows to be a means for the end, when a person is virtuous and his irrational faculties, which are capable of obeying reason (*EN* I 13), actually do follow its commands. The minor premise must indicate a "possible and useful action for achieving the end" and some passages in the *Metaphysics* speak of this action as a necessary condition for reaching the end:

> we say that something is "necessary" [. . .] if, without it, good cannot be generated or subsist, and evil avoided or destroyed; for example, it is necessary to drink the medicine in order not to be ill, and to sail to Aegina to earn money. (1015a 20–26)

Aristotle expressly distinguishes this type of necessity from that of inference or implication found in the scientific syllogism.[88] It seems clear that he is here thinking of a conditional necessity, or one ἐξ ὑποθέσεως[89]—a very difficult concept—and that the necessity mentioned in section 2.2. (cf. pp. 71–72), with regard to type (B) major premises, is a necessity of this kind.

This position of Aristotle's has been criticized by contemporary philosophers. Hare, for example, has maintained that here Aristotle does not pay sufficient attention to the distinction between necessary causes and sufficient conditions.[90] The link between the end and the intermediate terms appears to be necessary only if, in a given situation, there is one and only one way to obtain what one wants. Some, like Hintikka, accuse Aristotle of erroneously positing that every end can be reached by only one chain of means and successive specifications. Others hold that this is right, since with the appropriate restrictions and additional conditions it is possible to make necessary conditions out of these, which would seem to be only sufficient conditions.[91] Critics have debated this point at length, but it seems obvious (to take the usual example of a syllogism in *a. po.* II 11) that to achieve the aim of "staying healthy" after dinner one may take a walk, but one may also take a pill, eat lightly and so on; there is thus no need to choose any one means, not even in a quite specific situation.

Moreover, it should be observed that in *EN* Aristotle shows his awareness of the fact that often there are many ways of reaching the same end:

> and if it appears that [the end] can be achieved in many ways, they search for the ways in which it is achieved in the quickest and best way. (1112b 15–16)

At least in the case of the φρόνιμος, the two criteria are apparently to be used together. But this is not all: in other treatises, such as the *Rhetoric,* the *Topics* and at least one passage of the *Analytica Priora,* Aristotle gives useful advice on how to solve this problem. Let us briefly summarize some of his statements.

The *Rhetoric* devotes two chapters to deliberation (I 6–7). In them Aristotle's attention is concentrated mainly on the determination of what are the ends that can be proposed to the audience, in general, and to every particular audience. There are, however, some passages on the choice of "means," such as the following, which seem to anticipate Greenwood's distinction between "component" and "external means:"

> 'that which produces' is divided into three kinds: both as (1) being in good health produces health (τὸ ὑγιαίνειν ὑγιείας), and as (2) food produces health, and as (3) performing physical exercises produces health, because they generally produce health. (1362a 31–34)

Commentators have debated about which criterion Aristotle has used to construct this threefold division.[92] But to us it seems clear that (1) is a formal cause, necessary and sufficient, as the very choice of words used by Aristotle shows (ὑγιαίνειν = ὑγιείας). As for causes (2) and (3), they are distinguished from one another owing to the fact that one of them is defined as ὡς ἐπὶ τὸ πολύ, while the other one is not. They are therefore two efficient causes, one of which is necessary, while the other functions only in most cases: it is not possible to stay healthy without eating, but one can stay well without taking physical exercise. Neither of the two causes, however, appears to be sufficient. Thus Aristotle appears to be aware, in this passage, of the difficulty of positing a necessary chain linking ends, means and concrete action.

The text of the *Rhetoric* is amply echoed in the first three chapters of *Topics* III,[93] where Aristotle establishes how one can determine which of two or more entities is preferable, in those cases in which the most preferable is not immediately obvious (116a 4–9). Here we will not undertake a detailed analysis of the text; we only wish to mention that Aristotle gives various criteria for the choice of "means." He says, in fact, that the end is preferable to the means (116a 29, b 22), and that of two means the one closer (ἔγγιον) to the end is preferable. Of means, one that is useful for the general choice of life made by the agent is preferable to one that leads to a particular end (b 23–26); sometimes, too, the means for a very lofty end may be more important, and thus preferable, with respect to an end of minor importance (b 27–36). We may also observe the consequences (117a 5–7), in particular future consequences (a 7–15), since, as is obvious, the consequences of an act are evaluated with reference to the proposed end. The same argument is given in a mention of deliberation found in *De interpretatione* (9, 18b 32–33): "if we do this, this other thing will happen, and if we do not, it will not." What is appropriate to the present occasion or happens at the right moment (ἐν καιρῷ) is preferable, but even more so is what is always advisable (a 34–b 2).

We need not continue with this survey;[94] we may just mention that in 118b 27 et seq. Aristotle distinguishes what produces the useful from what produces the beautiful or pleasant, and he stresses the fact that what is preferable on the basis of more than one of these determinations is preferable to that which is preferable on the basis of a single determination. Hence what is both fine (noble) and pleasant is preferable to that which is only fine (noble). In this way any kind of asceticism is rejected.

In the *Analytica Priora* 68a 25 et seq., a rather complex procedure is given to show that it is preferable to reach an end, even one that is partly negative, rather than to reach only a means-for-an-end. The calculation of preferability is performed with a sole unit of measure, as is stated also in *de an.* 434a 7–12:

> indeed, [to decide] whether to do this, or this other thing, is the proper task of reasoning, and it is necessary that it be measured in relation to a single criterion,[95] since it pursues a greater good. So it can make, out of several images (φαντάσματα), a single thing. And this is the reason why [animals] do not seem to have [practical] opinion, i.e. they do not have an opinion that is derived by means of a syllogism.

This passage of *De anima* may help us to interpret the example that Aristotle gives in the passage of the *Analytica Priora,* which we have just mentioned. We do not intend to quote the whole of this rather long passage, in which Aristotle basically summarizes the first part of Plato's *Phaedrus* (230E–259B). We shall instead give a broad outline. Aristotle says that, if one uses a single unit of measure, one will have to add together (A) "the willingness of the beloved to give satisfaction" and (C) "the beloved's actually not giving satisfaction," in order to make, of the two φαντάσματα, a single thing, which will be contrasted with the sum of (D) "actually giving satisfaction" and (B) "unwillingness to give satisfaction," which are added together to make a single φάντασμα. One will then choose which of the two is preferable on the basis of the unit of measure, given by our proposed end. Therefore, whether we prefer the true end, viz. love and affection, or whether we invert the correct relation and take as our end the means for procuring affection, viz. sexual intercourse, will depend on the type of person we are (cf. Chapter 2). The choice of one or the other will depend on our character and our virtue, which will or will not lead us to find the mean in any given situation.

As we can see, in Aristotle there are various schemes and strategies for choosing from among different chains of means, all connected to a certain end. He also indicates the criteria to use in preferring one means over another. All these schemes are drawn from ἔνδοξα, but their presence in the discussions of *EN,* as for example in the famous chapter 1 7, where it is established that happiness is the supreme end, is evident. There is, in fact, no reason why τόποι of this kind, collected and elaborated to be used in dialectical discussions on ethics,[96] cannot be used also by those who deliberate and debate with themselves about how to act. This same possibility of twofold use of the τόποι is found in many orators of the time.[97]

Hence, between the premises of the PS, and between these and the conclusion, there is a composite link, just as, in general, the very nature of practical knowledge is also composite. As we saw in Chapter 1, practical knowledge in general is composed of λόγος + ὄρεξις. The link between the premises of the PS consists in the transmission of the ὄρεξις from one term to the other, from the ultimate end to the intermediate terms, down to the concrete action. But the desire is transmitted because there are clear rational links between the terms; it does not pass at random from one representation to another. Aristotle, for simplicity's sake, prefers to examine those cases where there is a single final chain that leads from the major premise to the action; but in his works one can also find clues on how to deal with those cases in which there are many possible choices. It appears that what must be chosen in any given situation is what is "preferable" from among the many possible intermediate terms, which give rise to various chains of means. "Being preferable" is related to a series of variables and historical conditions, but it is not assigned at random. In the *Topics* Aristotle develops a theory about this matter, which involves rules of the type "if an A is C to a greater extent than every B is, and no A is C, then no B is C." For example, if a science is better than any pleasure, and no science is a good, then pleasure is not a good (119b 7–21).

In our opinion, in order for there to be a transmission of desire and hence a correct PS, it is sufficient that a way of realizing the end should be either the only practicable one or else the one that is preferable. It does not seem indispensable that there be a strict logical necessity, since the characteristic that is transmitted from one premise to the other is not so much truth (even if it could be maintained that the means for an end that is a true good are themselves true goods), as it is desirability or preferability. It seems possible to state that, in order to have a true and correct PS, it is indispensable that the major premise be a good end and that the middle term be a specification of it, so as to give rise to an effective action. But for there to be a virtuous action, it is apparently not indispensable that the agent should grasp, in a given situation, absolutely the best means available. It is sufficient for him to grasp a really effective means, choosing the one that seems to him most suitable, from among the means that he is aware of.

Given that desire, in Aristotle's theory as also in Stoic philosophy, is also a physiological event, and involves movements of body organs such as the heart and the πνεῦμα, one may say, in von Wright's terms, that the link between the premises of the PS, and between these and the conclusion, is causal,[98] but that this causality does not exclude logical links between the premises: in fact, desire is transmitted on the basis of arguments, which may be true, false or debatable. Aristotle describes mainly the simplest case, the one in which desire is transmitted from the end to the means and to action on the basis of a single chain of arguments, which is correct and well devised. But we have seen on various occasions that in his works there are hints at a possible cataloging of the different types of error and deviation from the best form of practical reasoning (cf. Chapter 1 and Chapter 2, and, in this chapter, p. 77).

If there is no transmission of desire, the reasoning is not practical. Indeed, as we shall see, we can reason coolly about another man's choices and determine which action is preferable for a man in his position. But in this case the reasoning does not result in any action, and our limbs do not move, or abstain from moving, when they ought to.

5. The Conclusion Is an Action

The minor premise of the PS indicates a type of possible action, which depends on us, and is more useful than any other (so far as we know) for attaining an end; on this basis the desire for the end is transmitted to the act in question. It is therefore not strange, at this point, to affirm that the conclusion of the PS is an action and not a proposition. This does not at all exclude the possibility that the act may also be verbalized, as a hungry man does when, biting into his food, he mutters: "Now I'll eat you!" But the verbalization is not essential; it is the action that is essential. Aristotle says so explicitly in two passages. One of them is found in *de motu an.* 701a 10–13:

> but there [= in the theoretical syllogism] the end is a theoretical proposition. For whenever one thinks of the two premises, one thinks and puts together the conclusion. Here, instead, the two premises generate the conclusion, which is conduct (action);

and in *EN* VII 3, 1147a 25–28:

> the one is a universal opinion (δόξα), while the other regards particular cases, which are in the domain of sensation; when a single thing is generated on the basis of them, there [= in the theoretical syllogism] the conclusion must be affirmed by the soul, whereas in the case of practical [premises] one must act at once.

For a discussion of the interpretation of some concepts and terms in this second passage, see the Appendix to this chapter. Now, it is opportune to recall that many people have objected to the idea that the conclusion of the PS is an action. It is said that, if the PS is an intellectual process, its conclusion will have to be an act of the intellect, from which, later, an action may result.[99] To support this position (1) they quote passages in which Aristotle says that the conclusion is put into practice "if there is no impediment." This would lead us to think that the conclusion exists even before it is put into practice. (2) Others mention the fact that in *de motu an.* 701a 19–20, Aristotle states that the conclusion "I must produce a mantle" is an action; then, a little later, he gives another syllogism that takes as its major premise the conclusion of the previous one.[100] Therefore, they say, if it is a premise, the conclusion cannot be an action.

In general terms, what these interpretations posit as the conclusion of the syllogism is what we take as the minor premise, viz. the interpretation of a particular state of affairs, or plan of action, in view of an end. This makes it necessary, later on, to find a non-random connection between the conclusion of the PS and the action. The fact that, on this interpretation, the PS must be considered to conclude with a proposition that identifies a program of action does not suit Aristotle's explicit program of identifying the proper characteristics of the kind of thought that leads to action. As a first approximation, then, taking the action as the conclusion of the PS makes things simpler, since it eliminates the need for a further connection.

A second answer to objection (1) can be provided by a reading of *EN* 1112b 23–27, where Aristotle says that, when one comes across something that is impossible, one refrains from acting. If we apply this statement to the case of impediment, we may have two situations:

1. the agent, in completing the PS, regards as practicable a means that in reality is not (cf. *metaph.* 1048a 16–21): the PS is thus wrong in a banal sense, and the conclusion is not actually reached;

2. the agent regards as practicable a means that is so at the moment of deliberation, but is no longer practicable at the moment of action. In Aristotle's theory, deliberation and action are mutually exclusive and must be performed at different times, one after the other: when one deliberates, one does not act and vice versa. In this case it is very difficult to say that the agent, who makes a vain attempt to put the means into practice, does not act. It is more appropriate to say that his action is not successful owing to unforseeable external events.

As for case (2) given in *de motu an.* 701a 19–22, where Aristotle seems to contradict himself, taking something that he has defined as an "action" as the premise of another PS, it should be observed that Aristotle himself does not directly link the two syllogisms; one ends with the words "a mantle must be made, and this is an action" (a 19), and the other has as its major premise "if one has to make a mantle . . ." (a 21). The second syllogism illustrates the doctrine whereby one acts starting from an ἀρχή (a 21). In the terms of *metaph.* VII 7, 1032b 15, reflection on the ways of making the mantle is already part of the κίνησις, and of the γένεσις of it, since many processes occur by degrees and not all at once.[101]

In the case of these syllogisms, which regard the production of a mantle, we may note that, if the doer is an expert tailor he immediately begins to act, without having to redeliberate at every single step.[102] If, instead, the agent is a non-expert person, he will also perform the syllogism given in *de motu an.* 701a 21–22 ("if there is to be a mantle, first there must be this, and if this, then this other thing, and at once he makes this other thing"), after having deliberated and sought out the appropriate middle term. Behind this discussion lies the problem of how detailed the practical minor premise must be to result in an action. This cannot be determined *a priori*. As happens in the movies, the proposition "I have to break into this bank" may be the last practical premise of an expert bank robber, or the starting point for long periods of insomnia, worry and mulling things over (ζήτησις) for the novice who is short of money (and scruples).

To this it must be added that it is no accident that Aristotle, in *EN* III 3 and *EE* II 10, restricts the field of practical knowledge and deliberation to what depends on us. This restriction excludes from practical reasoning any kind of moral judgment on the behavior of others, unless it results in an action on the part of the deliberating subject (cf. 1112a 28–29). It implies a view of practical knowledge that is very different from ours today. Aristotle seems to exclude from practical knowledge in the strict sense all reflection, judgment and advice on situations that do not involve us. Such activities are relegated to a secondary form of knowledge, viz. σύνεσις, which deals with the same objects as φρόνησις, but differs from it (*EN* 1143a 6–8). Indeed, it knows only how to judge; it is κριτικὴ μόνον it does not give orders, as does φρόνησις, which is ἐπιτακτική, i.e. capable of giving orders (a 8–10). It is an "awareness" (συνιέναι), like what happens in the theoretical sciences. It is attained by means of δόξα, and is exercised on practical subjects "when someone tells us about them" (1143a 13–15). It thus differs radically from φρόνησις and the PS. Starting from a δόξα, σύνεσις results in another δόξα there is no transmission of desire. Probably the dialectical syllogisms about ethics referred to at the beginning are part of σύνεσις.

We are thus in a position to propose an answer to the question formulated in section 1, and which went like this: considering that the PS does not follow the rules of the *Analytica Priora,* is it possible to call it a syllogism anyway, understanding by this not a simple "argument," but something that falls within the scope of the definition given in *a.pr.* I 1? At this point the answer is in the affirmative, also because the definition mentioned is much more encompassing than the object described by Aristotle in the *Analytica Priora.*[103]

What is posited here is a succession of terms, each of which is composed of a value judgment that is accompanied by an act of desire; and because they are what they are, an action "necessarily" follows. This is Aristotle's position, but with the limitations we have observed: the necessity regards the one who deliberates, who, if he reaches a particular conclusion, must act; there is no obligation for that end, in that particular situation, to lead, necessarily and for everyone, exactly to that particular action. The fact that desire is not transmitted at random means that the double series of judgments (true/false, correct/incorrect) that we saw in Chapter 1 in regard to *EN* VI 2, 9 and 11 can be applied to such practical reasoning. Such judgments are used to determine the truth of the assumption of a good as a practical good, and the correctness of the identification of the appropriate means. It is only in the presence of a really good end, and of a correct behavior of desire, that a virtuous action can exist.

6. The Role of the Practical Syllogism

In our opinion, the PS is a concise way of expounding the main features of Aristotle's conception of practical knowledge. The aspects and characteristics of this syllogism harmonize with the general characteristics of φρόνησις as described above, as also with the importance of the role Aristotle reserves to nonrational, emotional factors in the determination of action.

Aristotle uses the vocabulary of the syllogism and analogies with theoretical reasoning to express the main features of practical reasoning. So-called practical syllogisms, then, are not a special part of practical reasonings, but they are practical reasonings themselves, reduced to the scheme of the syllogism, with all the necessary changes and adaptations; these changes and adaptations regard both the scheme of the syllogism, and the practical reasonings themselves. This complicates matters considerably, and the confusion has been compounded, in our view, by the fact that Aristotle wishes to express very many characteristics of practical reasoning through the scheme of the PS. Yet his attempt is not useless, and the same basic idea can consistently be found behind all the various passages where Aristotle speaks of the PS. These passages serve to make clearer the characteristics of practical knowledge that we outlined in Chapters 1 and 2, and to bring to light certain aspects of it.

Practical reasoning, since it is linked to the action it gives rise to, partly repeats the structure of such action. Just as acting is "doing something in view of something else"—in view of attaining an end—so too in practical reasoning the basic elements are the end and what-leads-to-the-end, the so-called means. And practical reasoning itself is, at bottom, only seeing "something," a practicable course of action, in the light of "something else," an end, and hence desiring (or not desiring) this "something." The field of practical reasoning is therefore everything that depends on us, including, as a first approximation, the production of objects (which is differentiated for other reasons, and not because productive reasoning is carried out on the basis of a different scheme from that of the PS), and excluding moral judgments on the behavior of others. We shall return to this point later.

"Positing an end" involves regarding a certain future state of affairs, or result, as being good and desirable; it means taking a practical principle on the basis of desire + opinion. We believe this practical principle is not given, in most cases, by noetic intuition, or by attending the schools of philosophers and participating in their discussions of the good. In this sense the *Nicomachean Ethics* does not set itself up as a treatise for teaching Aristotle's disciples the practical principles, even if, as we shall see, in the end it does recommend a certain model of life. Rather, *EN* is a treatise that exhorts people to act well, and makes it clear what acting well means. This is a different thing, because it is tantamount to clarifying already "given" notions. In fact, ends are the outcome of a training process, and are transmitted by social institutions such as the family (with its habits), the city (with its laws), and groups of friends, who choose to live together and share choices, pleasures and habits. Such ends are, in the best model, given by virtue, which is the result of training and habit; virtue is a habitual state of an individual, and is a mixture of reason and correct desire.

From the standpoint of the PS, the end is like a universal judgment about a certain future state of affairs; at least in some of Aristotle's formulations, it has an obvious relation with the theory of the mean. When one expresses the end of a deliberation, one states that for a certain kind of person a certain kind of thing or activity is a good (and hence the object of desire, if the person in question is not morally defective): "it behooves someone like me to do that." Aristotle thus recovers much of the ethics of the heroic age, which was typical of the Homeric poems and other literary expressions of the Greek people; in them one of the strongest ethical motives was a sense of *noblesse oblige*.

Sometimes it may happen that one immediately understands what to do, especially in ritualized behaviors or technical activities, such as writing, in which precise rules, handed down by teaching (διδασκαλία) and learned by heart, tell us at once which acts need to be performed. In most cases, however, although the end is the object of desire, it is not immediately practicable, but must be specified by one or more means.

Aristotle sees in deliberation the search for the middle terms that specify the end in relation to a given situation. At different times, according to the different contexts of discourse, these middle terms are viewed as redefinitions of the end, or as part of the action that the end consists of, or as external acts that are the efficient causes of the end, i.e. actual means. In any case they are future programs of action, at times expressed as mental images, programs that by their very nature can never be individual, but are always rather general. In fact, the specification of a program of action only occurs at the moment when the action is performed.

What is important is that such intermediate terms are the product of an analysis of the end in relation to a given situation, in which the end is taken as a good, and its goodness is not questioned. Rather, its practicability is examined, and one tries to see how the end can be realized. This deliberative analysis is made in the light of general norms of experience, which tell us what usually happens as the result of a certain course of action, and hence allow us to calculate what the consequences of one of our actions will be and to evaluate such consequences in relation to the end that we wish to reach. Deliberation gives rise to a chain of terms wherein each term is the end for the following one and the means for the preceding one; the terms become increasingly less general and more practicable, until we reach the last term, which can immediately be put into practice. An essential characteristic of these terms is that they are not desirable in themselves (otherwise they would be ends), but they are desirable only because they produce a certain result, the end, which is what we desire for its own sake. Deliberation thus produces a transmission of desire: when rational analysis demonstrates, to desire and to the emotional part of our soul, that a certain action is a way of bringing about a desired state of affairs, then that action itself becomes desirable. Deliberation therefore causes us to perceive something in a particular way, as being good and desirable; without deliberation, the same thing might seem indifferent to us, or even bad and repugnant.

Aristotle's works present a series of remarks on how to calculate the preferability of different ways of behaving in trying to reach the same end, so that the best one may be chosen. It is said that a course of action that achieves more than one end is better (e.g., it is both good and pleasant, and not merely good) or achieves nobler aims, and so on. But Aristotle is mainly interested in demonstrating the practical nature of the reasoning he is dealing with, and so usually he focuses on a simple model, one with a single chain of ends and means. He does not imagine that it may be necessary to calculate the best possible action in every given situation. Aristotle is rather tolerant, and regards as acceptable many behaviors that do not stray too far from the mean. Thus, in our opinion, he would consider to be acceptable different ways of reaching the same good end, even if not all of these options are the most "economical" or "elegant" solutions from the formal point of view. What he does insist on, however, is that the practical reasoning, if it is correct, and if one is not dealing with a case of "weakness of will," must give rise to an action. If one really desires an end, and if an immediately practicable course of action is seen as a means to that end, then that course of action is the immediate object of desire, and the action must follow.

We find here, too, the four possibilities of error that we analyzed in Chapter 2: one may make the practical calculation correctly or erroneously, and hence rightly understand that a certain action is a means for a certain end, or else one may be right or wrong in determining the end itself. But if the desire is correct—if, that is, it obeys reason and is channeled in the direction indicated by reason—it will move the limbs in the appropriate way, when the calculation is correct. The state of necessity regards the fact that, given an end and a practicable means of reaching it, an action must result; it does not mean that, starting from a given end, in a given situation one and only one type of action can occur.

There are thus considerable differences between Aristotle's PS and modern revivals of it, although Aristotle was the first to speak of the PS; even those who, nowadays and in various ways, have revived this concept base their work on Aristotle's. At this point, it may be useful to briefly summarize some of these differences, which correspond to important differences between Aristotle's general conception of practical knowledge and the modern positions.

Very briefly, we can say that, in Aristotle's conception of the PS, he is more interested in the efficacy of the reasoning than in its rigor and necessity. Aristotle offers us a conception of practical reasoning that is strictly linked to the action of an individual in a given context, and he structures the field of application of the PS in a significantly different way from today's thinkers. Some problems that are highlighted in our times are treated by Aristotle with less attention, or are completely absent in his works; on the other hand, he devotes much time to discussing some questions that are now considered of minor importance.

Most of Aristotle's attention in the *Ethics* is devoted to the ways of determining the end in concrete situations, the clarification of the nature of virtue and the description of individual virtues or of ethically significant factors such as friendship and pleasure. He does not give a logic of practical knowledge comparable to modern calculations, e.g. calculations that start from imperatives and not from judgments. Nor did Aristotle work out a propositional calculus that takes account of operators such as "it is obligatory that," etc.[104] Nevertheless, however schematic it may be, Aristotle's description of practical knowledge contains features of interest also for today's discussions; it is worth pointing out some of them. At first sight it seems possible to say that Aristotle, while maintaining a clear distinction between scientific and practical knowledge, both in relation to the ends they set themselves, and in relation to the emotional part of the soul (*EN* VI 2 and 3), does not make such a clear-cut distinction between them that they cannot be compared. Aristotle establishes the characteristics of practical knowledge starting from the theory of the syllogism, and takes the theoretical syllogism as his model. This model undergoes a whole series of modifications, inversions of priorities, and reductions in rigor, all of which are made necessary by the different object and the different end of it, but this still does not prevent the PS from being interpreted in relation to Aristotle's general theory of the syllogism.

Just as, in political theory, the description of the best state serves as a point of reference on the basis of which the various existing constitutions can be judged and described, so too in the field of practical reasoning Aristotle seems to want to understand the nature of the reasoning that leads to action by means of an analogy with scientific reasoning. But just as a plant or an animal species, when transplanted to a new environment, undergoes modifications that adapt it to its new situation, and differentiate it from the original model, so too the PS is an adaptation of the scheme of the syllogism to different tasks and needs. There is thus no identification between practical reasoning and the model of science set forth in the *Analytica*. There is not, however, the same difference between practical knowledge and science that could be posited today between, say, scientific research and aesthetic judgment, or poetic intuition.[105] There is, instead, a partial distinction, related to the end, within a common *genus*.

This is proved also by the relative proximity in which Aristotle puts production and action (cf. Chapter 1). These two fields are certainly distinct in his theory, but not so distinct as tends to be thought today, after twentieth-century criticism of the "inhumanity" of science and technology. Both the practical and productive types of knowledge have as their end an action, viz. a goal-oriented body movement, and they are both opposed to a purely contemplative ἐπιστήμη. Today we tend to detach productive activity from actual conduct, and to connect it rather with a concept of "science" that is very far from being that of the ancients. Thus comparisons between the two views of knowledge—that of Aristotle and that of us moderns—are very difficult to make, and often misleading. Undoubtedly Aristotle was the first to make a clear separation between actual conduct and production (cf. *EN* VI 3–4), but the difference between the two does not seem to lie in the logical structure of their reasoning, which is more or less the same, whether the end is an action or a product.

In conclusion, Aristotle underlines the peculiar features of the reasoning that gives rise to an action, or, more generally, to a goal-oriented body movement, whether it be the production of something or an action, and he conducts this examination within a single very general scheme of rationality. His scheme is symbolized by the concept of "syllogism"; this concept must certainly be understood in a rather general sense, but that does not by any means imply that the process is carried out on the basis of intuitive and emotional associations, or exclusively private and incommunicable perceptions, mystical revelations, or poetic or sentimental inspirations.

Appendix: Weakness of the Will According to *EN* VII 3, 1147a 24-b 5

According to the interpretation given here, the PS consists, in part, of the transmission of desire from an end to a concrete action, through one or more middle terms that indicate a good action as the specification of the end. The intermediate terms between the end and the action, seen from the perspective of the end, become, precisely for this reason, the object of desire. Aristotle says that movement derives from the minor premise, or also, if one so wishes, from both premises, but in a different way in each case, since the major premise is not a direct source of movement, except in special cases, when the minor premise is obvious. The major premise, instead, is the cause of the fact that we desire the means expressed by the minor premise (*de an.* III 11, 434a 16–21).

On the basis of our interpretation, we would now like to tackle a classic crux in the modern interpretations of Aristotle—the passage in *EN* VII 3 where he applies the explanatory scheme for action provided by the PS to the problem of ἀκρασία.[106] The thesis that Aristotle wants to maintain here is that ἀκρασία is also, in a certain sense, a form of ignorance and that, therefore, Socrates' identification of ἀκρασία and ignorance was not completely unjustified.[107] But, with respect to the scheme of the PS, this ignorance does not regard the major premise; what is not known in any significant way is the minor premise. There is a simple systematic reason for this statement: one who, in acting, does not know the correct major premise, i.e. one who does not set himself good ends, but pursues wicked aims, is not an ἀκρατής but a φαῦλος, an evil person.[108] It is not possible, in general, that ἀκρασία could ever be ignorance of the major premise and remain distinct from κακία, wickedness.

This general thesis is discussed in VII 3. Contemporary criticism is particularly divided about this text, and the debate is very heated; in the opinion of several scholars, in the course of his discussion—and particularly in the passage we intend to deal with here—Aristotle does not manage to maintain the thesis we sketched above, but is rather forced, by the very logic of his argument, to change his position. We do not here intend to rediscuss the entire question of ἀκρασία, about which there is an abundant literature; we only wish to uphold the position that those who affirm that Aristotle changes position in the course of Chapter VII 3, and that he does not maintain his identification of ἀκρασία with ignorance of the minor premise, neglect the possibility of interpreting the text in such a way as to make it a coherent and non-contradictory whole. The ambiguity that underlies the interpretations that we here intend to criticize is, in our opinion, mainly due to the tendency to regard the minor premise as only an assumption of factual data or empirical observations regarding a particular situation. It is, in fact, impossible to be ignorant of such data and still act; nor can this ignorance be called ἀκρασία, "weakness of will." To take Kenny's example, if a mature playboy, in a state of semi-drunkenness (*EN* 1147a 14), tries to seduce a friend's wife, the weakness of will does not seem to be that he has temporarily forgotten that "she is my friend's wife," but rather that he has temporarily forgotten that "she is to be left in peace."[109] The chapter is well outlined by Gauthier in this way: first, knowledge in action is distinguished from the mere possession of knowledge; then this distinction is applied to the PS, and it is shown that the knowledge not possessed in action is that summed up in the minor premise. Then Aristotle demonstrates how the incontinent man may know the minor premise, but not have it, so to speak, "on active duty"; and lastly he applies this scheme to the PS.[110] The application of the scheme of the PS to the problem of ἀκρασία is presented as an explanation φυσικῶς, conducted from the psychological point of view;[111] the scheme of the PS should serve to explain how it is possible that the ἀκρατής, even if he possesses the minor premise, may possess it as opinions are held by one who sleeps or is mad or drunk or is playing a part like an actor (*EN* 1147a 10–24). It appears that we are to understand that he may even know the correct minor premise "in words," but not know it in a practically relevant way, i.e. in a way that gives rise to εὐπραξία. The explanation of how this comes about goes like this:

> moreover, we could examine the cause from the psychological point of view as follows: one is a universal δόξα, the other regards particular cases, which are

> in the domain of αἴσθησις,[112] and when a single thing is generated from them, the soul must there affirm the conclusion, while, in the case of practical [premises],[113] it must act at once. For example, if one must taste every sweet thing, and this thing here is a particular sweet thing, then anyone who is able to and is not prevented from doing so must also, simultaneously, perform this action (τοῦτο . . . πράττειν). When, therefore, there is a universal that prohibits tasting, and another premise that 'every sweet thing is pleasant', and this thing here is sweet—this gives rise to action—if by chance ἐπιθυμία is present, the one says to leave this (τοῦτο),[114] and ἐπιθυμία drives one to taste it, since it can move each of the parts [of the body]. So it happens that one is incontinent, in a certain sense, on account of a λόγος and a δόξα, which are not contrary by nature, but by accident, to the right λόγος, for it is ἐπιθυμία that is contrary and not δόξα. This explains why animals do not have weakness of will, as they do not have universal ὑπόληψις, but only φαντασία and memory regarding particular cases. (1147a 24-b 5)

This text is divided into two parts. The first (1147a 24–31) expounds the correct PS; the second, introduced by a ὅταν οὖν (1147a 31–b 5), presents the PS as vitiated by weakness of the will. The two syllogisms that Aristotle contrasts with one another are contained, one in the first part and the other in the second part, and not, as almost all commentators affirm, both in the second part. There are two reasons for making this statement. In the first place, the function of the first part would otherwise not be very clear: often, indeed, commentators have remarked that here Aristotle would like to remind his audience of how the PS functions with regard to the problem of weakness of the will. But it is odd that this should be the case, since just a few lines earlier—in 1146b 35–1147a 4—he had already reminded his audience of how the PS functions with regard to the problem of weakness of the will. In that passage he had stated that it is possible to act against practical knowledge, if one does not make use of the minor premise; to explain this, he had formulated the following syllogism:

(1) Dried foods are good for every man
I am a man and this food is dry

[taste immediately].

Aristotle says: "either he does not have 'if this here is so-and-so', or it is not active" (1147a 7); this means that, if the just-quoted minor premise were present and active, the practical conclusion would necessarily result. This is exactly what has been repeated in the above-quoted passage, in lines 1147a 26–31. The two passages thus have the same content.[115]

In the second place, the traditional interpretation, according to which the passage 1147a 31 et seq. contrasts two syllogisms, one correct and the other incorrect, leads to paradoxical conclusions. Those who admit this generally think that in this passage there are two major premises, i.e. ἡ μὲν καθόλου . . . κωλύουσα γεύεσθαι (a 31–32) and πᾶν γλυκὺ ἡδύ (a 32–33).[116] These premises are said to give rise to two syllogisms called, usually, "syllogism of reason" and "syllogism of appetite," even if the latter expression must be considered a metaphor, since otherwise it would give expression to a contradiction in terms. If, in 1147a 31 et seq., there are two syllogisms, it is necessary to make τουτὶ δὲ γλυκύ (a32) the minor premise. The result is that we have the following two practical syllogisms:

(2) do not taste (anything sweet)[117]	(3) every sweet thing is pleasant
this thing here is sweet	this thing here is sweet
———————————	———————————
[he tastes it at once]	[he doesn't taste it]

Understood in this way, this example not only does not support the theory that Aristotle has outlined up to this point, but even refutes it completely: in fact, here we would have an incorrect syllogism (3), which should be that of the incontinent man, but in which, instead of having the same major premise as the correct syllogism (2) and a different minor premise, we have a different major premise and the same minor premise. Therefore, Aristotle—after having stated that he wants to give a psychological explanation of the cause of weakness of the will—would be contradicting what he said in lines 1147a 2–3,[118] where he states that one who does not control himself either does not have or does not apply the minor premise.

Before stating, as many others have, that here Aristotle changes his position, it is advisable to see if another interpretation of the passage is possible. And this should be done also because, as we mentioned earlier, syllogism (3) does not seem to be one proper to the ἀκρατής, but rather proper to the φαῦλος, who: (a) takes as valid a mistaken major premise, so that he takes as a true practical good what is only an apparent good ("every sweet thing is pleasant") and (b) has no inner conflicts.

We believe that in 1147a 31 et seq. only one type of practical reasoning is described, and it is that of the ἀκρατής. While Aristotle clearly states that "do not taste (anything sweet)" is a universal practical premise, "every sweet thing is pleasant" is presented as a universal δόξα but it is not said that, since it is a universal opinion, it is a practical premise—indeed, this is denied. Aristotle says that there is no contradiction καθ' αὑτήν (b 2) between this and the correct major practical premise, "do not taste (anything sweet)." He adds: "In fact, ἐπιθυμία is contrary, not δόξα." The contradiction could arise only if either "do not taste (anything sweet)" were only δόξα, or "every sweet thing is pleasant" were a major premise, i.e. a union of δόξα + ὄρεξις. But there is no contradiction between a practical premise and a mere opinion, since one may very well think that every sweet thing is pleasant to eat and yet refrain from eating it, in view of a superior good. There is no reason why a practical premise such as "do not taste (anything sweet)" may not be accompanied by many non-practical opinions regarding the kinds of things the premise is about, as e.g.: "every sweet thing is pleasant," "it is perishable," "it is expensive," etc. But the δόξα given above has a special role, although, in our interpretation, it is not a practical premise. We shall look at this role later on; this will explain why Aristotle mentions precisely this opinion out of all the possible δόξαι.

From the organization of the text, no matter how condensed and composite it may be, it is clear that the opposition is between the universal major premise and ἐπιθυμία. This is stated in 1147b 1–2, where it is clearly indicated that the opposition is between desire and correct λόγος. Aristotle, by using the same verb (ἐνῇ, ἐνοῦσα, a 32 and 34), underlines which two elements are present, in a significant way, in the soul of those who suffer from weakness of the will: a practical premise and a disobedient desire. In this way he picks up the terms and concepts of *EN* I 13 and II 1–3. But what is ἐπιθυμία applied to? Not to the δόξα that "every sweet thing is pleasant," for the reasons given above, but to the minor premise "this thing is sweet" (a 33).[119] This is made clear also in a later passage:

> instead, ἐπιθυμία, if only λόγος or αἴσθησις says that it is sweet, makes haste to taste it. (1149a 34)

Therefore, in the syllogism of the incontinent man, the minor premise, which causes the movement (a 33)[120] because it regards a concrete situation and is, so to speak, practicable, instead of subsuming the empirical fact under the correct major premise, proves to be ineffectual, because ἐπιθυμία opposes its force of rebellion. We mean that, because of the presence of an opposing passion, the perception of the state of affairs "this thing is sweet" is only verbally seen in the light of a correct general desire, in this case a φυγή that refuses to taste sweet things. In reality it is subsumed under the contrary impulse of ἐπιθυμία. The fact is perceived in two different ways, but only one of them gives rise to a practical minor premise. The correct minor premise is either not possessed at all, or is possessed only in words, and only in an insignificant way, while irrational desire is efficacious and pushes in the opposite direction.[121] This opposition is described by means of a careful choice of terms, in which only one element λέγει (says, *sc.* to do *x*),[122] and the other ἄγει, acts (a 34).

The cause that prevents the transmission of correct desire is ἐπιθυμία, which is thus the cause announced in line 1147a 25. In this way the passage that we are examining does not provide a different solution from that of the rest of the chapter; on the contrary, it appears to be well integrated into the context of the chapter (cf. the particle ἔτι, 1147a 24, which should be considered alongside the other instances of ἔτι in 1146b 35 and 1147a 10), and bases the general explanation of VII 3 on an analysis of the relevant psychological mechanism. Aristotle points out that the correct minor premise, "this thing here is sweet (and hence to be avoided)" is absent, or said as in a dream, or like the speech of drunkards and actors (1147a 12–14, 19 et seq.; b 9–12). Aristotle's series of examples, most of which regard the "theoretical" plane, should be transferred to the practical plane in order to be properly understood. The case of the actor seems to us the clearest one: he says to his antagonist "I hate you!" but he does not mean it seriously. In the practical context, these examples seem to us not to show that the knowledge of particulars is clouded over as knowledge (since one knows very well that "this is sweet"), but rather as a practical premise. It may therefore happen that an incontinent man has the correct opinion at the time when he acts, and while eating one sweet after another or playing havoc with one female heart after another, he repeats to himself, "I mustn't do it." But this opinion is not practical, or is not practically possessed, i.e. it is not accompanied by desire.

There is therefore a conflict, but it is not a conflict between two acts of desire regarding the same thing, since Aristotle—at least in this passage—seems to consider it contradictory to have two opposing drives, pursuing and fleeing, operating at the same time and from the same point of view, with regard to the same object. We shall see that on this point his *De anima* is partly different. It is, indeed, possible to react to a universal φάντασμα by rejecting it, though without managing to control oneself when faced with a concrete instance of the same object, if the desiring faculty does not constantly obey reason.

Aristotle presents a situation made up of five elements. Their particular relations explain the cause of ἀκρασία and show how it operates. They are:

I. a correct major premise, "do not taste," called also ὀρθὸς λόγος (1147b 3, cf. *EN* II 6);

II. a universal δόξα, such as: "every sweet thing is pleasant";

III. a statement regarding a particular state of affairs, stemming from αἴσθησις, such as "this thing is sweet";

IV. an ineffective minor premise, which says literally: "refuse it!";

V. an unreasonable act of desire, ἐπιθυμία, which impels one to accept it.

This situation leads to an action in contradiction with the major premise. In our opinion, using the elements given, one can put together the premises of a

PS, since in it there is a transmission—albeit a distorted one—of desire. We will thus have an erroneous PS, which is a formal representation of the psychological process characterising ἀκρασία. Hence it looks rather strange:

> (4) do not taste (anything sweet) <everything sweet is pleasant> (I+II)
> this thing is not to be tasted (it is sweet) {to be tasted} (IV + III + V)
>
> ---
>
> [it is tasted at once].

The above scheme is rather complicated and requires some explanation. Outside the parentheses we have written the parts of the PS affirmed by λόγος, then in parentheses we have added the specifications regarding the quality of the object. Alongside the major premise we have added, between the signs < >, the non-practical δόξα, according to which every sweet thing is pleasant. In the minor premise we have put the impulse of ἐπιθυμία between double brackets {}; it is opposed to the content of the practical premise, and actually causes the action, making the premise ineffectual. What we have said here will be clearer if we compare syllogism (4) with the "virtuous" syllogism illustrated in the first part of the passage, 1147a 24–31. It would go like this:

> (5) every sweet thing is to be tasted
> this thing is sweet (to be tasted)
>
> ---
>
> [it is tasted at once]. (a 29–31)

But since the syllogism of the ἀκρατής concerns a prohibition and not an order with respect to the same kind of action, for clarity's sake the comparison should be made by changing the sign of syllogism (5). We would therefore have a correct PS (5') which we can now contrast with (4) in the following way:

(4) do not taste (anything sweet)	(5') do not taste (anything sweet)
<every sweet thing is pleasant>	
this thing is not to be tasted	this thing is not to be tasted (it is
(it is sweet) {to be tasted}	sweet)
———————————	———————————
[it is tasted at once].	[it is not tasted].

In our opinion, this reconstruction, which summarizes the comparison made in 1147a 24–b 5, does justice to what Aristotle says in the whole of chapter VII 3. Here, in fact, we have an incorrect PS contrasted with a correct PS, containing the same major premise as the correct one, but having a different minor premise, in which the difference lies not in the perception of the state of affairs, but in the impulse given by desire. The particular thing is correctly perceived as something to be avoided, but ἐπιθυμία interferes and modifies the transmission of desire. Thus desire is not transmitted to the minor premise on account of ἐπιθυμία, which is the αἰτία of the error. And the error consists in not possessing at all, or not possessing in the appropriate way, the practical minor premise.

Two problems remain; one is related to element (II) and one to element (IV), which we have put into the final scheme of the wrong PS, and which in some way support and determine it. With regard to (II), we know that the δόξα present here is not a practical premise and is not accompanied by desire, since it is of universal scope. The incontinent man does not affirm that "every sweet thing is pleasant," but maintains, in complete good faith, that "it is necessary to avoid every sweet thing," with his desire in an attitude of obedience. Then he sees a sweet and eats it. But this does not involve a complete overturning of his practical principles, not even for a minute.[123] As a matter of fact, he rarely gives in to temptation, and when he does he regrets it. Even if it is not a practical premise, the δόξα mentioned in point (II) serves to direct ἐπιθυμία. This latter, which neither analyzes nor reflects, is activated only in the presence of a pleasant sensation, or one about which another faculty says, "It is pleasant," as is stated in *EN* 1149a 34–36 quoted above. The δόξα thus gives ἐπιθυμία an important piece of information, with regard to which unreasonable desire is automatically activated. But there is no PS between the universal δόξα in point (II) and the ἐπιθυμία in point (V), since the universal statement is not accompanied by desire and is therefore not a practical premise. Only the particular judgment, in which ἐπιθυμία "pushes" (ἄγει), is "on active duty," to use Anscombe's expression. Without δόξα (II), ἐπιθυμία (V) would not move, because normally, when we are presented with an unknown food whose effects on our palate are not known to us, our cupidity is not set in motion. On the other hand, without ἐπιθυμία no *akratic* action would be caused at all.

As for point (IV), to say, in words, that "this is to be avoided" is not a conclusion, συμπέρασμα, as many commentators have supposed, then pointing to this text to affirm that a PS does not always have an action as a conclusion. It seems, however, strange to maintain that Aristotle, after having twice repeated (1147a 2 and 28) in this chapter that the PS concludes with an action, now, just six lines later (a 34), expresses a judgment that implies that the conclusion of the PS is merely a statement. Point (IV) expresses an "aborted" practical minor premise, in which λόγος has quite coherently assumed a particular in the light of the universal, though desire has not followed it. It is therefore only "said" (a 34). Aristotle clearly states that this is a correct practical minor premise, but that it is absent, or present only "in words," in the reasoning of the ἀκρατής:

> since the last premise is a δόξα that regards sensible objects, and is the one that controls our actions, a person who is in a state of passion does not possess it, or possesses it in such a way that, as we have said, his possessing it is not knowing, but only empty speaking, like a drunken man who recites the words of Empedocles. (1147b 9–12)

The τελευταία πρότασις spoken of here, in a context where the technical language of the syllogism is quite noticeably present, can only be the minor premise.[124] Several recent commentators have tried to maintain that, by this expression, Aristotle is referring to the last phrase, i.e. the conclusion. This seems extremely doubtful, if we compare the two passages, *EN* 1147b 9–10 and *de an.* 434a 16–21 (quoted on p. 207). Both passages speak of a ὑπόληψις that regards particulars (τοῦ καθ' ἕκαστα, [τοῦ] αἰσθητοῦ) and that gives rise to movement (αὕτη κινεῖ, κυρία τῶν πράξεων). We are thus dealing with the minor premise, which is here not possessed in a practical way, and the reference to *De anima* makes it quite clear that a minor premise, and not a conclusion, is involved.

We therefore think that, in this passage, Aristotle is confirming his general doctrine, whereby the difference between a wicked man and a weak man lies in the different kinds of practical ignorance they are affected by. In accordance with Aristotle's usual tendency to schematize and simplify the differences, we may say that the two are differentiated in that the wicked man and the weak man are unaware, in a practically relevant way, of different practical premises. A wicked man does not know the major premise, and substitutes for it a general program of bad actions, to which he constantly directs his desire. A weak man sometimes does not know the minor premise and replaces it with an impulse of the appetite; this impulse can be represented as a minor premise that does not follow the major one and distorts the correct flow of the PS. Somehow there are mechanisms that do not work, in the transmission of desire, as Aristotle says in one of the most obscure passages of *De anima:*

> desire does not imply the deliberative faculty: sometimes it conquers and drives rational desire (βούλησιν), sometimes instead that [drives] this, just like a sphere; desire [conquers and drives] desire, when weakness of the will is generated. Instead, by nature, the superior desire always prevails and moves, so that it moves with three movements involved. (434a 12–15, manuscript text)

With respect to the passage in *EN* VII 3 discussed above, here Aristotle does not think that ἐπιθυμία immediately, and—as it were—without a struggle, takes the place of correct desire or βούλησις, but he thinks of a clash between the two (νικᾷ. . . καὶ κινεῖ) in which irrational desire wins. As for the sphere mentioned here, it is not clear whether Aristotle is thinking of the motion of the celestial spheres, in which the influences of the higher spheres converge, as some commentators have thought, or simply a marble bumped against by others, as some critics maintain. It is, however, clear that φύσει is the good and higher ὄρεξις that prevails, i.e. that of the major premise, but that sometimes (ἐνίοτε, a 12, as opposed to ἀεί, a 14) the mistaken ὄρεξις prevails over the reasonable ὄρεξις, or βούλησις, which is directed at the end of the major premise. Thus Aristotle can state that deliberation is not internal to desire and cannot command it so that it cannot rebel.

In this way, in our opinion, the PS used by Aristotle in the discussion of weakness of the will explains this phenomenon on the basis of an interruption in the correct transmission of desire from the major to the minor premise, and from this to action. This, we believe, confirms our basic hypothesis, viz. that the PS is the formal representation of practical reasoning as a mixture of reason and desire, in which both elements are important and lie on the same plane. The case described here falls under one of the four possibilities of error implicit in *EN* VI 2: it is a case in which the reasoning is correct, but the desire is not; hence desire does not pursue (or flee from) what reason affirms (or denies) is a good.

CHAPTER 4

ARISTOTLE'S CONCEPTION OF HAPPINESS

1. A Discussion of English-speaking Interpreters

Our study of the nature of Aristotle's wisdom could have concluded with the previous chapter, but the reader would have received a slightly distorted image of this form of knowledge. We would have run the risk of limiting wisdom's field of action to individual choices, and to particular moments of human life. We would thus not have done justice to Aristotle's conception of wisdom, an important element of which is the idea of "happiness."[1] Happiness is, indeed, the concept by which Aristotle tackles the more general problem of how to live well; but it is also, as being the ultimate end of human existence, one of the principles of practical knowledge, and as such it serves to identify the nature of wisdom according to Aristotle. For in Aristotle's philosophy a science or, more generally, a form of knowledge is first and foremost identified by making clear what its principles are.

Contemporary analyses of the Aristotelian concept of "happiness" are dominated by a distinction, which is both critical and explanatory, put forward by W. F. R. Hardie in 1965.[2] This is universally known as the distinction between an "inclusive" and a "dominant" conception of happiness.

Hardie maintains that one must not confuse two different ideas: one is that we should live in accordance with a rational plan that gives order to our ends and our desires; the other is that it is "necessary" to give a prevailing role to one single end over all others. It is, in fact, possible to have an ordered plan of life and still give satisfaction, either subsequently or simultaneously or alternately, to several mutually independent ends.[3] According to Hardie, Aristotle passes inadvertently from the former conception to the latter, and this confusion weakens his conception of happiness. He maintains that Aristotle begins by identifying happiness with a "second-order end," consisting in the harmonious gratification of the subject's main desires, insofar as this is possible. Hardie finds this conception expressed in *EN* 1094a 26–27, b 6–7, 1141b 24–26. But later on, he claims, Aristotle makes happiness a "dominant" or "prevalent" end, and identifies it with the object of the best desire, i.e. with doing philosophy. Aristotle's error and confusion are, he says, particularly evident in *EE* I 2, where he wonders which of the things at our disposal happiness consists of. Hardie feels that nothing is so important that it can be identified with happiness, i.e. it can make a man happy even when it is acquired at the expense of every other good. The orderly attainment of the main ends of human life, and the sacrificing of everything for a single aim are, in effect, two very different things, and if this confusion were to be found in Aristotle, Hardie would be right to take exception.

The subsequent debate[4] has partly modified and simplified the terms of the discussion. Almost all the authors who have contributed to the debate have adopted Hardie's terms, "inclusive" and "dominant" (except for Hardie himself, who, as we shall see, in 1968 changed his vocabulary). They have used these terms to characterize the two conceptions of happiness said to be present in Aristotle.

Many of them have further radicalized the opposition between the "inclusive" and "dominant" conceptions. The inclusive conception has been viewed as one that makes happiness a complex set including "all the host of life and human actions" (Nagel), "everything that is *per se* desirable" (Ackrill), "the possession of everything that, at a given moment, one desires" (Engberg-Pedersen). In a word, according to the "inclusive" conception, happiness is said to be, as in the *Definitions* of Pseudo Plato, "A good compounded of all goods" (412d 10). The "dominant" conception, instead, has always been viewed as that which identifies happiness with philosophical contemplation.

This simplification has aroused opposition. Some (Clark, Wedin) have underlined the fact that the "inclusive" conception of happiness, if taken literally, is an absurdity: no one can identify happiness with the sum of all goods; if anyone did so, the lack of one single good, even a minimal one (Clark mentions cream chocolates) would suffice to make him unhappy. Others, more correctly, have identified the "inclusive" conception of happiness with the sum of various interests and various types of goods (Cooper, Wilkes), or with the exercise of all the moral and intellectual virtues (Kenny), and not with the sum of "all" goods.

In reaction to these developments, as we said, Hardie[5] changed his vocabulary, no longer speaking of "inclusive" and "dominant," but rather of a "comprehensive" plane and a "paramount" object. The change is explicitly designed to deny that the tension between the two different perspectives makes Aristotle's position inconsistent or contradictory, or that there is a change of position in the different texts that Aristotle devotes to this problem. Hardie does not believe that Aristotle, when he makes θεωρία the essence of a happy life, is suggesting a fanatical and exclusive dedication to contemplation. According to Hardie, Aristotle identifies happiness with a complex set of ends and interests in which philosophical θεωρία is the main component; in different texts he points out different aspects of this conception, i.e. its being "a complex," a composite set, and having a "main component." Still, in Hardie's opinion, this does not absolve Aristotle of all criticism: he has not told us what criterion oversees the organization of the whole, nor what relation there is between the pursuit of contemplation and the exercise of the other virtues. Aristotle seems to have thought that it is sufficient to set oneself a principal end and aim at that, and he has not succeeded in providing convincing reasons for the absolute pre-eminence of philosophical contemplation with respect to every other end.[6] So much for Hardie.

Hardie's position seems more acceptable than some of those that his approach gave rise to. The gap between contemplation and the exercise of the ethical virtues that he points out had been also noted by many of the main interpreters of Aristotle. For example, in 1928 Jaeger, discussing Greenwood's opinions, stated that "it is not easy to find in *EN* what properly the internal dependence of moral virtue on scientific knowledge still consists of."[7] Jaeger says "still" because, according to his reconstruction, this dependence clearly existed in the *Protrepticus* and the *Eudemian Ethics,* works in which mystical contemplation, he said, was posited by Aristotle as the criterion by which to measure earthly values.[8]

Those who have insisted on the incompatibility between the "inclusive" and "dominant" conceptions have contrasted texts containing the former position with other texts containing the latter.

To tell the truth, Ackrill tried to interpret the whole of *EN* I in an "inclusive" sense, but his attempt did not succeed. In fact, *EN* I is clearly linked with *EN* X 6–8, where the "dominant" conception is expounded in the most detailed fashion. Instead, Cooper and Kenny, in two recent books, have set *EE* against *EN*. In the former text they have seen a work in which happiness is described in an "inclusive" and open manner, and in the latter a work in which happiness is viewed in an "intellectualistic" and dominant manner. The just criticism of Jaeger's "theonomic" interpretation of *EE,* together with a more careful consideration of the arguments of *EE* I, have led to a paradoxical reversal of Jaeger's scheme; and some scholars have begun to maintain that, after all, *EE* is to be considered Aristotle's best treatise on ethics, the more recent and philosophically more important text of the two.

It seems to us that there is not such a sharp opposition between the two treatises, and it seems that the discussion of εὐδαιμονία in *EE* I–II is compatible with that in *EN* I, even if at times the points of departure are different, and even if Aristotle, in the two works, emphasizes different sides of his conception of the happy life. Indeed, the two analyses seem to us to lead to more or less the same result. As for *EN* X 6–8, its relation with *EN* I and with other proximate texts will be discussed with care below.

It is therefore necessary to see if both an "inclusive" and a "dominant" conception of happiness are really present in Aristotle and, if they really are present, we must see whether they are really incompatible, as some maintain, or whether, though compatible, their joint presence involves various theoretical difficulties and obscurities in important points of the doctrine, as others believe. To investigate the matter it is necessary to examine the origin of these concepts, their degree of adherence to Aristotle's text and the historical and philosophical background that lay behind the development of Aristotle's position.

2. Some Observations on the Foregoing Discussion

As is well known, the terms inclusive/dominant or comprehensive/prevalent are not to be found in Aristotle's text, and Aristotle never conducts his discussion of happiness on the basis of this distinction. Indeed, Hardie has insisted on the fact that Aristotle is not aware of mixing two different conceptions in his theory—conceptions which can be identified by means of the distinction he has drawn. In this way a distinction developed in another philosophical environment is applied to Aristotle's text.

A recent survey by den Huyl and Machan[9] provides useful information on the origin of the distinction. The distinction between an "inclusive" and a "dominant" end seems to have been elaborated in the ambit of utilitarian ethics, with regard to problems in interpreting the thought of Jeremy Bentham and John Stuart Mill. In these authors, pleasure (equivalent to "happiness") can be considered either as a particular state of the soul, or as a complex whole composed of different activities. In the former case the ultimate end is conceived in a monistic way, while in the latter it no longer has the role of a dominant end, but is seen as an inclusive, second-order end, of which activities such as aesthetic and, in general, intellectual enjoyment are parts. D. den Huyl and Machan note that the discussions about Mill and about Aristotle are carried on in the same way and start from similar problems.

It is not necessarily wrong to apply to a philosopher a conceptual distinction that is foreign to him; indeed, it may help to make the position of the author being studied clearer and more understandable. But when the result of such an application is to impute obscurity and confusion to the author studied, it is legitimate to doubt the advisability of using a distinction which forces him into the Procrustean bed of an opposition invented by others.

The difficulty in applying the inclusive/dominant distinction to Aristotle's conception of happiness is clearly shown by the problems that many contemporary commentators have had in pointing to texts that are manifestly "inclusive," to be set against other texts that are patently expressive of the "dominant" conception. Let us illustrate this with a recent example.

Some scholars, such as Cooper and Kenny, have considered the definition of happiness that Aristotle gives in *EE* II 1, 1219a 38–39, as being typical of an inclusive conception. It runs like this: "Happiness will prove to be the activity of a complete life in accordance with complete virtue (ζωῆς τελείας ἐνέργεια κατ' ἀρετὴν τελείαν)." This has been set against the definition of happiness given in *EN* I 7, 1098a 16–18, where the expression of a "dominant" conception of happiness has been seen. It goes like this: "[Happiness is] an activity of the soul [. . .] in accordance with virtue" and "in accordance with the best and most perfect [virtue] (κατὰ τὴν ἀρίστην καὶ τελειοτάτην)." We would thus have, on the one hand, an activity in accordance with the whole set of human capabilities or, better, a set of moral and intellectual activities, and, on the other, a single activity, that of the most perfect virtue. The inclusive/dominant opposition is said to be expressed by the contrast between τελείαν and τελειοτάτην.[10]

Kenny cites a couple of texts to support his thesis that happiness, in *EN* I, is exclusively activity in accordance with the best and most perfect virtue (*EN* I 13, 1102a 5–7 and 1103a 2–10), but in our opinion these very texts prove the contrary. Indeed, they show that in *EN* I Aristotle has no intention of affirming that happiness corresponds to performing only one kind of activity, i.e. philosophical contemplation. To understand this, it is necessary to take account of other passages, in addition to the ones mentioned.

1. In *EN* I 8, 1099a 29–30, it is said that happiness is equivalent to the best activities, ἄρισται ἐνέργειαι, or to a single one of them, the best (τὴν ἀρίστην), without choosing between the two possibilities;

2. later on, in 1099b 26, it is said that happiness is "a certain kind of activity of the soul in accordance with virtue," κατ' ἀρετήν, without any further specification;

3. in 1100a 4–5, Aristotle states that, "as we have said,"[11] to be happy there must be "both complete virtue and a complete life (καὶ ἀρετῆς τελείας καὶ βίου τελείου)." This passage is important; it is part of *EN* and yet it shows striking similarities with *EE* 1219a 38–39 (quoted above); it gives, as features of happiness, both a "complete life" and "complete virtue," exactly as in *EE*. There are some differences, to be sure, such as the substitution of βίος for ζωή, and the absence of any indication that happiness is activity in accordance with complete virtue (κατ' ἀρετήν), but these seem to us to be of minor importance;

4. in 1100b 11–13 Aristotle reminds us that, according to his definition (λόγος), happiness consists of "activities in accordance with virtue (ἐνέργειαι κατ' ἀρετήν)," and it seems to us that here he is referring to different kinds of activities and not to repeated acts of the same kind; indeed, Aristotle posits different degrees of honor (b 15) for these activities;

5. again in 1101a 14–16 Aristotle says that there is no reason not to call happy "one who acts in accordance with complete virtue (τὸν κατ' ἀρετὴν τελείαν ἐνεργοῦντα)," is endowed with sufficient external goods, and not for a short period, but for an entire life (ἀλλὰ τέλειον βίον). This formulation, too, is practically identical to the one in *EE* II 1, though with certain additions and expansions whose importance we shall discuss later.

This is the main point of our argument: we have noted that there are no important conceptual differences between *EE* and *EN*, inasmuch as the terms and expressions used in the definition of happiness given in *EE* II 1, 1219a 38–39, repeatedly appear also in *EN*. The word τέλειον, which is present in these passages of the two *Ethics*, must be interpreted in the same sense in both books. There is no reason to assume that, in expressions so similar, it has different meanings, as for example that in one place it is closer to the meaning of "complete" and in the other it has the meaning of "perfect."

Therefore, in tackling the reading of *EN* I 13, there appears to be no reason to set this text against what is said in *EE*. Aristotle states, as in *EE*, that happiness is "a certain activity in accordance with complete virtue (κατ' ἀρετὴν τελείαν)" (1102a 5–6)—and not "an activity in accordance with a certain virtue"—adding that there are two kinds of virtue, ethical and dianoetic. At the end of the passage,[12] he says that "also" the wise man—one who possesses intellectual activities—is to be praised, and that therefore also the habitual states (ἕξεις) such as wisdom, and understanding, are virtues. We have discussed this passage elsewhere, as it is important for determining the nature of φρόνησις[13] here it suffices to observe that Aristotle does not at all maintain that "only" the wise man is to be praised, or that only his ἕξις is virtue. The complete virtue of

1102a 5–6 evidently includes both the series of ethical virtues and the series of dianoetic virtues.

In our opinion, then, on account of the foregoing reasons it seems clear that the definition of happiness as "activity in accordance with complete virtue" and the definition of happiness as "activity in accordance with the best and most perfect virtue" are not mutually incompatible. Aristotle clearly shows that he understands the two definitions in a sense that makes them equivalent in many ways; he passes indifferently from one to the other in the final part of *EN* I. Still, it is not clear how this is possible, nor what may be the similarities and differences between the two definitions, in Aristotle's eyes, since it is not a question of opposing a life in conformity with all human abilities and excellences to a life devoted only to contemplation.

3. Happiness According to Plato's Academy

One way to solve the problem could be to compare Aristotle's position with that of the other disciples of Plato, in order to see the degree of his originality and coherence on the basis of the discussions of the Academy. This is not a new approach; it was already suggested by Burnet and later picked up by Dirlmeier and Gauthier.[14]

Fortunately, all the definitions of happiness given by the first scholarchs of the Academy have been preserved. Clement of Alexandria devotes Chapter 2 22 of the *Stromateis*[15] to a comparison between the Academic and Christian conceptions of the highest good (*summum bonum*). He holds that Plato, who he believes took the essence of his thought from the philosophy of Moses, identifies happiness with "assimilation to God insofar as this is possible for man." Halfway through the chapter Clement opens a parenthesis—which is of great importance for us—in which he briefly expounds the opinions of the early disciples of Plato on the nature of happiness. The parenthetical nature of this passage is confirmed by the fact that Clement does not bother to criticize these authors, and puts off the discussion of their positions for another, more opportune occasion (II 22, 134, 1 : it is not clear what text is being referred to). The passage goes like this:

> (4) Speusippus, Plato's nephew, says that happiness is a perfect disposition (ἕξιν . . . τελείαν) in the things in conformity with nature, or a disposition related to goods. All men have a tendency (ὄρεξις) toward this way of being (κατάστασις), but it is good men who achieve the absence of troubles (ἀοχλησία). In his opinion the virtues generate happiness. (5) Xenocrates of Chalcedon defines happiness as possession (κτῆσις) of the virtue proper (to each, οἰκεῖα), and of the capacity that serves to put it into practice (ὑπηρετική).

> (6) Moreover, he clearly says that [1] that in which it comes about is the soul; [2] that by which it comes about are the virtues; [3] that on the basis of which, *qua* parts, it comes about, are [3.1] noble actions, [3.2] dispositions (ἕξεις), [3.3] [mental] states (διαθέσεις), [3.4] movements (κινήσεις) and [3.5] honest attitudes (σχέσεις); [4] that without which it does not come about are [the goods] of the body and external goods. (7) Polemo, a disciple of Xenocrates, clearly means that happiness is self-sufficiency in all goods, or in the most numerous and greatest of them. He also lays it down that happiness never exists without virtue, and that virtue is sufficient for happiness separately from the goods of the body and external goods. (II 22, 133, 4–7)[16]

To sum up: (1) *none* of Plato's disciples *identifies virtue with the possession of all goods.* All of them, on the contrary, following in Plato's footsteps (2) *closely link happiness with virtue.*[17] As Aristotle says in the *Elegy to Eudemus* (fr. 673 Rose), Plato was the first to show with examples and arguments how a man becomes both good and happy. Speusippus says that the virtues produce happiness; Xenocrates says that happiness consists in possessing virtue and knowing how to put it into practice, and that it is generated by virtue; lastly, Polemo makes the virtues the necessary and sufficient cause of happiness. All of them (3) *make happiness consist in a "state" or in a "way of being":* Speusippus speaks of ἕξις, διάθεσις, κατάστασις Xenocrates makes it a κτῆσις and Polemo a state of αὐτάρκεια. Virtuous actions are not mentioned by Speusippus, who rather speaks of "tranquillity" and "absence of troubles" (ἀοχλησία, ἀλυπία, cf. fr. 60D Lang = 112 Isnardi Parente), in conformity with his doctrine, which posits pleasure and pain as two opposing evils. Instead, for Xenocrates virtuous actions are one of the parts (μέρη) of happiness, and, again, Polemo does not mention virtuous actions as a part of the self-sufficiency (αὐτάρκεια) of the happy man; (4) as for external goods, some critics[18] feel that Speusippus considers these goods to be not irrelevant to the state of happiness, even if they are not expressly named in this passage; Xenocrates takes external goods as a necessary but not sufficient condition of happiness, while Polemo does not even feel that they are a necessary condition for being happy. On this point, their disagreement is explicit.

As we have seen, they all believe that happiness is a complex whole that includes some goods and excludes others. Its nature as being τελειότης (completeness, perfection) does not mean that all goods, of all kinds, are part of it. In particular, for Xenocrates external goods, such as wealth and honors, health and strength, are not a constituent part of happiness, but a necessary condition for it, while for Polemo they are not even a necessary condition for being happy.

Xenocrates' position is the most complex. It is divided into a "definition" of virtue as the "possession" of two different spiritual qualities, virtue and the ability to put it into practice, and a "further analysis" distinguishing the "site" of happiness, "what produces it" and its "parts"; these parts are five in number, and include states and movements. Virtuous actions have a pre-eminent place in the listing of the parts of virtue.

4. Aristotle's Critique

Aristotle takes over many of the Academic positions, both in this and in other aspects of his discussion of ethics. In a previous chapter we saw that Aristotle ascribes even his definition of ethical virtue to his contemporaries (1144b 21: καὶ γὰρ νῦν πάντες, an expression usually used to indicate the philosophers of the Academy; cf. *top.* 104b 25). But in other respects Aristotle develops an original position, which in the end proves to be very different, and almost opposite, to the one he started from.[19] The passages which most clearly contain a criticism of the Academic positions mentioned above are some parts of *EN* I 8 and *EE* I 4, which we must now examine.

In *EE* I 4, Aristotle states:

> most of the obscure points and doubts will be clear when we have clearly defined what εὐδαιμονία should be thought to be—whether, that is, [it consists] only in the soul's having a certain character, as some philosophers, and some of the most elderly, have believed, or whether, although one must necessarily have a certain character, it is above all necessary that one's actions should have such a character. (1215a 20–25)[20]

Like Xenocrates, here Aristotle makes happiness consist of a certain good state of the soul, together with a certain kind of actions. What is typical of Aristotle's position, here, is the fact that he says that the thing that is "above all (μᾶλλον) necessary" is that good actions should occur, while for Xenocrates it is more important for the soul to be in a certain state.

In *EN* I 8, 1098b 22 et seq., Aristotle cites the opinions of others to confirm the validity of his argument. As in *metaph.* II 1, also here (b 23–29) he says that all his predecessors, despite their differing opinions, grasped some part of the truth. He agrees with those who identified happiness with virtue, or with a certain virtue, but he qualifies this agreement, and expresses his own opinion: happiness can be identified with virtue only if one accepts the thesis that the most typical characteristic of virtue is to cause right actions.[21] We shall see that it is these, above all, that happiness consists of, and that Aristotle connects virtues and actions much more closely than the Academics did, as the following passage makes clear:

> It certainly (ἴσως) makes no small difference whether one considers the greatest good [= happiness] to consist of possession (κτῆσις) or of use (χρῆσις)—a

> habitual disposition (ἕξις) or an activity (ἐνέργεια). It is possible that the disposition may be present without leading one to do anything good, for one may be asleep or inactive in some other way, whereas this is not possible for the activity. It will necessarily act, and act well. Just as, at the Olympic games, it is not the strongest who are crowned, but those who compete (in fact, some of these win), so it is those who act correctly who attain the fine and good things of life. (1098b 31–1099a 7)

The key terms of Speusippus' and Xenocrates' definitions are mentioned, viz. disposition and possession (ἕξις, κτῆσις), and they are replaced by new key terms, χρῆσις and ἐνέργεια, use and activity. The essential change[22] in perspective consists in identifying the happy man as an active person, and not one who lives in a state of ataraxia, apathy or immobile tranquillity. Happiness thus consists of a sum of "certain" goods, viz. fine actions and praiseworthy deeds. This is why Aristotle often says that εὐδαιμονία is εὐπραξία, correct behavior (*phys.* 197b 3–5; *pol.* 1325b 18–21; 1325b 14: εὐπραγία *rhet.* 1360b 14).

In *EE* II 1 Aristotle resumes the discussion of the Academic position, and defines happiness as the "activity of a complete life in accordance with complete virtue" (1219a 38–39). We have already mentioned this passage in the preceding pages. Keeping in mind the comparison with the Academic positions, let us now re-examine this definition of "happiness," which is, according to Cooper and Kenny, the definition closest to an "inclusive" conception.

The structure of this chapter has been discussed by many recent authors, and many apparent obscurities and difficulties in the text have been clarified.[23] Aristotle's procedure is rather rigorous; the demonstration is based on a series of assumptions, justified on the basis of their being self-evident, or by induction, or by reference to previous discussions; and from these assumptions Aristotle deduces his definition of "happiness."

As far as we are concerned, this text is important mainly because in it Aristotle demonstrates his thesis that activities and actions are greater and better than states and dispositions; in this way Aristotle defends his decision to define happiness in terms of ἐνέργεια and not of ἕξις.

The part of the discussion that most interests us begins at line 1218b 35 where, after distinguishing between the various kinds of good, Aristotle says:

> of the things that are in the soul, some are habitual dispositions (ἕξεις) or capacities (δυνάμεις), while others are activities (ἐνέργειαι) and movements (κινήσεις). (b 35–36)

Here the opposition is between two classes of reality, and not four different components of the soul, as some have thought.[24] On the one hand, there are "habits or capacities," terms that are used almost as synonyms, and on the other "movements and activities." It is not necessary to find any particular distinction between these last two terms. In *EN* 1098b 31, quoted above, the opposition was between possession or habit, on the one hand, and use or activity, on the other, and it was not necessary to distinguish precisely between the two terms used by Aristotle to mark the two sides of the opposition.[25] This division of psychic realities is not the "official" division of Aristotelian ethics (cf. *EN* 1105b 20: the soul contains "passions," "capacities" and "habits"), and it is clearly constructed in relation to the Academic definitions of the concept of "happiness."

After this first assumption (ταῦτα δὴ οὕτως ὑποκείσθω, 1218b 37), it is posited that ἀρετή, "in the things for which there is a use or an ἔργον"[26] (b 38–1219a 1), is one of the "habits or capacities," which are "states" or "modes of being." This statement is based on a brief induction (a 1–5), which we here omit. If we apply the second assumption to the soul, which is one of the things that have an ἔργον (a 5), we obtain the following position: virtue of the soul (from now on we shall simply say: virtue) is the best ἕξις of the soul. Yet, starting from these arguments, Aristotle does not consider it necessary to reach the conclusion that happiness is, first of all, the possession of virtue, and only subsequently the putting into practice of it, as Xenocrates did. Instead, he shows that the mere possession of virtue is not happiness. The demonstration is based on the identification of "happiness" with the "supreme good of man."

A first and still preliminary step is contained in lines 1219a 6–8; Aristotle states that the ἕξεις, and the "works" (ἔργα) that derive from them, can be arranged in two parallel columns (συστοιχίαι), with the following relations obtaining between them:

1. the ἔργον of the best ἕξις is best, and, more generally,

2. the relation that the (ἕξεις) have with one another is identical to the relation that the ἔργα have with one another.

By means of these assumptions, Aristotle excludes the possibility that, if a capacity (*x*) is, let us say, of less worth than a capacity (*y*), the actualization or ἔργον of (*x*) is of greater or equal worth to the actualization of (*y*). In the two columns, obviously arranged on the basis of their "worth" or "goodness," every ἔργον is, so to speak, on the same level as the ἕξις it is derived from.

The second stage in the demonstration is to establish what kind of value relation there is between the entire column of capacities and states, and the entire column of movements and activities. The principle that solves the question is that by which "the ἔργον is the end of every thing" (a 8): in fact, as an end, it will be superior to the capacity from which it derives. Aristotle adds:

> It is therefore clear, from what has been said, that the function of the best state is better, as it is an end; for it has been posited that the best thing and the extreme, that toward which all other things tend, is the end. (a 9–11)

This passage sums up the hypotheses formulated earlier and reaches a conclusion. Some of the concepts used here are not provided with any foundation, but they must have been dialectical principles about which it was easy to obtain the listeners' assent.

Later on, Aristotle states that the principle just formulated, viz. that the ἔργον is better than the disposition, holds true for all the meanings of ἔργον. Indeed, this term may indicate either a sensible object or an activity: both a house and the activity of seeing are ἔργον. Aristotle is mainly interested in the second of these senses, the one indicating an activity. Thus the previous conclusion is particularized:

> So that it is necessary, regarding the things whose ἔργον is a use [χρῆσις, cf. *EN* 1098b 31 et seq.], that the use must be better than the habit. (a 17–18)

This is followed by a passage that to some has seemed to be an unnecessary addition,[27] though it is quoted in the recapitulation of the whole subject made by Aristotle at the end of this discussion. Therefore Aristotle must have considered it an integral part of his argument. It is probably the answer to a possible objection: "but is the ἔργον, the work of a being to which a state of excellence or virtue (ἀρετή) is attributable, the same, both when it is in a state of ἀρετή and when it is in an inferior state?" As such, the question does not appear in the chapter, though the answer is given in lines 1219a 18–23. Aristotle says that it is the same ἔργον: the difference between an ordinary shoemaker and the best one in town does not lie in the fact that the one makes shoes and the other makes something better than shoes. The best shoemaker in town will obviously make the best shoes in town. Thus, in this passage Aristotle applies principle (2) above to the case of ἀρετή, so that the best ἕξις comes to have the best ἔργον from among those of the same type.

As was done before, at line 1219a 5, here too the distinctions made in the case of the soul are applied:

> moreover, let it be supposed that 'causing to live' is the function of the soul (and the function of this is a use and state of wakefulness, as sleeping is inaction and rest); therefore, since the function must necessarily be one and the same for the soul and for virtue, the function of virtue will be a virtuous life. This, then, is the perfect (τέλεον) good which, as we have established, is happiness (εὐδαιμονία). (a 23–28)

The English translation, which necessarily has to give ἀρετή the meaning of "excellence, perfection" when speaking about shoes or the shoemaker's art, and that of "virtue" and "virtuous life" when speaking of the soul, partly obscures the perfect correspondence that Aristotle wishes to establish between the two cases ("the same criterion holds good also for the other cases," as he says in a 23).

It was, in fact, said that, of all goods, the best, and those from among which happiness must be identified, are the goods of the soul; that the realities of the soul are modes of being and activities; and that activities are better than modes of being, since they constitute the end of such states of the soul. Happiness, as a perfect or complete (τέλεον) good, does not include all goods, but only the best. The use of the term τέλεον does not suffice to lead us to conclude that happiness is an all-inclusive set within the category of "goods." On the contrary, it is a very selective set; only fine actions are component parts, μέρη, of it. The dispositions and habitual states from which fine actions are derived are goods within the soul, and must necessarily be present for fine actions to exist. If the virtue of the soul is lacking, a fine and noble action can be performed only by chance or accidentally, and is thus not truly virtuous. But this is not enough to make dispositions and mental states a part of happiness, even if they are more than mere external necessary conditions, such as health and wealth.[28]

Aristotle thus restricts the choice of what is to be considered a "part" of happiness. Xenocrates had taken as "parts" of it both states and the acts resulting from them; what is more, he put the "capacity-to-realize" at the service of virtue. Aristotle's restriction with respect to the Academic positions is clearly expounded in the summary Aristotle makes in lines a 28–35:

> this is clear from our hypotheses; as indeed it was said that happiness was the best thing [cf. 1214a 7–8] and that the ends within the soul were the best of goods [1218b 32–35], <that the things in> it[29] are either habitual states or activities [b 35–36], and since [1] an activity is better than the disposition from which it comes, and [2] the best activity is proper to the best habitual state [1219a 6–8, 9, 11–13, 17–18], then the activity of virtue is the best thing in the soul.[30] And it was said that happiness was the best thing [here he repeats a 29]; therefore happiness is the activity of a good [= excellent, virtuous] soul.

The fact that happiness is something complete, τέλεον (a 28), does not mean that it is composed of anything besides activity; it only means that happiness is composed of all virtuous activities. This is said immediately afterward:

> and since it was said that happiness is something perfect (τέλεον), and it is possible that a life may or may not be complete (τελέα), and this is true also for virtue (as in the one case it is complete, while in the other it is partial), and the activity of incomplete things is incomplete, happiness will be the activity of a complete life in accordance with complete virtue. (a 35–38)

We have dwelt so long on the analysis of this chapter because it seemed necessary to do so, as this text has usually been considered the one in which an "inclusive" conception of happiness is most clearly expressed. In reality, however, its intention and aim are, so to speak, exclusive. Aristotle reserves the role as "parts" of happiness to a much more limited series of goods than that allowed by his predecessors. A similar tendency to limit and distinguish what is a part from what is not can be found in some passages of the *Politics* and *EE* I, which we shall examine in the next section.

5. The "Parts" and Necessary Conditions of Happiness

To understand Aristotle's distinction between what is, and what is not, a part of happiness, we must carefully examine the concept of "to be a part of."

The discussion contained in *pol.* VII 8–9 is important for our purposes. In it Aristotle wants to determine what must be the parts (μέρη) of the city, as distinguished from the necessary conditions for it. Aristotle here takes up, and develops in an original way, a theme that was already to be found in Plato's dialogues.[31] He states:

> since, as happens in the case of all the other natural compounds, those things without which the compound cannot exist are not, themselves, parts (μόρια) of the whole, so also it is clear that we cannot consider as parts of the πόλις the things that must necessarily belong to it; and [it is also clear] that this holds true for every other community from which something single in kind is formed, since there must be something that is one, common, and the same for [all] the participants, whether they participate in it equally or unequally. (1328a 21–26)

It follows then (1) that the parts of organic compounds are different from the necessary conditions of them; in the case of the city this diversity comes from the fact that the "parts" possess some characteristics that the "necessary conditions" cannot share; (2) that, however, it is not necessarily true that all the parts possess, to the same extent, the characteristics that make them "parts." We shall see these two principles operating also in the case of happiness.

The reason why necessary conditions are not parts is based on the distinction between ends and means.

> when one thing is for something else, and that thing is the objective [end], there is nothing in common between them, except the fact that one produces and the other receives. I mean, as in the case of the tool seen in relation to the work that is produced with it and to the craftsmen: for a house and its builder have nothing in common; rather, it is the craft of the builder that has the house as its end. (1328a 28–33)

In the *Politics* this principle is applied to the case of happiness, not the happiness of the individual but that of the πόλις. In any case, the two concepts of happiness are identical (cf. *EN* 1094b 6–7), because the city is a community whose end is the best life, i.e. the happiness of its citizens (a 35–37),

> which is the activity of virtue, and a complete use of it; it happens that some can have a part in it, and others only slightly or not at all, and clearly this is the cause behind the creation of various kinds and differences [of states], and of many constitutions. (a 37–41)

Participating in the activities of the πόλις and aiming at the best possible life is what it means to be a μέρος, part, of the city. There can be different actualizations of this "being part"—some better, some worse, depending on the type of constitution. In all of them, however, there is participation in the common good. In Chapter 9 of the *Politics* these general observations are applied to the best πόλις (1328b 33–34). In it, the citizens must partake of a life lived in accordance with virtue, in freedom, without being tied to productive activities (1328b 35–1329a 2). It is possible to participate in the life of the πόλις with different functions, such as that of warrior, or that of councillor, and both are ways of being "part" of the city, though endowed with different τιμή, honor and prestige. For a city to be happy, it suffices that all the human beings who are part of it should be more or less happy; it is not necessary that the others be happy (a 21 et seq.).

The concept of "necessary conditions" is discussed in *EE* I 2, a passage which, as we have seen, aroused Hardie's protests. Aristotle says:

> He who can live according to his own choice must[32] posit some sort of aim of living well, be it honor or fame or wealth or education, in view of which he performs all actions (as it is a sign of great senselessness not to arrange one's life in view of some end); above all, one must first determine within oneself, without haste or negligence, what, of the things that depend on us, living well consists of, and [what is] that without which it cannot belong to men. (1214b 6–14)

The expression "aim of living well" is quite imprecise, as it could give the idea of an ulterior aim, of which living well is the means. Instead, as Aristotle makes immediately clear, this σκοπός is equivalent to establishing in what (ἐν τίνι, b 12) living well consists. The list "honor, fame, wealth, education" merely provides examples[33] and indicates a series of possible realizations of the vague idea of living well. As we already know, Aristotle has in mind his definition of happiness as "activity in accordance with virtue."[34] This does not mean that in this chapter such a definition is already presupposed, but only that here nothing is said that makes it impossible, later on, to define happiness in this way. And, in relation to this idea, it is useful to distinguish at once the components (ἐν τίνι) and the necessary conditions (τίνων ἄνευ . . . οὐκ ἐνδέχεται, b 13–14). As a matter of fact:

> that without which it is not possible to stay healthy, and staying healthy, are not the same thing, and this is true for many other cases; so then living well and that without which it is not possible to live well [are also not the same thing]. (b 14–17)

The definitions of happiness mention only the component parts and not the necessary conditions.[35] Aristotle, after having, in a parenthesis (b 17–24), differentiated the necessary conditions of living well from the necessary conditions of living in general, underlines the importance of the distinction between parts and conditions of happiness; he states that the two things must not be confused:

> as these are the things that cause disputes regarding happiness—what it is, and by what means it is generated—for some people think that the things without which one cannot be happy are parts of happiness. (b 24–27)

This distinction reinforces the idea that Aristotle's definition of happiness has not been conceived as a mere theory, but is also intended to have a practical value: it aims to distinguish, in the ends that men set themselves, the good ones (those which are really a part or a specification of happiness) from the mistaken ones (in which the relation between ends and means is misrepresented). This same distinction lies, for example, behind the criticism of the blind pursuit of wealth in *pol.* I 9.

In conclusion, therefore, it is possible to maintain that in the life of an individual, or in that of a city, the necessary conditions (that without which the whole does not exist) are not on the same plane as the parts of the compound (what the whole consists of) . On the other hand, not all the parts are equal to one another, although they have a common element which their being part is based on. "To be part" means to take part, "to a certain extent," in the life of the whole; the exact extent may be greater or lesser in the diverse cases. In the life of the city, being a citizen entitles one to a certain degree of honor and power, but not to the same degree as everyone else. Likewise, in the life of an individual not every virtuous activity has the same importance, but some virtues are more important than others, though they are all parts of the happy life.

6. Happiness as the Supreme Good

It is useful to compare the conclusions reached so far with other passages of *EN* and *EE*. Let us briefly sum up: happiness is a good composed of parts; these parts are virtuous actions, or activities in accordance with complete virtue; in this way not all goods are included in the concept of happiness, and Aristotle proposes a restriction with respect to the Academic positions. By means of this restriction he obtains a tool with which to evaluate the current opinions on happiness, and which he can use to guide his disciples toward the best choices. The passages we shall now refer to deal directly with the concept of happiness, and usually studies of Aristotle's idea of happiness start with them. We, however, deemed it useful to have at our disposal some explanatory hypotheses such as those described above, before tackling these passages.

It has been already noted[36] that in *EN* the treatment of happiness is a particular element in a general distinction of goods, and that Aristotle speaks of "happiness" only after having dealt with the concept of "highest good," with which happiness is identified.

Happiness, however, as it is the highest good, also falls into the broader divisions of the general concept of "good" that Aristotle posits, since all goods are contained in them. This is a subject that we cannot deal with adequately here;[37] we shall just give a brief outline of it.

In *EN* I 1 Aristotle starts from the broadest possible definition of "good" as an end, i.e. as "that toward which all tend" (1094a 3); this is to be understood not in the sense that there is only one end for all actions (it would be strange if Aristotle made such a weighty statement right at the beginning of his discussion) but, as Thomas Aquinas takes it, in the sense that every human choice, action, art and research tends toward its proper good (*EE* 1218a 30; *top.* 116a 19). Thus in *EN* I 1 Aristotle takes a good as an "end," and proceeds to distinguish various kinds of ends. This distinction is not the only one possible, however; elsewhere he distinguishes a "true good" from an "apparent good" (cf., for example, *top.* 146b 36), or "absolute good" from "relative good for someone" (e.g., *top.* 116b 8, *EN* 1113a 7). Conceptually, the two distinctions are not equivalent, though at times they are confused (cf. *EN* III 4).

In *EN* I 1, then, Aristotle distinguishes various kinds of human ends and tries to identify the highest of these ends. As in *EE* II 1, the ends may be activities (ἐνέργειαι) or works (ἔργα) that are the result of activities (1094a 3–6). This distinction is interwoven with that between goods-in-themselves (ends) and goods-for-something-else (means) (cf. *top.* 106a 4, 116b 32, 37); thus we can distinguish ends and means among both works and activities[38] (1094a 16–18). This passage makes it impossible to reduce productive activities to a mere means for ethical-political activities.

A peculiar move, and one typical of this passage, is the connection of the distinction between ends and means to the distinction between forms of knowledge. It is not strange that Aristotle should develop the subject in this way, in a chapter that is a general introduction to a treatise on practical knowledge; but it is important to underline this, because it determines, to some extent, the whole subsequent discussion.

Aristotle distinguishes various sorts of ends and various kinds of knowledge related to these ends; the forms of knowledge are mutually related in ways similar to those of the ends they aim at. Just as there are some ends that are subordinated to others, so also there are "architectonic" sciences and "subordinate" sciences. The general principle of the distinction is that no science has more than one end, but every end has its own proper science. The situation at the end of *EN* I 1 is that of a plurality of "architectonic" sciences, each with a different end. Every science and every end are the leaders of two distinct chains of sciences and ends, which are respectively subordinate (a 14–16).

The next chapter, I 2, is clearly devoted to making a further unification of aims. But the opening passage of it is very obscure, and has been much discussed, especially by recent critics. It goes like this:

> If then (εἰ δή) [1] there is an end of our actions that [1.1] we desire for its own sake, and [1.2] [we desire] everything else for it, and [2] we do not desire every thing for another thing, as in this way [2.1] we would go on endlessly, so that [2.2] desire would be useless and vain, it is clear that [3] this would come to be the good and the best thing [. . .], and if this is so [4] we must try to give a broad outline of [4.1] what it is and [4.2] what science and capacity it is the object of. It would seem to be [5] the object of the most important (κυριωτάτης) and most architectonic (science). [5.1] Politics is obviously such a science. (1094 a 18–29)

This is followed by a passage in which various arguments are advanced in support of the idea that politics is the most important and architectonic science of all, as it appears to comprise within itself (περιέχοι ἄν, b 6) the ends of the other sciences.[39] Aristotle adds that, even though the supreme end is the same for the individual and for the πόλις, it is preferable to pursue the good of the city (b 7–10). We cannot dwell on this point here. But we may note at once that in this chapter Aristotle holds fast to the principle that for every end there is a science; thus, having affirmed the existence of a supreme end, two questions are necessarily raised: (4.1) what it is, and (4.2.) what science it is the object of. There has been much discussion in recent years about the logical structure of this chapter,[40] but it has not taken into account the factor indicated here.

Usually the passage is understood as a hypothetical argument of the type: if (1) and (2), then (3). But also the coda of the passage is important; it has the following structure: if (3), then (4), on which (5) depends. Now, it is clear that in order to establish (3), (1) is sufficient; if there is something that is desired for its own sake, and everything else is desired for its sake, then it is obvious that this is the good and the best thing. But what is (1) based on? Gauthier maintains that here Aristotle does not want to demonstrate his thesis, but only to repeat a common opinion of the Platonic school.[41] On the contrary, exegetes such as Burnet,

Léonard and Joachim[42] have claimed that (2) was the demonstration of (1), from which (3) is then derived. To strengthen their interpretation they have linked proposition (2.1), "in fact, in this way we would go on endlessly," with a passage in the *Metaphysics* (II 2) in which Aristotle states that it is not possible to regress infinitely in causal chains, and this is true also for ends (994a 8 and b 7). It is thus not possible to say that one takes a walk in order to stay healthy, that one stays healthy in order to be happy, and that one is happy for another end "and, in this way, that one thing is always done for another" (a 10). On the contrary, for a human action to be undertaken there must be a πέρας, a limit and an ultimate end to be pursued (b 14). This end "is what does not tend toward anything else, but other things exist for it" (b 9–10). Therefore, in the *Metaphysics* Aristotle deduces, from the very structure of human action, which is a "doing something for something,"[43] the existence of an ultimate end in the chains of motivation of action.

But all this is not sufficient to demonstrate (1). In fact, this connection with the *Metaphysics* makes Aristotle's argument fallacious. What is established in *metaph.* II is that every chain of ends must have "a proper" ultimate end, but from this one cannot deduce what is stated in (1), viz. that there is "only one" ultimate end toward which all causal chains converge. This has been pointed out by many authors, including Geach, Anscombe, Kenny and others. It has also been observed that (1) and (2) are linked by the word καί (and) and not γάρ (for) or similar particles; hence it is difficult to admit that (2) justifies (1)—though this is not utterly impossible (Wedin). Others have suggested that the contrary could be true, i.e. it could be (1) that establishes (2) (Williams), or else that (1) and (2) could be two mutually independent conditions, which jointly determine (3).[44] However, the first of these two hypotheses, i.e. that (1) is a justification of (2), seems rather improbable, since the two propositions (2.1.) and (2.2.) are introduced by a γάρ and are therefore the clauses that justify (2).

In our opinion, this text serves as an introduction to the rest of *EN* I. It is thus unlikely that Aristotle would have wanted to demonstrate, in these first few lines, one of his fundamental ethical doctrines, viz. the uniqueness of the supreme good. Indeed, later on (1095a 15, 1097a 15) he returns to this point. Still, it is clear that he intends to unify the chain of ends and not stop at the situation described at the end of *EN* I, where various architectonic sciences had various ultimate ends as their objects. In our opinion, then, what we have here is an argument made ἀπὸ τῶν ἐπιστημῶν, starting from the sciences; it is, moreover, based on the principles of correspondence between each science and its object outlined above.[45]

Aristotle's reasoning can be interpreted in the following way: if (1) is true, and the situation described in (2) does not hold, we can affirm (3), from which a program of investigation (4) is derived. This program is subdivided into two points (4.1) and (4.2), and we see at once (5) that the answer to (4) is clear and manifest. There is, in fact, a science that has the characteristic of being the most important and architectonic one, and also has the function of establishing the ends of the other sciences: politics. Point (5.1) makes a statement of fact: from it one can infer the existence of the object described in (3). If, in reality, what is described in (3) is the object of a science like that described in (5), and such a science exists, then it is reasonable to admit that also the relevant object exists. This interpretation can be supported by two other passages of *EN* in which Aristotle seems to proceed in the same way. The first of these, *EN* I 9, makes explicit reference to *EN* I 2 and strictly ties the existence of the supreme good to the existence of a science such as politics:

> these things agree with what was said at the beginning; in fact, we took the end of politics as being [the] 'best thing' [and politics] takes great pains to give the citizens a certain character, and to make them good and capable of performing fine actions. (1099b 28–30)

The expression τὸ γὰρ τῆς πολιτικῆς τέλος ἄριστον ἐτίθεμεν leads one to think that Aristotle took the existence of political science as the basis for affirming the existence of the supreme good, and not vice versa.

A similar position is found also in a preceding passage, *EN* I 4, where Aristotle explicitly discusses the problem posed in (4): "what it is and what science and capacity it is the object of." It was established in (5) that the supreme end is the object of politics, but what it is was not specified. Now Aristotle resumes the discussion:

> to begin again, let us say: given that all knowledge and every choice tend toward a certain end, what is [6] the end that we say is pursued by politics and [7] what is the greatest of all practical goods? (1095a 14–17)

Here, quite clearly, the object described in (6) and that described in (7) are the same thing, and the two propositions indicate two aspects of the supreme good.

It is only at this point, after a very general and abstract discussion, that in *EN* I the term εὐδαιμονία (happiness) is introduced. It is a widespread opinion, Aristotle assures us, that happiness is both (6) and (7), the object of politics and the highest good. A formal and abstract description is given a concrete content, taken from the sphere of opinions (but, as is well known, for Aristotle this sphere does not coincide at all with the sphere of pure appearance). The opinion that happiness means "living well and acting well" (a 18–20) is equally widespread. But in this way we have merely found a name (a 17), and it is still not clear what happiness consists of (a 20–22). Hence the information given so far is true, but not clear, and not precise enough to be put into practice. However, it has already been said that happiness is a "way of living." This notion proves to be crucial in an important part of the discussion, both in *EE* and in *EN*. We must therefore devote a special section to it.

7. Happiness as a Way of Life

We shall now take a look at the texts of *EE* and *EN* in which Aristotle interprets the notion of happiness as a kind of βίος. In some of these texts he does not investigate the internal structure of the happy life in relation to its parts and necessary conditions, but rather various types of life are examined, to see which of them coincides with the happy life.

EN I 5 sets out to determine what, in actuality, in terms of content, the human good and happiness are, starting from common opinions (1095b 14–16).[46] The chapter moves forward by a process of elimination, as will happen later in *EN* X; many of the arguments against identifying happiness with the political life, adduced in that text, are already present in this chapter. Aristotle, in 1095b 16–22, excludes the idea that a life of pleasure gives happiness, because such a choice is fit for slaves and animals, although some powerful people have chosen to live like this. Political life, whose end is honor, is considered a rather superficial (ἐπιπολαιότερον, b 24) choice. In fact, this choice presupposes that honor is not entirely the ultimate end, since one tends to be honored in order to have external confirmation of one's own virtue: "it appears that it (honor) lies more in the one who honors than in the one who is honored, and yet we perceive (μαντευόμεθα) that what is the good for one is personal and inalienable" (b 24–26). The true end of the political life, then, is not honor but virtue; but we know that it is a constant doctrine of Aristotle's that just to be virtuous does not at all mean to be happy, because the mere possession of virtue does not imply putting it into practice: "as it appears (φαίνεται), this, too, is insufficient, since it is thought that one may happen to be asleep or inactive all one's life, and also to undergo the worst evils; and whoever lives in this way would be considered happy by no one, except to maintain an *a priori* thesis" (b 31–1096a 2). Here Aristotle's polemic is directed against the Academy, as we know; he says he has expounded these topics more fully in his published discourses (ἐν τοῖς ἐγκυκλίοις, a 3). Not much is said here of the contemplative life, which is only mentioned (a 4–5); but a life devoted to accumulating riches is roundly rejected, with the air of one who is stating the obvious in denying that it can be happy.

In *EE* I 3 it is said that the aporia regarding ways of living is proper (οἰκεῖα, 1215a 4) to this treatment. In fact, refuting mistaken opinions concerning the best life is equivalent to demonstrating the right opinion. Here a typically Aristotelian dialectical procedure is theorized; it is present in all his greater works, and is the main method used to arrive at first principles in every form of knowledge, be it theoretical or practical (cf. *de cael.* 279b 5–8). The fact that a principle is arrived at in this way does not mean, as many people seem to think, that it is merely debatable or merely likely, but only that the ὁδός that leads one to grasp the principle proceeds via the discussion and refutation of the most widely accepted and most probable opinions. (a 5–7)[47]

This chapter establishes in the most precise way what the subject of the discussion is:

> moreover, it is important that such things should not remain obscure, [but][48] above all the thing [1] toward which every study must tend, [i.e.] [1.1] what is the starting point from which it is possible to participate in the good and the good life—if it is too great a cause of envy to say the 'blissful life'—and [1.2] regarding the hope of attaining each of the appropriate things.[49] (1215a 8–12)

The practical question of how to attain the principles of a happy life depends on determining what these principles are. The more practical question is important, but the theoretical one comes first (*pol.* VII 1324a 13 et seq.). With regard to the distinction made in 1214a 10 et seq., to the effect that some things are sought only for the pleasure of knowing while others are sought for practical purposes, it is clear that here one is asking what happiness is in order to be able to attain it, and Aristotle says that, of happiness, one must know "what it consists of and how it is acquired." Indeed, if happiness were a gift of fortune, or if it were innate like having blond hair, the whole discussion would be useless; but if it consists of something else, then the investigation is useful (1214a 15; 1215a 12–15).

Aristotle tackles this practical problem from the standpoint of his well-known principle that the exercise of virtue is more important than the mere possession of it:

> but if [the good life] consists of a certain character belonging to the individual and his actions, the good will be both more common and more divine.[50] More common, because it will be possible for a greater number of people to share in it, and more divine, because it can be attained by those who are prepared to bestow a certain character on themselves and their actions. (1215a 15–19)

In Chapter *EE* I 4, which we discussed above, Aristotle posed the question whether happiness means to possess a certain personal quality or to perform certain actions. That passage is followed by a distinction between different kinds of βίοι, on the basis of the ends pursued and the characteristic actions performed: satisfying the needs of life, or tending toward happiness. The passage is structurally complex, though the meaning is clear:

> as the different ways of living have been dealt with, and since some do not even strive after a well-being of this kind, but are engaged in order to obtain necessary things, such as those [ways of living] devoted to the common business and those devoted to making money and earning a living [. . .] while, regarding the others,[51] aiming at the conduct of a happy life, there are three goods—also mentioned earlier—[and] they are the greatest goods for men: virtue, wisdom (σοφία) and pleasure. Thus we see that there are also three ways of living that are chosen by all who can: the life of the statesman, that of the philosopher, and that of pleasure. (1215a 26—b1)

Much of the discussion in *EE* I 4 and 5 consists of a comparison of the ways of living, on the basis of the dominant end of each (contemplation and truth, fine actions, bodily pleasures, cf. b 1–5).

Each of those who choose a certain βίος thinks that the happy life is something different from what the others believe. Aristotle quotes Anaxagoras, for whom to be happy does not mean to have external goods—greatness, beauty, wealth—but to have internal goods:

> certainly (ἴσως) he thought that whoever lives free of troubles[52] and without blemish where justice is concerned, or takes part in some divine contemplation, enjoys bliss insofar as this is humanly possible. (b 11–14)

Here happiness is located, with indifference, both in the theoretical life and in the practical one; but the discussion is just beginning, and this passage is not decisive for choosing the best from among all the possible βίοι. Aristotle does not choose between theoretical and practical modes of living, and does not even say that happiness is a mixture of the two; he simply sets them both against a life dedicated only to exterior goods.

Chapter 1 5, instead, gives a more precise idea of the subject. Here Aristotle tries to find out which of the objects of desire can satisfy every appetite, since—as is well known—happiness is self-sufficient.[53] The three types of happy life are present in this chapter in the persons of their champions, Anaxagoras, Sardanapallus and Smindrydes of Sybara, and "certain others," who prefer above all else actions deriving from virtue, not for the good reputation caused by them, but for the actions themselves. These are the "true" statesmen, who are set off from current politicians (1216a 11–27). This passage is followed by another, in which the life of pleasure is rather hurriedly eliminated from the roster of candidates for the role of "happy life," and the choice between the other two possibilities is left open:

> first of all we shall investigate virtue and wisdom, [trying to find out] what the nature of each of these is, and whether they are parts (μόρια) of the good life, or rather the actions that derive from them; for they are taken to be parts[54] of happiness, albeit not by all men, but at least by all those who are worth mentioning. (1216a 37–b 2)

The question as to what the "parts" of happiness are is obviously only mentioned here, and is not solved, but the presence of such an ἔνδοξον is a good sign of how affairs really stand (cf. *EN* 1172b 36–1173a 2).

The activities of ethical virtues and those of intellectual virtues must be parts of the happy life, while physical pleasure is not, *per se,* a part of happiness, but is replaced by those more refined pleasures "on account of which they rightly think that a happy man lives pleasantly and not just without pain" (b 35–36). The μὴ μόνον (not only) in this quotation is designed to rule out Speusippus's position: pleasure, in some form, is not excluded from the makeup of the happy life. But it is not physical pleasure; rather, it is the pleasure that accompanies, perfects and refines the higher activities:

> therefore, whether there is only one, or whether there are several [activities] of the perfect and blessed man, the pleasures that complete and perfect (τελειοῦσαι) these activities are called in the proper sense (κυρίως) the 'pleasures of man' and the remaining ones [are pleasures] in a secondary and inferior sense, just like the activities [they belong to]. (1176a 26–29)[55]

The happy life will thus be composed of ἕξεις such as virtue and wisdom (σοφία), or, better, of the actions derived from them, plus the pleasure that accompanies and perfects such actions. These are the parts of happiness, the elements that enter into its makeup.

In the *Topics* Aristotle seems to have adopted, at least in part, a position in favor of a composite conception of the happy life. This is seen in an argument against Xenocrates contained in *top.* VII 1, 152a 5–30.[56] Xenocrates had maintained that the happy life and the virtuous life were the same thing, because, if it is possible to say of two entities that they are, from the same point of view, something "in the highest degree," then the two entities are identical. And the virtuous life and the happy life are both desirable in the highest degree. Aristotle objects that the criterion used by Xenocrates does not hold for complex entities, but only for individuals. For example, he adds, it is possible to say that both the Peloponnesians and the Spartans are brave in the highest degree, but this does not mean that Peloponnesians and Spartans are identical, because the Spartans are a part of the Peloponnesians (together with the Achaeans, the Argives and many others). According to Aristotle, Xenocrates' argument falls into the same error, since between the happy life and the virtuous life there is the same relation that there is between Peloponnesians and Spartans:

> and for this reason not even Xenocrates managed to prove his point, since the 'happy life' and the 'virtuous life' are not single entities, and therefore it is not necessary for them to be the same thing, but one is included in the other.[57] (a 26–30)

The argument given here does not exactly coincide with what we find in the *Ethics*—and in a previous chapter we saw other cases of the "evolution" of Aristotle's position from the *Topics* to the later treatises—but the sense seems fairly clear. The life of virtue is not identical with the happy life because the happy life is only one of the possible kinds of virtuous life. It is not enough to possess virtue, or to act virtuously, in order to be happy, if external goods (such as health and some degree of financial well-being) are completely lacking, or if one is afflicted with misfortune. A virtuous life may also be conducted by one who behaves well in adverse circumstances, but such a life could not be called happy.

The idea that the happy life is a complex set of different activities is suggested also by the term βίος used by Aristotle. Usually dictionaries[58] distinguish between the two Greek words meaning life, βίος and ζωή, holding that the latter refers mainly to biological life, and the former to one's manner of living, as in the expression "a risky life." It is mainly human beings who possess a βίος, but the word can also be used of animals, as happens, for example, in Aristotle's biological works. However, the texts of the *Ethics* that we are now examining show that Aristotle uses the two terms interchangeably, and attributes to ζωή the meaning of "manner of living" (cf. *EE* 1215a 4–5, and Bonitz, *Index, s.v.*). It is less common, however, to find in Aristotle the word βίος used to mean biological life, and when he discusses the traditional subject of "modes of life"[59] he speaks of βίοι and not of ζωαί.

Now, a person who conducts a certain kind of life does not thereby perform only a single kind of action. Nomadic or herbivorous animals do not devote every single minute of their day to wandering around or chewing grasses; in the same way hunters do not only hunt nor do fishermen only fish. At a higher level, a civil community such as the πόλις of the Spartans is characterized by a βίος στρατιωτικός, a military life (*pol.* 1270a 5), but this does not mean that the Spartans devote every minute of their lives to marches, military exercises and battles. They also sing, and take part in symposia, pray to the gods, marry, listen to the lectures of the sophist Hippias and do many other things. Nonetheless, in some way their lives are organized around war as their principal activity. It is thus our opinion that a βίος is a way of life, and as such it is composed of a series of different activities,[60] but it is characterized by one predominant type of action, which to some extent determines all the rest, and enables us to distinguish one βίος from another.

This interpretation, however, does not hold for certain texts by Plato, who describes types of βίος comprising only one kind of activity. For example, in the *Phaedrus,* 248a, the divine βίος is composed solely of contemplation, and in the *Philebus* 20E et seq., he describes a βίος ἡδονῆς and a βίος φρονήσεως, the former consisting of nothing but pleasurable activities without the use of the intellect, and the latter of nothing but intellectual activities without any form of pleasure. But in the same dialogue (22A)[61] it is said that the best life is a mixture of the two things. The *Philebus* presents a rather abstract model; instead, the *Theaetetus* (173C–174A) describes a more concrete model of βίος. Plato outlines a life dedicated to philosophical reflection in which, though admitting that alongside intellectual activity there must be others, he clearly intends to "maximize," so to speak, theoretical activity at the expense of all others, and in particular to the detriment of social relations. Plato says that those who have been educated to undertake philosophical reflection devote as much time as possible to contemplation and neglect all the rest: they stay away from the marketplace and from political life; they do not concern themselves with the traditional social life, such as large-scale dinners and spectacles, and they are unable to recognize the differences in honor and dignity among citizens. A famous example of this βίος is Thales, who fell into a well while contemplating the stars.[62] Below, we shall compare this description of an absentminded professor with the celebration of the contemplative life that Aristotle makes in *EN* X 6–8. In the meantime, we wish to point out that Plato does not have only such a narrow conception of βίος, but that, when he uses the term in the usual way, he thinks of more subtle forms of life. For example, in *apol.* 38A, when Socrates says he wants to continue living a life devoted to the discussion of virtue and similar subjects, he obviously does not mean a life in which one does nothing but that; and in *resp.* 582 B–D Plato says the philosopher leads a life that includes not only the pleasures enjoyed by normal citizens, such as earnings and honors, but also intellectual pleasures, which are unknown to ordinary people.

Before tackling the reading of the texts in *EE* and *EN* where Aristotle compares the main βίοι, we deem it useful to compare this concept with that of a "rational plan of life" (hereafter: RP), introduced in recent years by J. Rawls,[63] and used by various modern scholars to interpret Aristotle's notion of happiness. According to Rawls, an RP is basically a way of planning one's present and future with reference to a series of desires and preferences, which vary from person to person. The function of this plan is to divide the main human resources of time and energy in pursuing the various ends, in accordance with the intensity of the needs that such ends satisfy. In an RP one tries to make room for those ends that are more compatible with all the other ends that are actually desired, and to exclude those that prevent one from obtaining other satisfactions. The purpose of the RP is the harmonious realization of the main aspirations of an individual; according to Rawls, this harmonious realization is what corresponds to the term "happiness." An RP is "rational" because it is based on certain principles of efficacy and practical rationality: how to find the most efficacious means, preferring strategies that involve the satisfaction of a greater number of main ends, as well as strategies that have a greater chance of success. All RP's have the same moral value; they are all distinguished from disorderly and self-destructive ways of organizing one's life, but it is explicitly stated that no RP is superior to any other, provided they all satisfy, coherently and rationally, an individual's desires and aspirations. So much for Rawls. It therefore seems possible, at least theoretically, to find some RP's that are completely acceptable, according to the definition given, and also totally wicked. Rawls's notion of happiness is one of those that does not allow us to make judgments about what others mean by the happy life or to prescribe one kind of life in preference to another; herein lies the difference between the RP and conceptions such as Aristotle's.

The notion of βίος described above presents important similarities and differences with respect to Rawls's conception of a "rational plan of life." First of all, a βίος is not necessarily rational, and indeed it is even attributed to animals. In the case of humans, a βίος may be chosen out of fidelity to tradition, because of one's social condition, or owing to a personal inclination; only in a few cases is the choice the result of deliberation and educated awareness. In any case, it always indicates the organization of all activities around a particular class of actions that have a predominant role and, like a general light, illuminate the other activities. Unlike the notion of "RP," the notion of βίος enables us to evaluate the kind of happiness chosen by an individual, when the activities characterizing the various forms of life are compared. For example, one who devotes his life to caring for lepers, and is happy in doing so, is better and more worthy of esteem than one who organizes satisfactorily his life around poker games. The βίοι, then, can be arranged on a scale of increasing value, depending on the value of the actions that characterize them. This is not possible in the different RP's, where the value obtained is basically a certain harmony in the satisfaction of a number of ends; the precise number and nature of these ends varies from one individual to another, for reasons that are not made clear. Though useful for a renewed philosophical approach to the discussion of justice, the idea of an RP does not (in our opinion) sufficiently clarify things if superimposed onto the Aristotelian concept of "happiness."

In a similar fashion to what he says in his biological treatises and in the *Politics,* and even in the *Ethics,* Aristotle considers the βίος to be a way of living characterized by a predominant kind of activity. Thus many βίοι are possible, and each of them will be characterized by a different predominant activity. It is, however, impossible for the same person to live more than one βίος at a time; furthermore, the idea of βίος seems to imply a certain duration. It is thus just possible that the same person may, in the course of his existence, devote himself to more than one βίος. But there are sound reasons for doubting that he can seriously lead different types of life simultaneously.

8. The Definition of Happiness in *EN* I 7. Part One.

This section and the next one differ from the previous ones in being somewhat more technical in their treatment. This is necessary because of the difficulties encountered in I 7. Moreover, in these sections no new results will be arrived at, nor will new elements be found to shed light on Aristotle's conception of happiness. The purpose of this discussion is to put our interpretation to the test, in order to see if it succeeds in explaining and clarifying in an acceptable way the official definition of εὐδαιμονία given in *EN.*

The passage that goes from 1097a 15 to 1098b 8 has always been considered the centerpiece of Aristotle's discussion of the concept of happiness, although there has been a recent increase of interest in *EE,* in particular *EE* II 1, a text we have already examined. In Bywater's scansion, chapter 1 7 is divided into two parts. The first, 1097a 15–b 21, starts from the idea of supreme good and restates in a new way the argument of *EN* I 1–2, reaching the conclusion that εὐδαιμονία has the characteristics of "perfection" (τελειότης) and "self-sufficiency" (αὐτάρκεια) proper to the supreme good; the second, 1097b 22–1098b 9, tries to establish in a more precise way (ἐναργέστερον) what happiness is, starting from the notion of ἔργον (work, function) which is peculiar to man *qua* human being. This second part is closer to *EE* II 1, but—as we shall see—there are very noteworthy differences in the process of demonstration, although, in our opinion, as we tried to show earlier, there is not a radical difference in the conclusions arrived at.

Partly repeating the discussion in *EN* I 1–2, Aristotle again states, at the beginning of *EN* I 7, that every kind of activity and every entity tend toward their own end, which is their proper good, in view of which everything else is done (1097a 15–22). Having established this, as in *EN* I 2, Aristotle advances the possibility of unifying all these ends:

> so that, if there is something that is the end of all actions, it will come to be the practical good; if there are several ends, they will be such goods. (a 22–24)

Contemporary critics have often appreciated these lines, in which they have glimpsed the possibility of an "inclusive" conception of the supreme good, i.e. a consideration of the ultimate end as being composed of many ends. And they have set this passage against other parts of *EN* I 7, in which a "monolithic" or "dominant" conception of the supreme good is said to be expressed. This does not appear to be justified by the text itself, in which Aristotle says that the passage 1097a 22–24, quoted above, and what we stated earlier, in *EN* I 2, are the same thing: "changing the argument, we have reached the same conclusion [as before]" (a 24).[64] The change with respect to *EN* I 1–2, which appears in the λόγος given here, consists in its no longer being based on the relation between an ἐπιστήμη, or a δύναμις, and its related end, but in its being based only on the concept of end. Therefore also the unification of the various ends in an ultimate end must take place in different ways, if it is true, as we have maintained, that in the unification of *EN* I 1–2 the concept of "form of knowledge that pursues an end" is central. And just at the beginning of *EN* I 7 Aristotle explicitly says that he wants to re-examine the question of what the sought-for good is (a 15–16).

It is not very clear what it means to say that, if there is an end of all actions, this is the practical good and, if there is more than one, they are all such practical goods, since this statement is too general. It therefore needs to be clarified, i.e. made more specific (a 24–25), and the next passage, 1097a 25–b 1, is explicitly devoted to clarifying the relations that exist between the ultimate ends of human actions. The new analysis is based on the concept of τελειότης, which we here take to be "perfection" or "completeness." Aristotle establishes that:

1. if there are many ends, some of which are ends in themselves, and others ends for something else, the former are more perfect, and it is among them that the best thing, the supreme good, which is something perfect, is to be found (a 25–28);

2. if there is only one perfect and complete end, it will coincide with the supreme good and the best thing; if there is more than one, the best thing, which is perfect, will coincide with the most perfect and complete of them (the passage specifies this at a 22–24 and clarifies it at a 28–30).

Therefore the practical good coincides with the ends; and the highest, most perfect practical good coincides with the most perfect end. There seems to be no contradiction between lines a 22–24, where it is admitted that there may be more than one practical good, and lines a 28–30, where—using the criterion of τελειότης—the most perfect end is taken to be the supreme practical good (τὸ ἄριστον, a 28).

Still, this difference is not yet clear, and Aristotle in a 30–34 explains what he means by "more perfect." He uses three criteria:

3. an end pursued for its own sake is more perfect than one that is a means for something else (a 30–31, which repeats a 25–28);

4. an end that is never pursued for the sake of something else is more perfect than one that is pursued both for its own sake and for the sake of something else[65] (a 31–32);

5. an end that is always pursued for its own sake and never for the sake of something else is absolutely (ἁπλῶς) perfect (a 33–34).

Points (4) and (5) are important: here things that belong to the category of ends-in-themselves are contrasted; these are the practical goods of line 24. A distinction is made between them, and it is stated that "only" the end described in point (5) is the best thing and the supreme good. It is added (a 34) that, according to a widespread opinion, happiness has the characteristics described in point (5), but no argument is presented to affirm that only happiness corresponds to this description. This probably results from the fact that Aristotle does not admit that there can be more than one supreme good which is absolutely perfect, always pursued for its own sake and never sought for the sake of something else.

The ends described in point (4), those that are pursued for their own sake and also for the sake of something else, are very important. Aristotle's text does not say that at times they are pursued for their own sake and at other times for the sake of something else, but rather that they are pursued for both reasons. How this happens and what it means are made clear both in the following lines and in an important passage of the *Topics.*

In the following passage of *EN* I 7, Aristotle says:

> happiness above all else seems to be of this type [5]. Indeed, we always choose it for its own sake and never for the sake of something else, while honor, pleasure, intellect and every virtue are chosen partly for their own sakes, since we would choose each of them even if nothing came of it, [but] we choose them also for the sake of happiness, believing we shall be happy by means of them. Instead, no one chooses to be happy for the sake of those goods, nor in general for the sake of anything else. (a 34–b 1)

The difference between happiness and honor, then, is that honor is pursued both for its own sake and for the sake of happiness, while happiness is pursued only for its own sake and not also for the sake of honor. Some commentators have felt that this means that only happiness is pursued for its own sake, and they have made it the ultimate end of all goods, as in Plato's *Symposium* (205A).[66] Others, as we have said, have thought that honor and other such goods are sometimes pursued for their own sake, and sometimes for the sake of happiness.[67] If these interpretations imply that practical goods such as honor and pleasure are to be understood as means for attaining happiness, or that, when they are pursued for the sake of happiness, they are valuable only as means to it, they do not seem acceptable. Ends of the kind described in (4) are not desirable because of something else, and are not to be pursued only insofar as they lead to something else, like true means, but they are desirable in themselves, and are to be pursued wholeheartedly. This is the meaning of the expression "we would choose each of them even if nothing resulted from it" (b 3–4).

This sentence can be explained by comparison with a passage of the *Topics*, VI 12, in which Aristotle gives, as one of the incorrect modes of definition, taking what is an end-in-itself as an end-for-something-else. For example, one must not say that justice is "what saves the laws" or that wisdom is "what produces happiness," as in this way justice and wisdom are considered means for the laws and for happiness (149b 31–34). Also in the *Topics* Aristotle holds that we pursue these goods for their own sakes, as well as for the sake of something else, with these words:

> or rather nothing makes it impossible that what is preferable for its own sake may also be preferable for the sake of something else; nonetheless, whoever has defined in this way what is desirable in itself has committed an error. In fact, the best aspect of anything lies in its essence (οὐσία), and it is better to be desired for oneself than for the sake of something else; therefore, also the definition should indicate this aspect. (b 35–39)

It seems clear, on the basis of this passage, that goods of type (4) cannot be reduced to means for happiness, and are to be pursued in their own right, whether they result in happiness or not. But they are not the highest good, since happiness derives from them, albeit not "in an essential way"; and they can be pursued either only for their own sake, or both for their own sake and also for the sake of happiness.[68] The degree to which such goods are to be pursued does not depend on the extent to which they help to foster happiness; this is the important point, the reason why these goods differ from means. Virtuous acts are good in themselves and are to be performed even if they do not bring happiness. Happiness, in its turn, is the best thing and the most perfect good; here there is no opposition between one particular activity and others, because being happy is not a special type of action; rather, it is "living well and acting well." The opposition lies, in the realm of ends-in-themselves, between less perfect ends and the most perfect end in the sense stated above.

The passage so far examined, 1097a 15–24, was intended to confirm the results reached in *EN* I 1–2 and to develop them further. The next passage, 1097b 6–21, is meant to confirm what has been said in this same chapter, in lines 1097a 24—b 6. Aristotle says: "It is clear that, on the basis of autonomy, one arrives at the same conclusion, since the perfect good is held to be self-sufficient" (b 6–8).

Here Aristotle applies a general principle, which we find expressed in a simple form in *rhet.* 1364a 5–6: "What has less need of another or of others is a greater good, as it is self-sufficient."

Just as earlier the criteria for identifying the most perfect end were given, so now a definition is provided of what is meant by "self-sufficient" (b 8–9: τὸ δ' αὔταρκες λέγομεν). It means "what suffices for a life that is not solitary (μονώτην), but lived in relation with others" (b 9–14), which thus comprises at least the social virtues, since "man is by nature a social animal" (b 11).[69] The possession of happiness thus must not make one incapable of conducting a life of relations with one's parents, children, wife, and, in general, friends and fellow citizens. Indeed, it is said that "what is self-sufficient is what, by itself, makes life desirable and has no need of anything" (b 14–15). And from this viewpoint, too, happiness appears to be the supreme good. We read:

> we hold that happiness is constituted in this way (τοιοῦτον, b 15). Moreover, it is the most desirable thing of all, without being counted together with anything else (μὴ συναριθμομένην) and if it were counted together with something else, it is clear that it would be more desirable with the addition of even the smallest good. What is added together is always an addition of goods, and, of goods, the greater is always to be preferred. Therefore it seems clear that happiness is something perfect and self-sufficient, as it is the end of actions. (1097b 16–21)

In the interpretation of this whole passage it should be kept in mind that it explicitly aims at confirming the results of the previous section of *EN* I 7, i.e. that happiness is the τέλος of all human actions (a 20–21) in the sense made clear above, that it is the most perfect of all goods, and that it is perfect in an absolute sense (a 30, 33, 34). Happiness is chosen only for its own sake, while the other goods-in-themselves are chosen also "for the sake of happiness." And it suffices for a self-sufficient life, which includes the various human relations.

Now, the principle introduced in 1097b 16–21, viz. that "of goods, the greatest is always preferable" also appears in *EN* 1172b 27–28, in *top.* 117a 16–21 and in *rhet.* 1363b 18–21. These texts should be kept in mind, since the above-mentioned passage, 1097b 16–21, is one of the most widely debated texts in the whole of *EN* I. In the *Rhetoric* it is only said that the sum of many goods is better than a single good, or a few goods. In the *Topics* this principle is mentioned, and Aristotle adds:

> objection: if one thing is a means for another, it will not at all be possible to pursue both of them rather than one only; for example, as regards getting well and health with respect to health, since we choose to get well for the sake of health. (a 18–21)

Alexander of Aphrodisias[70] seems to have interpreted the passage of *EN* I 7 quoted above in the light of this text from the *Topics*. In fact, in commenting on the *Topics,* he says that, in the chains of means and end, the means are not added to the end, but the end alone is preferable, "and not even happiness together with the virtues is preferable to happiness alone, since in happiness also the virtues are included (περιέχονται) [. . .]; in fact, one does not add to the things that include those that are included under them, as has been said in the first book of the *Ethics*" (247, 4–10). He seems to believe that it is not possible to make happiness preferable by adding anything to it, because it is the end of all virtuous actions (which in their turn have, as a necessary condition, the possession of a certain quantity of external goods); hence the possession of happiness is self-sufficient and is the supreme good, while possession of the other virtues would be desirable only as, and to the extent that, they serve to make one happy. This is Alexander's interpretation, which is adopted by various ancient and modern commentators.[71] In our opinion this interpretation does not fit the distinctions made in the first part of *EN* I 7, because it reduces ends-in-themselves to the status of mere means. It is tantamount to admitting that virtuous acts should be performed only insofar as they contribute to happiness, and this goes against Aristotle's opinion. He maintains that virtuous acts must not be performed only for the sake of happiness, but also not only for their own sake, irrespective of any consideration of one's happiness. They are to be performed for their own sake, and also because they lead to happiness, of which they are a part.

Ackrill has held that nothing can be added to happiness because it includes within itself every desirable thing, i.e. it is the sum of all goods. We discussed this interpretation at the beginning of this chapter, and we mentioned the criticisms made of it by those who consider it absurd that happiness can be a good composed of all goods, as in this way the subtraction of even the smallest good would suffice to destroy it.

The point that Aristotle wants to make here is that happiness is indifferent to additions and subtractions. If it were the sum of all goods, it would be preferable to the sum of all goods and some non-good, or the sum of certain goods could be preferable to the sum of all goods plus some non-good. The rest of the passage of the *Topics* (cf. a 117a 21–24) denies that happiness is like this. Against the above hypothesis, Aristotle says:

> and there is no reason why some non-goods may not be preferable to goods;[72] for example, happiness and something else which is not a good, [may be preferable] to justice and courage.

Non-goods are not preferable for their own sake, but only accidentally, inasmuch as they are joined to εὐδαιμονία, which is self-sufficient,[73] not perturbed by non-extreme evils and suffices to make life desirable. This does not mean, however, that in a happy life[74] every least desire is satisfied, or that a slight dissatisfaction suffices to destroy happiness. Happiness is something stable and by no means easy to change (cf. 1100b 2–3). If happiness depended on external events, which give and then take away certain goods, the same person would become happy and then again unhappy many times, "making the happy man resemble a chameleon and based on rotten foundations" (1100b 6–7). But happiness does not consist of external goods and the vicissitudes of fate, which indeed are nothing but external conditions (1100b 8–10), while other kinds of goods are important. Possessing these, the happy man is able to bear the events of life nobly and with moderation (1100b 20–22). Hence the existence of some unsatisfied desires does not destroy happiness:

> and since many things happen by chance, and differ from one another in size and degree, it is clear that small successes have no importance for our life, and likewise small failures; instead, important things that occur in large numbers, if they go well, make a life happy [. . .] if, instead, they turn out badly they distress one and ruin one's bliss, as they bring displeasure and hinder the carrying out of many activities. (b 22–30)

Therefore, to be happy it is important to have a certain amount of external goods, so that one can practice the various actions it consists of, but it is not necessary that every wish should be fulfilled (cf. also 1101a 8–13).

It thus seems possible to refute both the interpretation that makes "happiness" the ultimate end of all actions, in the sense that all other ends become mere means for it, and the interpretation that makes it the sum of all goods. From *EE* II 1, we know that "happiness" is the activity of the soul in accordance with virtue; hence, we can understand these statements of Aristotle's as meaning that happiness implies the existence of a series of external goods, which are necessary conditions for it, and a series of other and better goods (virtuous actions, which presuppose the existence, in the soul, of virtue and good dispositions), which are its component parts.

But, in the order of exposition in *EN* I 7, this result has not yet been reached. Aristotle is now, in the first part of this chapter, proceeding formally, without yet saying what the content of the notion of "happiness" is, i.e. what it consists of. Instead, the second part of *EN* I 7 will be devoted to establishing the content of this concept; here the definition of "happiness" is completed. What we know so far is that happiness is something perfect, self-sufficient, and the highest end of actions.

9. The Definition of Happiness in *EN* I 7. Part Two.

The last part of *EN* I 7, 1097b 22–1098b 8, partly corresponds to *EE* II 1, and has always aroused great interest. With respect to *EE*, the demonstration contained in *EN* appears less technical and logically less rigorous; while the former text is based on the results of the previous book, *EE* I, as well as on a series of concepts derived from Academic discussions, this text is presented almost as a new beginning which, starting from a series of apparently self-evident observations, reaches conclusions that are by no means common. We might explain this by supposing that it is addressed to a wider audience than that of *EE*, an audience similar to that of *resp.* 352D–353A (a text that closely resembles I 7, 1097b 22–1098b 8, both in its structure and in its arguments). On account of these characteristics, the demonstration contained in it makes it possible to conduct a freer and more accurate theoretical discussion of what human happiness is.

A brief introduction, 1097b 22–24, picks up the statement made previously, to the effect that everyone agrees that happiness is the best thing (cf. 1095a 17). Then Aristotle adds that we will have more information about happiness if it is clearly established what the ἔργον of man is. In *EE* II 1, in a polemic directed against the Academy, the superiority of the ἔργον was shown by means of a long and quite technical discussion (1218b 38–1219a 11). Here such a discussion is taken for granted, and we have only its conclusion, expressed by a syllogism of this kind:

> for all things that have an ἔργον, this is the good
> man has an ἔργον
> ―――――――――――――――――――
> for man his ἔργον is his good.[75]

The major premise is justified by a very brief induction, like that in *EE* 1219a 1–5.[76] The minor premise is introduced as a hypothesis (εἴπερ), which is justified in lines 1097b 28–33:

> [1] are there then functions and actions proper to the carpenter, and the cobbler, but for man there is none, he being generated for no purpose? [2] Or rather, just as there is clearly a function for the eye, the hand, the foot and in general for each of the parts of the body, so also could one not suppose there is an ἔργον for man that goes beyond these?[77]

This argument has not convinced everyone. Of the most recent critics, Léonard has raised objections, and Hardie has added even more radical criticisms, while Clark and Hutchinson have essayed an important defense. The criticisms and objections are based on different interpretations of the text. It is, therefore, first of all necessary to establish what kind of argument Aristotle is advancing here, and then discuss its validity.

Léonard and Gauthier think that here Aristotle is proceeding by means of subtraction, i.e. by excluding one human function after another, until he finds the one and only function typical of man not *qua* architect or shoemaker, but man *qua* man. In this way the activity typical of man would be identified with only a part of what man does, and the objection has, rightly, been made that one could, instead, identify the activity typical of man with the whole set of things that men do. On the contrary, paying closer attention to the logical structure of the argument, Burnet and Kullmann see in passages (1) and (2) a double induction, in the form of rhetorical questions. Hardie has criticized the validity of this double induction, which in his opinion risks reducing man to a mere tool. He maintains that it is by no means obvious that man *qua* man has a function; he assigns "functions" only to tools, and to those who, within the human community, carry out an ἔργον such as fighting, producing, governing and so on. According to Hardie, this criticism does not spare even the passage of Plato (*resp.* 353 A) that inspired Aristotle.

In many of Aristotle's texts, as has been correctly pointed out, it is possible to note the function of a being only in the framework of a complex system, in which the being has a basic role for the very subsistence of the system. Nussbaum takes the heart as an example; its function is to pump blood. In this way it is possible to analyze a living organism, identifying the aims and roles of its different constituent parts. On the other hand, there are also places where Aristotle not only speaks of the function of a being that is part of an organic whole, but also of the function, or ἔργον, of an entire living complex. For example, in *de gen. animalium*, 731a 28 et seq., he speaks explicitly of the ἔργον of living organisms, and not of simple parts. One can thus say that the ἔργον of a plant is to produce seeds, while the ἔργον of animals involves more than just generation, including also the partaking of knowledge, to some extent. In these passages the ἔργον is understood to be the distinctive characteristic that differentiates one complex organic system from another; the criterion used is the determination of its specific or distinctive activity. Something is said to belong to the plant or animal kingdom on the basis of the presence or absence of such functions, such as whether it has perceptions.

In *EN* I 7 the procedure is very similar to that of the biological passages we are referring to. It is therefore not necessary to suppose that, when Aristotle speaks of the function, or ἔργον, of a being (e.g. the "first philosophy," *phys.* 194b 15 or dialectic, *top.* 183a 39 and b 4), he has in mind an organic context, whether real or imaginary, that such a being is part of,

The role of ἔργον in Aristotle's doctrine of the supreme human good can be better appreciated if Aristotle's theory is compared with some recent discussions on the concept of "good." Here we shall again refer to Rawls's theory, since others, too, have found it useful to compare Aristotle's position with this recent theory in order better to clarify it.[78] Rawls maintains that he is a continuer of a tradition that started with Aristotle; he understands "good" in the simplest way, as follows. We say that a being *a* is a good *x* if and only if it possesses, to a more than average extent, the characteristics and properties that *x* can be reasonably expected to have, after we have established the general role of *x,* i.e. what *x*s do. Here the concept of "role" is rather close to Aristotle's notion of ἔργον. The criterion of reasonableness is also present in Aristotle, e.g. in *EN* III 4 and in *top.* 145a 25–27, where it is said that the definition of a being is linked to the good use that the science of that object and the φρόνιμος as such would make of it.

With respect to Rawls's definition, Aristotle's position is marked by the absolute pre-eminence given to the notion of ἔργον, and hence to the "function" of a being with respect to all its other characteristics and properties. This is clearly due to Aristotle's doctrine of the priority of act over potential, as is stated in *metaph.* IX 8. In this latter text, the idea that the ἔργον is more important than the potential, and the idea, referred to the substance (οὐσία), of the superiority of act over potential are explicitly linked. The end of a capacity is actualization, and not vice versa. This was said earlier, in *EE* II 1, and is repeated here:

> the ἔργον is the end, and activity is action (ἔργον), and for this reason, also with regard to its name, the activity (ἐνέργεια) is called after the action (ἔργον) and leads to the act (ἐντελέχεια). (1050a 21–23)

According to Aristotle, the good of a being lies mainly in the activity and being-in-act of the being itself. This is what the substance and the essence of every being mainly consist of. The importance of an ἔργον thus does not lie in its being part of an organic context, nor in its being valuable as a tool, but rather in the fact that it is mainly through its ἔργον that a being expresses what it is. In the *Metaphysics* Aristotle explicitly connects this doctrine to the idea of "happiness":

> where there is no other ἔργον except activity, it lies in the agents; for example, vision [is] in those who see, contemplation in those who contemplate, life is in the soul, and hence so is happiness, since it is a kind of life[79] (ζωὴ γὰρ ποιά τίς ἐστιν). (1050a 34–b 2)

The doctrine of the *Metaphysics* is clearly similar to that of *EE* II 1 and reaches the same conclusion. In *EN* I 7 Aristotle tries to argue in favor of this theory in a more "exoteric" way; the two brief inductions given in lines 1097b 25–26 and 28–33 are certainly insufficient to establish the doctrine that the ἔργον is the most important feature of a being, and is its specific good. They only serve as two series of examples, by means of which Aristotle tries to make his position plausible. Aristotle thus resumes the discussion starting from the biological concept of life, to identify the specifically human element:

> what then can it be? On the one hand, 'living' is obviously (φαίνεται) also common to plants, while we are looking for man's proper function. We must therefore leave aside the life of nutrition and growth; then there might be some kind of life of sensations, but this too is obviously shared also by horses, oxen and every other animal. What remains is a sort of active life (πρακτική τις)[80] of the part endowed with reason. And, of this part, one part [is rational] because it obeys reason, while another part is so because it possesses reason and is a thinking being; since also this [latter] has two names, it is this that must be exercised, since this is what is called [rational][81] in the proper sense of the word. (1097b 33–1098a 7)

Here Aristotle does not distinguish between different "types of soul," but rather "types of psychic life"; indeed, he is discussing what the ἔργον[82] of man is, and the ἔργον here coincides with a certain kind of psychic life. It is the individual who lives, although the principle of life in him is the soul (cf. *EE* 1219a 24: "The ἔργον of the soul is to cause to live").

It would once again be possible to interpret Aristotle's procedure as a progressive elimination of functions. In this sense, the one specifically human activity is the only one that he does not share with any other animal. One could object that this interpretation does not take account of the composite nature of man, who is not a pure, bodiless intellect. Even if the quest is for the ἴδιον, the proper trait of man (b 33), it is not necessary to identify this ἴδιον with purely rational activity. Even Aristotle, in mentioning the "part capable of obeying reason," makes man's ἔργον include also that part of the soul linked to the emotions and desire. In this connection, commentators generally refer to the doctrine of *de an.* II 3, whereby the higher faculties potentially include within themselves the lower ones, as the triangle is included in the quadrilateral. This is usually interpreted to mean that the rational soul does not remain separate from the rest of the psyche, but penetrates and informs the lower faculties, or at least some of them. There is thus a specifically human way of living the vegetative life—the life of growth, sensation and desire—which is added onto rational life in the strict sense. A good man is he who fulfils this ἔργον well, so that he is worthy of the recognition and esteem of his fellows.

We are now ready to read the lines that follow, 1098a 7–20, which are rather close to the main part of *EE* (1219a 9–39), and go like this:

> and if the function of man is activity of the soul in accordance with reason or not without reason, we may say that, in general, the ἔργον of anything and the ἔργον of that same thing in a state of excellence (σπουδαίου) are the same, as in the case of a cithara player and of a great cithara player; and, in an absolute sense, this holds true for every case, since the additional good [cf. 1097b 28] provided by its being in a state of excellence (ἀρετή) is added to the

ἔργον. Indeed, it is natural for the cithara player to play the cithara, and for an excellent player to play it well. (1098a 7–12 [cf. *EE* 1219a 18–23])

Here it is pointed out that there is no difference in kind between the function of a being and the function of the same being in a state of ἀρετή. But some abbreviated expressions that Aristotle uses here deserve to be elucidated.

The ἔργον of man consists in activity of the soul in accordance with reason. Now, on the basis of 1097b 25–28, we know that the good of everything that has an ἔργον is the ἔργον itself, but not every "activity of the soul in accordance with reason." In fact, the ἔργον of an ordinary man and that of an excellent man are identical only "in a generic way" (a 8), and do not have more restricted forms of identity (cf. *top.* 152b 31–32). This corresponds to what is said in *EE* II 1219a 19–20,[83] i.e. that the ἔργον of a craftsman is the same as the ἔργον of an excellent craftsman, "but not in the same way." Here we are dealing with the difference between a kind of action and the perfect way of being of this kind of action. The final part of Aristotle's demonstration is based on this distinction:

and if this is so, and as we have posited that the function of man is a certain kind of life [cf. 1097b 33–1098a 4], and we have said that this life is the activity and action of the soul accompanied[84] by reason [cf. 1098a 4–7], and that this happens in the best and finest way (εὖ ταῦτα καὶ καλῶς) in the virtuous man—indeed, the good of each thing is fulfilled in accordance with its own proper virtue [cf. 1098a 7–12][85]—if this is so, human good is the activity of the soul in accordance with virtue, and if there are more virtues than one,[86] in accordance with the best and most perfect one. And this, moreover, in a complete life.[87] (1098a 12–18)

The good of man consists of the "best activity of the rational soul in accordance with virtue." This is Aristotle's answer to the question raised in 1097b 23 ("it is still necessary to say more precisely what it is"). The structure of this part of *EN* I 7 is very similar to that of *EE* II 1. In both chapters Aristotle's theory is expounded after a long recapitulation that summarizes the preceding text. As in *EE* II 1, Aristotle speaks of the ἀρετή of the soul, meaning by this the best habitual disposition, which gives rise to the best ἔργον. This ἔργον is a certain type of activity, defined in *EE* II 1 as ζωή σπουδαία, "virtuous, excellent life"; here, in 1098a 14, it is defined as the life σπουδαίου ἀνδρός, i.e. of the excellent or virtuous man. In lines 1098a 4–5 we distinguished between two kinds of life of the rational soul, one "as obeying reason" and one "as possessing reason." These kinds of activity correspond to two different habitual dispositions, i.e. two different kinds of virtue, as well as two different parts of the soul.[88] These two types of virtue consist of, first, the habitual disposition to listen to reason, and, second, the habitual disposition to exercise one's own rational faculty. The second of these dispositions is the more perfect one, τελιοτάτην, 1098a 17. The fulfilment of it, viz. the use of the properly rational part of the soul, is human happiness, which is a certain kind of activity of the rational soul "as possessing [reason] and reflecting" (1098a 4–5). Human happiness cannot consist of the activity typical of the habitual disposition that is only capable of obeying λόγος, e.g. obeying the orders given by other people. If this were the case, even children and slaves would be happy.

The interpretation advanced here is different from the one normally given of lines 1098a 12–18. Often the distinction between the virtues of the rational soul and the most "perfect and complete" (τελειοτάτη) of them is not connected to the idea of ἀρετή as the "excellence" of the human soul, but as "virtue" in the usual sense, i.e. as one of the virtues, in particular one of the intellectual virtues, θεωρία.[89] We feel, instead, that ἀρετή must be understood in the same sense throughout this passage, and that the most perfect ἀρετή is, generically, the activity of the soul that possesses reason and reflects. This appears to be confirmed by *EN* I 9, as well as by a passage in the *Politics* (VII 14 1333a 19 et seq.) which we shall return to later (pp. 168 et seq.). In *EN* I 9 Aristotle says:

> we have said that [happiness] is a certain kind of activity of the soul in accordance with virtue [. . . .] It is therefore obvious that we do not call happy an ox, or a horse, or any other animal, since none of them is capable of participating in such activity. And it is for the same reason that children are not happy either, as they are incapable of performing such actions on account of their age [. . .] what is needed, as we have said, is both complete (τελείας) virtue and a complete life. (1099b 26–1100a 5)

We know that the reference ("we have said") in this passage is to 1098a 12–18 quoted above, and in particular to line 1098a 17. Also in *pol.* 1259b 30 et seq. Aristotle says that children and women do not possess complete virtue, since they have not sufficiently developed the "authoritative" part of the rational soul (cf. also *EN* 1111a 26). The "complete virtue" of the above-quoted passage, like the "most perfect, or complete virtue" of the previously quoted passage, is not contemplation, but the virtues of the adult man, who can govern himself and those who depend on him:

> it is for this reason that one who commands must have complete (τελέαν) ethical virtue, as his task is architectonic to the utmost, and it is λόγος that functions as architect, while each of the others has just the amount that befits him. (*pol.* 1260a 17–20)

Women, children and slaves all have, albeit to differing degrees, fully developed that part of the soul that can obey the voice of reason, but they do not have at all, or have only in a weakened form, the truly rational part of the soul. They therefore cannot be truly happy.

This explains what was said previously, in the same chapter (*EN* I 7), about the αὐτάρκεια of happiness, which includes relations with family members and friends, and also the remarks in *EN* I 2 about the architectonic function of the kind of knowledge whose object is the supreme good. It thus seems to us that the most perfect virtue mentioned in 1098a 17 is the virtue of the most important part of the rational soul, that it includes both σοφία and φρόνησις, and that it is not at all just θεωρία.

In this chapter, *EN* I 7, happiness has been defined as the highest and most perfect human end, better and more complete than any other end; it is self-sufficient, i.e. indifferent, at least to some extent, to the addition or subtraction of particular goods, and comprises within itself, as parts of itself, virtuous actions. Such actions are desired and carried out for their own sake, in cases where happiness does not stem from them, but they are desired and carried out also for the sake of happiness, that is to say—as we understand things—as parts of a complex whole which is happiness considered as a way of life. Happiness, then, is the virtuous and excellent life of the rational soul, and above all of the most properly rational and "architectonic" part of it. This explains why only free, adult, male citizens are truly happy.

10. More Remarks About the "Parts" of Happiness

Book VI reconsiders the activities of the rational soul as parts of the happy life. In Chapter 12 Aristotle asks what is the use of σοφία and φρόνησις, since the object of the former is not the things that make a man happy, and the latter seems not to be indispensable for acting well (1143b 18 et seq.). We have already discussed this text, but we skipped over 1144a 1–9, which now interests us. Aristotle maintains that σοφία and φρόνησις are useful, for two reasons:

> we say [. . .] that they are desirable in themselves, as each of them is the ἀρετή of its respective part, even if neither of them produces any result. (a 1–3)

Σοφία and φρόνησις are thus ends in themselves, as are honor and virtue in *EN* I 7, and not means for something else. It is therefore not correct to approach the question by just asking what they are "useful" for. Their desirability does not stem from the fact of their producing anything, but first of all from the fact that each is the excellence and perfection of a "part" (of the soul). Here the term "parts" of the soul is used in a slightly different sense from that encountered in *EN* I 7 and 13, where the parts considered were the rational part, the irrational part that was, however, capable of obeying reason, and the vegetative part. Here, instead (cf. *EN* VI 2), Aristotle is speaking of what composes the rational part of the soul, commonly called the "rational soul"; it is composed of two parts, one "scientific" and the other "calculating," of which σοφία and φρόνησις are the respective ἀρεταί, virtues or excellent dispositions. As such they are to be pursued for their own sake, even if nothing results from them, as in *EN* I 7.

But, just as in *EN* I 7 and *top.* VII 1, here too Aristotle adds that, although they are not means, but ends, the virtues (in this case, intellectual and rational ones) do produce something, viz. happiness:

> in the second place they do produce something, not as medicine produces health, but as health does;[90] so wisdom [produces] happiness, since it is part of complete virtue—it makes a person happy by the fact of being possessed and by its action.[91] (a 3–6)

This passage has been much discussed,[92] and those who feel that Aristotle, in general, identifies happiness exclusively with the theoretical life have thought that here Aristotle overturns his theory of happiness (Ross) or that he confuses "part" and "means" (Greenwood). Gauthier and Hardie hold that here Aristotle is using "part" in the sense of "form"; they, too, consider θεωρία to be the only component of a happy life. These are all attempts to find here a position similar to the one that many scholars attribute to *EN* X 6–8, i.e. a position that identifies happiness with θεωρία alone, but they do not seem acceptable on the basis of the most natural reading of the text, which has justly been defended by Cooper. Cooper points out that the expression "complete virtue" (ὅλη ἀρετή, a 5) indicates a whole, as in the corresponding passages of *EE* 1219a 37 and 1220a 2–4; σοφία is one part of this whole, and φρόνησις is another. "Theoretical wisdom" and "practical wisdom" are thus two intellectual virtues, whose activity is part of the complex whole called the "happy life." In this passage happiness is a whole composed of parts, virtuous activities, including the activities typical of theoretical and practical wisdom. This does not mean, however, that they are parts in the same way as the others, or that they are on the same plane and have identical roles.

The relations between σοφία and φρόνησις are clarified only at the end of Chapter VI 13, where a relation of subordination is posited for the two virtues. This relation also involves the virtues of character, or ethical virtues, since, as we know, φρόνησις is both an intellectual virtue and the rational element of the ethical virtues. In this very same Chapter VI 13 Aristotle says that to possess φρόνησις means to possess all the virtues. Once again Aristotle uses the comparison of medicine and health:

> yet [φρόνησις] is not the mistress (κυρία) of theoretical wisdom, nor of the best part of it, just as medicine is not the mistress of health. Medicine does not

> use health, but sees how it can generate health, and gives orders in favor of it (ἐκείνης ἕνεκα), not to it. It would be just as if someone said that politics commands the gods, because it gives rules for all the things pertaining to the city. (1145a 6–11)

Practical wisdom does not dominate the theoretical virtue of σοφία. Indeed, σοφία is the end of practical wisdom. This does not mean, in our opinion, that the exercise of φρόνησις necessarily becomes a mere means for θεωρία, as some have believed.[93] Practical wisdom is not desired or exercised only because it fosters θεωρία, but also in its own right; whoever possesses only practical wisdom and the related ethical virtues is, as we shall see, happy, though not completely happy, since he lacks the best and most pleasant activity. If, however, we ask what the relations between φρόνησις and σοφία are, then we see that there is a relation of subordination. We shall see later that the two choices of life, theoretical and practical, are both forms of the happy life, though they do not both have the same value; within these choices, the relation between φρόνησις and σοφία is defined differently, although, in our opinion, φρόνησις is never reduced to a mere means for θεωρία. Therefore, one who leads a "political" life does not make the same mistake as one who lives to get rich; that is, he does not take the means for the end, nor does he overturn the natural order of actions, even if he is not fully and completely happy.

EE VIII 3 deals with the concept of complete virtue, or καλοκἀγαθία. In this text it is said that καλοκἀγαθία is what results from the sum of the partial virtues, ἀρεταὶ κατὰ μέρος a very schematic and incomplete treatment of this important subject is given.[94] Aristotle here discusses καλοκἀγαθία almost exclusively from the point of view of its relation with natural goods, such as health or wealth. To be a noble man necessarily means to have all the specific virtues (cf. 1248b 11–13), just as being completely healthy implies not having any part of the body in bad condition:

> in fact, in the other cases things cannot be otherwise, since no one [can] be healthy in his entire[95] body and not be healthy in the parts of it, but all the parts, or the most important ones, must be in the same condition as the whole. (1248b 13–16)

Thus complete virtue is not an added ἕξις, but the whole set of all the virtues of the intellect and of character: theoretical and practical wisdom, courage, temperance, generosity, affability and so on, the exercise of which constitutes happiness. It is characteristic of the noble man that he performs fine actions for their own sake (b 35–36), and for this reason he is the only one, or the one most able, to use external and natural goods in an appropriate way; he best knows how to use honor, wealth, good health, fortune and power. Being endowed with all this, he is able to put into practice all his virtuous dispositions. The model of the noble man outlined here is rather abstract and schematic, and, on account of its excessive perfection, it seems to be the consequence of a deduction, rather than the description of a possible model. Just as Midas turned everything he touched into gold, so the noble man makes all his actions noble:

> [such men] choose fine and noble actions, and not just these actions; they also [do] things that are not by nature noble, but are natural goods, since for them they are noble. (1249a 2–5)

Natural goods become noble because they are used as means to accomplish noble actions: "in fact, material goods are noble when the things for which [they] act and choose are noble" (1249a 5–6). The noble man's virtue is therefore a harmonious whole of high quality.

In this short section we have looked at a few texts that suggest some important information on the internal structure of the happy life: it is a complex of activities in accordance with virtue, in which every activity is an end in itself and thus desirable in itself; but this does not mean that they are all on the same plane, nor that the exercise of the virtue of theoretical reflection has the same importance as the exercise of the virtue of affability with friends. An internal hierarchy of virtuous activities seems implicit in Aristotle's position, and some activities are more important and valuable than others. In our opinion, this does not necessarily mean that some virtuous activities become mere means, and should be exercised only to the extent that they foster intellectual activities, or encourage only θεωρία, nor does it mean that θεωρία is, in the final analysis, the only component of a happy life. We shall examine this point more closely in the next section.

11. The Definition of Happiness in *EN* X 6–8 and in *EE* VIII 3. Part One.

The text of *EN* X 6–8 is very well known and is commented on in almost all the main studies of Aristotle's ethics. Many authors find in it an occasion to express, more or less openly, their incredulity with regard to Aristotle's recipe for a happy life. According to a widespread opinion, which we have already mentioned, for Aristotle, as for Plato in the *Theaetetus,* happiness means just doing philosophy, and every action and every single choice in a good life should aim at the exercise of contemplation as the ultimate end.[96] This poses some quite serious problems, for the doctrine seems to become paradoxical. If contemplation is the only true component of a happy life, in every single choice he makes the Aristotelian man will have to ask himself what series of actions can help to increase his chances of contemplating, and every other truly virtuous activity will become impossible, or will be possible only by accident and as a means, not as an end in itself (cf. *pol.* VII 8, quoted above p. 124).

The idea that only those who devote themselves to a life of contemplation are happy is regarded by many people, in the best of cases, as being an unwarranted generalization, and a mistaken elevation of Aristotle's personal preference to the status of a general principle, to be considered valid in most cases. The type of life conducted in the schools of philosophy would thus become, improperly, the model of the happy life for all.[97] Now, it is certainly not possible to deny that the Aristotelian doctrine of happiness shows clear signs of intellectualism, and from this standpoint the common opinion of scholars is surely justified. In our opinion, however, a careful consideration of the text can do away with the greatest oddities and the most implausible theses that are ascribed to Aristotle, without, however, imposing on the text exclusively modern criteria of reasonableness and acceptability.

In the following pages we do not intend to give a detailed reading of these chapters, as there are ample illustrations of them both in the general comments on *EN* and in specific commentaries;[98] rather, we shall concentrate our attention on some points of interest for our problem.

EN X 6–8 is a section of *EN* that is explicitly devoted to establishing what happiness is. The discussion begins with an introductory section divided into two parts, whose function is that of concluding the entire *Ethics* with the description of happiness (1176a 30–b 9). Happiness is set as a subject to be discussed after the virtues (*EN* II–VII, first part), after friendship (*EN* VII–IX) and after pleasure (*EN* VII, second part, and X 1–5). Secondly, Aristotle's main doctrines on happiness are summarized, so as to show that these chapters follow and complete[99] what has gone before: it is recalled that happiness is not a habit or a habitual state (ἕξις), that it does not coincide with the mere possession of virtue, but that it is an activity. It is then stated that happiness is not an activity necessary for survival, but is a complete activity, performed for its own sake, and self-sufficient, which coincides with performing actions in accordance with virtue "inasmuch as performing noble and virtuous actions is one of those things chosen for its own sake" (b 8–9). There follows a rather long discussion (1176b 9–1177a 11) tending to exclude amusements (παιδιά) from the components of happiness. Amusements are activities that are only apparently performed for their own sake, or are chosen for their own sake only by worthless people; serious people use them as moments of repose (ἀνάπαυσις) which are necessary if one is to be able to dedicate oneself to more important things.

In *EN* I 5 Aristotle had distinguished three βίοι: the life of pleasures, the political life and the life of contemplation. Here amusements take the place of the life of pleasures, though they are not the same thing, but only one part of pleasures. Amusements and pleasures are assimilated to one another in the concluding lines of the passage (1177a 6–9); but in general this text cannot be read as a criticism of the βίος ἀπολαυστικός, the life devoted to pleasures. The life of pleasures has been excluded from the roster of possible candidates for the role of "happy life" in the preceding chapters, *EN* X 1–5, which deal explicitly with "pleasure" as such. The question treated here is residual and of secondary importance.

On the contrary, the beginning of Chapter X 7 is very important:

> If happiness is activity in accordance with virtue, it is reasonable that it should be in accordance with the highest virtue, and this will be the virtue of the best part. Therefore, whether it is intellect or something else that is considered to dominate by nature, to guide us and to have an idea of things noble and divine–whether it is itself something divine, or the most divine part that exists in us[100]—it is the activity of this, in accordance with its proper virtue, that will constitute perfect happiness. It has been said that it is contemplative [activity]. And this would seem to be in agreement both with what was said earlier and with the truth. (1177a 12–19)

The confidence with which Aristotle puts forward his thesis has seemed disconcerting to some people.[101] Aristotle says that the identification of happiness with the activity of the intellect is in agreement with the truth and with what was said in *EN* I. Neither of these two statements seems obvious to the reader.

In this connection it should, however, be said that probably the expectations of the modern reader are different from those that Aristotle intended to satisfy. Today, those who tackle the reading of *EN* X with the aid of contemporary criticism and exegesis want to know what is the internal composition of the happy life, and how its various components must be mutually balanced. In the text quoted at the beginning of this chapter, Hardie expresses this need in the most precise way. As we shall see, Aristotle does mention this problem, but clearly the focus of his interest lies elsewhere. The practical aim of the treatise, which is repeatedly proclaimed in the course of *EN* I, can be seen very plainly here. Aristotle does not just describe the various forms of the happy life, or establish a hierarchy among the various human activities, but he advocates a certain type of life as being the best, and engages to demonstrate the superiority of the intellectual life over the life of the politician. In this way he makes more specific the general definition of happiness as the "activity of man in accordance with complete virtue" by indicating the various ways of acting in accordance with complete virtue; by means of this specification, he makes more feasible, and hence highly "practical," the supreme good, which is a practical principle and the object of rational desire. In our chapter on the practical syllogism, we saw that the specification of a practical end, and object of desire, is necessary if one is to pass from an appropriate but vague end to a more specific end, which makes it possible to draw up a plan of action. And certainly for Aristotle's audience it must have been easier to understand the advice to organize one's existence around a concrete model of life, the βίος θεωρητικός, than to organize it around the abstract formula that happiness is the "activity of man in accordance with complete virtue." We shall return to this point later.

The specification made here, however, does not involve any identification of the "happy life" with the "philosophical life," as Aristotle never operates such an identification. Instead, he identifies "contemplation" with "perfect happiness" (1177a 17 and b 24), and says that a man who lives in this way is "very happy" (1178a 8). In our opinion, perfect happiness is not identical with mere happiness; rather, it is the best way of being happy.[102] The subject discussed in *EN* X 7–8 is the contrasting of two modes of living,[103] two complex sets of virtuous actions, each characterized by a main activity, which dominates the others but does not exhaust them, as Hardie well says. The problem we have to examine, then, is what is the composition of the theoretical life, and what is that of the political life. We must see if Aristotle intends to contrast a life of pure philosophical reflection with a life of pure realization of the virtues of character, as Plato does in the *Theaetetus,* or if there is not, rather, a basis of social and community virtues, such as justice, modesty, affability, temperance, courage and so on, which are implicitly contained in both βίοι.

In *EN* X 7, 1177a 19–b 26, Aristotle gives a series of arguments in favor of the thesis that contemplation is the most important and best (κρατίστη) activity, the most continuous, most pleasant and most independent; it thus possesses the features of happiness in a special way. This is supported by a description of θεωρία for its own sake, leaving aside all comparison; then, from 1177a 30 on, Aristotle develops a comparison with the other virtues. Contemplation is thus compared with justice, temperance and courage.

> since, as regards the things necessary for living, both the wise man and the just man, as well as all others, need them; but of those people who are sufficiently well supplied with them, the just man will need other people toward whom, and in the company of whom, he can be just, and the same holds good for the temperate man (σώφρων), the courageous man and each of the others. But even if he is alone a wise man can contemplate, and the wiser he is the more he can do so. Probably (ἴσως) it is better if he has fellows, but in any case he will be supremely independent (αὐταρκέστατος). (1177a 28—b 1)

Here the difference between intellectual and ethical virtue is more one of degree than of kind, though it seems possible to glimpse a more restricted meaning of the concept of αὐτάρκεια (independence) than that defined in

EN I 7 and in *EN* 1129b 30–33. There the independence of the happy man did not exclude, but rather comprised, his ethical relations with relatives, friends and fellow citizens. Here, instead, it appears that αὐτάρκεια consists of being independent of everyone.

At line 1177b 1, Aristotle begins to contrast the "theoretical life" with the "political life," and this subject dominates the rest of the discussion. These are, in fact, the only two candidates for the role of "supremely happy life." The terms of comparison are here explained quite clearly: it is not a question of setting the exercise of theoretical virtue against the exercise of the virtues of character (plus φρόνησις, which is closely linked to them). Instead, the opposition lies between a life in which the interest in science and philosophy is paramount, and a life in which the predominant interest lies in τιμή and participation in power struggles, in conformity with the morality prevailing in Athenian democracy in Aristotle's day.[104] *In our opinion this means that the moral virtues typical of social life, such as generosity and justice, are fully legitimate parts of both these* βίοι. This can be derived from some remarks made in *EN* X 8, which we shall now examine, and can be confirmed by some passages of *pol.* VII, which will be discussed in the next section.

The first reason for the superiority of the philosophical life over the political life is that nothing results from θεωρία except the very activity of thought, while politics gives rise to "good action" and something else besides (1097b 2–4). It should be noted that here Aristotle does not state that this "something else" is θεωρία he is not here examining the relations between the dianoetic virtues φρόνησις and σοφία, and their respective realizations, as in *EN* VI 13; rather, he is contrasting two ways of living, the "philosophical" and the "political." One may presume that in the "political life" the drive for political power excludes the practice of contemplation.

Aristotle contrasts political activities with θεωρία, as they are inconvenient and time-consuming (ἄσχολοι), both in peacetime and in war. That political activities are so in wartime is clear, since war is a means and not an end: "in fact, no one chooses to fight for the sake of fighting, nor to prepare for war for war's sake" (b 9–10; would Alexander the Great have agreed?). But also in peacetime virtuous activities are the opposite of σχολή (= ease, freedom, leisure time). The politician must procure for himself both power and honor, and hence he has to depend on others. Here (b 12–14) Aristotle directly picks up what he had said about the political life in *EN* I (1095b 22–26), but a certain difference with respect to *EN* I can be observed. In *EN* I (1094b 7–10), as we have seen, the end of the political life, viz. to ensure the citizens' happiness, was said to be a finer and nobler thing than obtaining one's own welfare and happiness. Here, on the contrary, the fact that politics has an end other than that of the action itself is taken as a sign of the inferiority of politics with respect to philosophy. The reasoning is turned upside down, with respect to the first remarks of *EN* I. Now Aristotle says that one's own happiness and that of one's fellow citizens is, in any case, something different from political action in and of itself, and is sought after precisely because it is different (b 14–15). "Therefore, if of all the virtuous activities political and military activities are the best in terms of nobility and greatness, they are nevertheless inconvenient and time-consuming, and aim at [another] end, and are not chosen for their own sake" (b 16–18). On the other hand, θεωρία fully possesses all the traits proper to happiness: "instead, the activity of the intellect, which is contemplation, seems to surpass others in dignity,[105] has no end outside itself[106] and has its own peculiar pleasure" (b 19–21). Aristotle here shares the tendency to praise ἀπραγμοσύνη which was already present in some circles of Athenian culture:[107]

> and independence, comfort and leisure time, freedom from work (insofar as this is possible for a man), and all the other characteristics we ascribe to one who enjoys a state of bliss, are evidently found in connection with this activity. It will prove to be a man's perfect happiness, when it encompasses a complete life. For nothing incomplete is to be found among the elements of happiness. (b 21–26)

This is followed by a section criticizing the traditional opinion that this life is beyond human capabilities.[108] Against this ἔνδοξον Aristotle uses his theory, whereby a divine element is present in man (b 26–1178a 8, cf. 1177a 12–19), and he takes this element as representing what "being human" mainly consists of. In these lines "being human" is used in two different senses. On the one hand, "being human" is spoken of as "being mortal," in contrast to divinity (b 27, 30–32; 1178a 10, 14). On the other hand, "being human" is spoken of as "being a compound entity whose main part is a divine intellectual element" (1178a 6–7). From this point of view, the higher life is one lived in accordance with the divine element (cf. *protr.* fr. 6 Ross), and the greatest happiness is one achieved κατὰ τὸν νοῦν, in accordance with the intellect.

So far Aristotle has shown the advantages of the theoretical life. In the following chapter he resumes the comparison between the theoretical life and the practical life. In it we will find some useful hints for a solution to the problem that most interests modern commentators. We shall see this in the next section.

12. The Definition of Happiness in *EN* X 8–11 and *EE* VIII 3. Part Two.

Chapter X 8 opens with the statement that a life in accordance with the remaining virtues is a secondary form of happiness.[109] Here Aristotle is no longer speaking of the politician, but rather of the virtuous life of citizens in general. The ethical virtues, and the φρόνησις connected with them (1178a 16–19), are related to the sphere of the body and its passions, and are the virtues of man as a composite being:

> as these [virtues] are connected with the passions, they will regard the composite whole, and the virtues of the composite are human; hence so is the way of life, and happiness in accordance with such virtues. (a 19–22)

Instead, the life of νοῦς is separate (a 22–23). We then get a comparison of the "theoretical life" with a "life lived in accordance with the remaining virtues"[110] from the standpoint of external goods. As we know, there is one part (A) of external goods that are indispensable for every form of happy life (a 23–27: health and the necessaries of life; and also in this case the theorist has fewer needs). The ethical virtues require other external goods (B), such as wealth, strength and freedom of action—things that the theorist can largely do without (a 27–34). And the greater and finer the actions are, the more necessary the goods of type (B) will be. Instead, such things may even give annoyance to one who contemplates. This point is very important: Aristotle states that one who lives the philosophical life is not a god, whose life consists only of contemplation (as in the *Phaedrus,* 248A 1). The "philosophical life" of man is a complex whole made up also of the ethical virtues:

> but since he is a man and lives together with many others, he chooses to act in accordance with virtue; he will therefore need [goods] of that kind [B] in order to live as a man. (b 5–7)

The point is like that made in *EN* I 7: one who lives the happiest life cannot dispense with relations with others. The life lived in accordance with the virtue of the "philosophical" man is not aimed at "maximizing" contemplation, but is rather related to the fact that man is a being endowed with a wide range of capabilities for action, and his happiness consists in the realization of them, each to a degree commensurate with its worth. The virtuous actions of the philosopher are thus neither accidental nor instrumental.[111]

A new section of an exhortative type, parallel to that in Chapter 7,[112] repeats the idea that θεωρία is the proper activity of the gods, and that animals are not happy because they do not contemplate.[113] In reality θεωρία is the activity that, more than any other, possesses the characteristics of happiness; therefore, it is clear that the more one contemplates, the happier one will be. Aristotle even goes so far as to say:

> since for the gods the whole of life is blissful, while for men it is so only insofar as there is some resemblance to such activity, and none of the other living

> beings are happy, since they do not contemplate at all. Indeed, the more extensive θεωρία becomes, the more extensive happiness is too; and those who contemplate most are also most happy, not by accident, but because of such contemplation [. . .] . Therefore happiness must be a certain [activity of] contemplation (θεωρία τις). (b 25–32)

The expression θεωρία τις found in line 32 does not, in our opinion, indicate some kind of mystical contact with the divinity, but a kind of activity consisting in theoretical reflection and not action. Aristotle, here, says nothing about the objects of this activity, although the divine and eternal beings are some of the chief and most worthy objects of θεωρία. Nonetheless, it does not seem possible, on the basis of this passage, to deduce that Aristotle opposes theology (which, in the opinion of some, is indicated by the vague expression "a certain [activity of] contemplation") to the other theoretical sciences. Rather, he is contrasting the practice of the theoretical sciences with other, vaguer, meanings of θεωρία and θεωρεῖν (cf. Bonitz, *Index,* p. 328a 4 et seq.).[114]

At line 1178b 33 Aristotle returns for the third time to the problem of external goods, reaffirming that, as a man, the philosopher needs external goods in order to contemplate, and that, unlike the gods, he requires nourishment, health and other such things (b 33–35, cf. 1178a 25–27). Then, starting in line 1179a 1, he poses the problem of measuring external goods:

> but it should not be thought that one who is happy needs a lot of great things, just because it is not possible to be blessed without external goods. Indeed, independence and action are not based on excess, and it is possible to perform noble actions even without dominating the earth and seas;[115] and indeed, even with limited goods one could act in accordance with virtue. It is possible to see this clearly: in fact, private citizens are not thought to perform honest actions any less than the powerful, but even more than they. It is sufficient to possess a certain measure [of goods]: for the life of one who acts in accordance with virtue will be happy. (1179a 1–9)

We think that this passage is extremely important, and deserves more attention than it has so far been given. Aristotle here is not merely repeating things already said, but is articulating his ideal model of the happy life more clearly. This model is confirmed by citing authorities such as Solon (whose words were taken as the gospel truth by the Athenians) and Anaxagoras, whose authority was perhaps a little dubious. Solon is mentioned for his aversion to excessive wealth, and Anaxagoras is quoted as having said that the happy man is neither rich nor powerful, and would seem strange to the masses (a 9–16, cf. *EE* 1215b 6).

The mention of Anaxagoras clarifies what kind of βίος Aristotle is talking about. Dirlmeier[116] holds that here we are dealing with the amount of goods needed to conduct the βίος πολιτικός, or life in accordance with the ethical virtues. This is strange: if this were true, it would mean that Aristotle, after having maintained, in the two previous sections devoted to the subject of external goods, that one feature of a life lived in accordance with the ethical virtues is precisely the need for more external goods than those needed for the theoretical life, is here maintaining, on the contrary, that, for a life lived in accordance with only the ethical virtues, at bottom very few worldly goods are needed. The whole opposition on which the hortatory nature of these chapters is based would thus vanish. It is more probable that here Aristotle is talking about the man who lives the βίος θεωρητικός.[117] This position is supported by his extraordinary defense of the life of a private citizen (ἰδιώτης, a 6–7) as against that of a powerful man.[118] The man Aristotle is talking about performs virtuous (a 5–6) and honest (a 7) actions; he acts in accordance with virtue (a 8–9), as did the man devoted to a life of contemplation in 1178b 5–7. Moreover, the passage 1179a 1–9, which we are discussing, is sandwiched between two texts that are certainly speaking about the "philosopher" (1178b 33–35 and 1179a 9 et seq.), and the argument seems well connected. It is thus not likely that in this section Aristotle would change the subject of his discussion; the argument flows more logically if we understand Aristotle as here describing the philosophical life.

If this is true, Aristotle's model of happiness is clear: the happiest man is a private citizen who is moderately well-off and in good health, who acts properly and correctly in his relations with others, especially family members, friends and fellow citizens, who stays out of the struggle for political power and devotes himself, insofar as possible, to the life of contemplation, exercising his faculty of theoretical reflection. As can be seen, the upshot of the discussion of *EN* X 6–8 is a particular model of happiness, and not a general theory of the relations between the component parts of the happy life in all possible models.

The general definition of the happy life, i.e. that a life is happy when one acts in accordance with complete virtue, can be put into practice in various ways; such ways are not to be considered as being all on the same plane, depending on each person's preferences, but are to be ranked in order. Evidently, complete virtue includes the exercise of θεωρία but this exercise entails certain conditions that considerably limit the exercise of the other virtues. Instead, the kind of life that promotes the exercise of the political virtues necessarily either severely limits or completely prevents the exercise of contemplation,[119] and it is a second-rate kind of happy life, though still a happy one. In Aristotle there is no imperative to maximize θεωρία, nor any duty, in the strong sense, to contemplate; rather, he proposes a model whose realization depends on more or less favorable circumstances. In our opinion, this is confirmed and amplified by an important passage in *pol.* VII.

Before looking at *pol.* VII, however, we must compare what Aristotle says in *EN* 1179a 8–9 with the famous passage that concludes *EE* VIII 3.[120] In *EN* 1179a 8–9 Aristotle says that it is not necessary that a happy man should be rich or powerful, but it suffices for him to have enough goods to be able to act in accordance with virtue. In *EE* VIII 3, 1249a 21–b 23 the same problem is discussed, viz. that of the limit (ὅρος) of external goods needed. This limit is given by the σκοπός one aims at (1249b 24–25), since external goods are obviously means and not ends in themselves. The most important part of the text goes as follows:

> in previous [texts] it was said 'as reason [prescribes]';[121] this is as if one were to say, in treatises on diet, 'as medicine and its λόγος prescribe.' This is true, but is not clear. Hence it is necessary, as in the other cases, to live with reference (πρός) to the dominant element, and in accordance with the habitual state and activity[122] of the dominant element, as for example the servant [who lives] with reference (πρός) to his master, and every being according to the principle appropriate for it. And since man, too, by nature is composed of a dominant element and a dominated one, and each[123] of them must live with reference (πρός) to its own proper[124] principle. This is said in two senses; for medicine is a different kind of principle from health, as it exists for health's sake; and with regard to the contemplative[125] faculty, this is also the way things stand. For the god[126] is not an imperative commander, but is rather the end in consideration of which wisdom[127] commands. The objective has two names (they have been distinguished elsewhere),[128] for that [the god] has no need of anything. Hence the choice and purchase of natural goods that produces the greatest contemplation of the god—a [choice] of bodily goods, wealth, friends and other goods—is the best, and this is the noblest criterion. Instead, any choice that, by defect or excess, prevents one from serving the god and contemplating is bad. That is how things stand for the soul,[129] and the best criterion for the soul is to take as little notice as possible of the irrational part[130] of it as such.[131] (b 3–23)

The reasoning is elliptical, and probably the text contains a premise that is not finished ("And since men too . . ."); many points are doubtful, but Aristotle's general theory is rather clear: Aristotle concludes his treatment of the virtue of a noble man (καλοκἀγαθία) from the perspective of its relation with external goods, stating that contemplation, with the amount of external goods useful for it, is more important than the other virtues, and the amount of external goods useful for them. From this point of view, the argument contained in *EE* VIII 3 is not very different from that contained in *EN* X 8 and *EN* I, which we have seen in the previous pages. All these passages state that the best quantity of external goods is a moderate amount, and they estimate this "moderate amount" in relation to the needs of θεωρία. But in neither of the two passages is it said that the other virtues are only means for contemplating as much as possible. The object of θεωρία is here indicated as "the god" and in *EN,* 1177a 15, as "the noble and divine realities." In spite of Jaeger's famous thesis that *EE* and *EN* are in mutual opposition, it does not appear that the positions of the two treatises are very divergent.

Difficulties in interpretation arise mainly starting from lines 1249a 9–16 ("And since man, too [. . .] that is how things stand"). In our opinion, Aristotle is here summarizing elliptically and obscurely a theory that can be found elsewhere in a complete form. It is this: man is composed of a dominant [rational] part and a dominated part [which is irrational, but capable of obeying reason]. Each of the two must obey its proper principle [which, for the latter, is the former; the former, then, is subdivided into two other parts, the calculating one and the scientific one. The calculating part is practical, but does not command the scientific part; rather, it commands in consideration of it]. The two parts are related to one another like health and medicine. This is also true for the theoretical part. [This, too, is for the god's sake], not in the sense that the god needs to be contemplated, nor that the god gives orders, but in the sense that this theoretical part tends toward him as toward its proper object [i.e., the sought-for cause. In this broad sense, then] the god is the end for which practical wisdom [the virtue of the calculating part] gives orders.[132]

Here in *EN* Aristotle speaks of the moderate amount of goods that enables one to act in accordance with virtue, in a life seen as a complex set of activities, which includes θεωρία. The latter, owing to its very nature and inherent superiority, conditions all the rest; it requires independence and ease, and thus precludes participation in political strife. Likewise, in *EE* Aristotle speaks of the amount of goods needed for contemplation, considered as the most important element in the complete virtue of a noble man. Keeping in mind these two passages, Aristotle's position seems to be the following:

1. the happiest life is an active life in accordance with virtue and in a complete way;

2. it therefore also includes θεωρία

3. the amount of external goods needed for θεωρία is different from that needed for the unconditioned development of the other virtues;

4. therefore it is possible that the attempt to obtain those goods that are indispensable for the exercise of the political virtues, such as honor and power, may be harmful to θεωρία

5. it is therefore necessary to choose the amount of goods that, first of all, makes θεωρία possible, and not that which allows only other virtues;

6. the choice indicated in (5) does not prevent also the exercise of the virtues of character, since, apparently, private citizens act more honestly than do the powerful.

Hence the philosophical life does not prevent one from also putting into practice the other virtues. Aristotle's theory of happiness has a formal part, which consists in the identification of happiness with a βίος, which is active and not limited to the mere possession of the virtues, and in the distinction between the component parts and the necessary conditions for a happy life. But, aside from the formal part, we also find in Aristotle a "substantive" (or content-oriented) theory of happiness, which provides indications regarding what the most important of all the virtuous activities is, what the best βίος of all happy lives is, and what is the most appropriate amount of external goods or necessary conditions for happiness.

All this is confirmed and further elaborated, from the standpoint of political constitutions, in *pol.* VII. We shall look at this text in the next section.

13. Happiness and the Best Constitution

Like Plato in the *Republic,* so too Aristotle in *Politics* VII states that the criterion by which we can determine what the human good is remains the same for individuals and for the πόλις. But the similarities between the two texts are more apparent than real, since Plato considers it possible to make the political community happy without making individual citizens happy, whereas Aristotle denies this, in clear opposition to his master (*pol.* 1264b 17 et seq.). According to Aristotle, the best constitution is certainly the one that reproduces, on a grand scale, the model of happiness described in the *Ethics;* but it is also the one that in practice gives the individual citizen a chance to attain happiness and to act in accordance with complete virtue (1324a 23–25). Such a way of acting is possible only in a political community, and not when living in isolation; on the other hand, the purpose of the political community and the reason for its existence is just to make possible the good life for individuals.[133]

In *pol.* VII 1–3 Aristotle discusses authoritatively, and with many repetitions, the question as to which kind of life is preferable (αἱρετώτατος βίος, 1323a 15–16) and what is the best political system (1324a 13–19). In the section composed of chapters VII 13–15 he again discusses, in greater detail, what is the best constitution from the point of view of its end and the kind of life it leads to. Here we shall briefly summarize the content of these chapters, focusing our attention only on those passages that most closely regard our research. In Chapter 1, in referring to the so-called "external discourses" (λόγοι ἐξωτερικοί, 1323a

22–23), he states that in order to know what the best constitution is one must first establish what the best way of living is (1323a 16–20), and see whether it is identical for the individual and for the πόλις. This last question is answered in the affirmative several times in the course of this book (1323a 20, b 29–31, 33, 34–36; 1324a 7–13; 1325b 30–32; 1334a 9 et seq.). As for establishing what kind of βίος is best, one must start by determining the goods that compose it. Now, as we know, and as Aristotle repeats here, there are three types of goods: external, bodily and spiritual. Of necessity the happy life is composed of all these types of goods, at least to some extent (1323a 24–27). It is not possible to be happy without virtues such as courage, temperance, justice, wisdom or while being hungry or living completely without the light of (practical) reason (a 27–34). The problem, however, regards the amount of goods, since many people would be content to have even very little virtue, but desire very great wealth (a 34–38). We come back here, as can be seen, to the problem discussed in *EE* I 2. Using both facts (ἔργα) and arguments (λόγοι), Aristotle restates his well-known position: the virtues are ends and external goods are means; therefore, such goods have a limit, while the goods of the soul are to be possessed to the greatest possible extent, inasmuch as happiness consists of them (a 38–b 21). Hence happiness is a sum of different kinds of goods, some of which are to be possessed to the greatest possible extent, and others only insofar as they suffice for the first type:

> let it therefore be established that each will have as his lot as much happiness as he has virtue and wisdom, and insofar as he acts in accordance with them; we may take the god to witness, as he is happy and blessed not because of any external goods, but for his own sake and because he possesses a certain nature. And for these reasons good fortune must necessarily be different from happiness. For chance and fortune are the cause of the soul's acquiring external goods, but no one becomes just or temperate by luck or on account of fortune. Then [let it also be established], on the basis of these same arguments, that also the happy πόλις is the best one, and one that acts nobly. (1323b 21–29)

The best constitution will therefore be the one that encourages good behavior and the performance of noble actions; both for the individual and for the city, such actions consist of putting into practice the various virtues. Thus, a πόλις and a man considered to be "happy" will both be wise, just and brave, and will not depend on external goods, just as the god does not depend on them (1323b 31–36). Obviously, in the case of the πόλις, being wise, brave and so on is to be understood in a rather metaphorical sense,[134] since the πόλις as such does not act; it only acts through its citizens, individually or all together. Aristotle's position is to be understood in a weak sense; he believes that the end of the constitution is the happy life of the community, which he identifies with the happy life of individual citizens, and not of all the inhabitants of the city (VII 8). This life consists in acting nobly and not in amassing wealth at any cost.

Chapter 2 recapitulates many of the problems discussed in Chapter 1, but from a new standpoint: Aristotle now asks himself what the best kind of virtuous life is;[135] hence he no longer sets a "life devoted to earning" in opposition to one "devoted to the exercise of virtue"; rather, within the second category, he contrasts the βίος πολιτικός and the βίος θεωρητικός, just as in *EN* X 7 and, to some extent, in *EE* VIII 3. Here the theoretical life is described in a rather negative way; as in the model of the *Theaetetus,* it appears to be a life "as foreigners" in one's own city,[136] and the life of politics—in the sense that this term has when it is used pejoratively—is viewed as a life devoted to external goods (*EE* VIII 3, 1248 b 25 et seq.), or to power struggles. Those who wish to excel in virtue choose these two models of life (1324 a 25–32), and in doing so they are partly right, but also partly wrong (a 16–24), according to Aristotle.

We shall not try to retrace here the whole long and complex argument used by Aristotle. It continues up to Chapter 3, and concludes with a (rather surprising) argument in favor of the life of contemplation. In general, we may say that for Aristotle a life devoted to the quest for power is not the best life, neither for an individual who lives in the πόλις, nor for the πόλις that acts in the context of Greek civilization and the Greek commonwealth.

In Chapter VII 3, Aristotle proposes a solution that is, apparently, a middle ground between opposing theses, but is, in reality, a defense of the life of contemplation against the life of politics. From the fact that happiness is mainly composed of fine and noble actions, it is wrong to draw the conclusion—typical of the Athenian culture of the time—that the best thing to do is to try to obtain as much power as possible in order to perform many fine deeds (1325a 34 et seq.). Aristotle proposes a solution that many have praised, but which in reality is quite disconcerting, and recalls certain dialectical *tours de force* by Socrates in the early dialogues of Plato. In the final part of *pol.* VII 3, he admits that the best life for the individual and for the πόλις is an active life, since happiness is acting well (εὐπραγία, 1325b 15, cf. a 22). Then, however, he redefines the term πρᾶξις, blurring the opposition described up to this point. In the discussion of modes of living, πρᾶξις was a special kind of ἐνέργεια or activity, and consisted in performing virtuous actions; it was contrasted both with θεωρία and with ποίησις. Here, instead, πρᾶξις is directly identified with ἐνέργεια or activity,[137] and it is made to include both πρᾶξις proper and θεωρία. In this way Aristotle can even affirm that the most practical reflections are not those that lead to behavior toward other people, but those whose end lies in themselves, and that theoretical reflection can be interpreted as a πρᾶξίς τις (1325b 16–21).

What has been said so far holds true mainly for the individual; it is only from line 1326a 23 on that the results of this investigation into human happiness are applied to the whole city. Also in the case of the πόλις, the most perfect praxis consists of activities that are not directed externally but have their own end in themselves. But the body politic cannot perform the same kind of actions as an individual, and contemplate.[138] Aristotle is quite vague on the matter:

> and it is not even necessary that the cities that are isolated [from others] and have chosen to live in this way should be inactive, since [acting well] may even occur according to the parts (κατὰ μέρη). In fact, there are many reciprocal social relations (κοινωνίαι) between the parts of a city. The same happens in the case of any individual, for, on the contrary, the god and the entire cosmos would hardly be in the best condition, since they have no external activities, but only those proper to themselves (τὰς οἰκείας τὰς αυτῶν). (1325b 23–32)

The comparison with the god and the cosmos is rather exterior, based only on the fact that they, too, have no external relations. But this gives no inkling of what this activity "according to the parts" may be—an activity proper to the cities that have no "foreign policy." Since this activity is praised by Aristotle, it is unlikely that it is the city's "internal policy," in the sense of power struggles within the πόλις. It must rather be the virtuous actions that the citizens do to each other, as the term κοινωνίαι seems to suggest, or else the "cultural" activity of the city, consisting of ceremonies, spectacles and games.[139]

The problem of which is the best state is discussed again, from the standpoint that interests us, in *pol.* VII 13–15. Instead of quotations from external sources, as in *pol.* VII 1, here we find two quotations from *EE,*[140] whose theories are amply summarized. Aristotle repeats that external goods are indispensable conditions of happiness, but are not part of it (1331b 40–1332a 2), and that happiness is the practical actualization of virtue (1332a 7 et seq.). A long section (1332a 28–b 11) is devoted to the necessary conditions for a good constitution: external goods, good character and correct habits on the part of the citizens and the domination of reason in all choices made in common. Chapter 14 deals with the problem whether the education of the governed and of the governors is the same (1332b 12–1333a 16); then it returns to a discussion of the subject that most interests us. Aristotle refers to his theory of the parts of the soul (1333a 16–b 5): "there are two different parts of the soul; one of them has λόγος within itself, while the other does not have it within itself, but is capable of obeying λόγος" (a 16–18). The human virtues are virtues of these two parts of the soul (a 18–19), but the τέλος is found mainly in the highest part, which is again divided into two: "it is divided into two parts, precisely as we are accustomed to making the distinction; the one is practical λόγος, the other theoretical λόγος. In the same way, then, it is necessary to divide also this part [of the soul]" (a 24–27). Using this distinction, we can determine which actions constitute a happy life:

> and we say that also actions are related in the same way, and those of the naturally better part must necessarily be preferable, for those who are able to perform them, either all [three] of them, or at least the two [lesser ones],[141] since for everyone the highest thing he can attain to is always what is to be preferred. (1333a 27–30)

This passage makes it clear that not all the inhabitants of the city who take part in the happy life—i.e., citizens in every sense—need to contemplate. Many of them will stop at the virtues of character and practical λόγος, without attempting θεωρία. For these people, this is the best end, and this is their happiness. But this is not in contradiction with *EN* X 6–9, where the highest type of happiness was described.

Whoever can, however, must put into practice all the virtues, and in this case θεωρία is to practical wisdom as peace is to war. Here Aristotle repeats the comparison made in *EN* X 7 (cf. also *pol.* 1333a 30–b 3). Inasmuch as the legislator must organize the state with a view to assuring the happiness of its citizens, he must give them the possibility to exercise the highest possible degree of virtue. However, even those who reach the highest type of virtue will perform lower-level actions, as well as those actions required to obtain the well-being indispensable for contemplation. This is stated both in this chapter, and then, even more clearly, in the next chapter. Let us take a look at these two passages, one after the other:

> all of life is divided into ἀσχολία and σχολή, and into peace and war; some practical actions are aimed[142] at necessary and useful things, while others aim at noble things. It is necessary that, with regard to these things, there should be the same choice that there is with regard to the parts of the soul and the actions proper to them. The end of war is peace; the end of ἀσχολία is σχολή, and the end of necessary and useful things is noble things. It is the statesman's task to keep all these things in mind when giving laws, in relation both to the parts of the soul, and to the actions proper to them, and above all to the best things and the ends. He must act with regard to life and practical choices in the same way, for one must be able to be engaged in making war, but above all in enjoying peace and leisure. Necessary and useful actions must be performed, but noble ones even more. (1333a 30–b 3)

And in Chapter 15 he adds:

> since the human "end" seems to be the same for the individual and the collectivity, and there must be the same criterion (ὅρος) both for the best man and for the best constitution, it is clear that the virtues required for σχολή must be present in them, since, as has been said several times, the end of war is peace,

> and leisure is the end of necessary occupations. Of the virtues that are useful for σχολή and διαγωγή, there are some whose work (ἔργον) is carried out in σχολή and others [whose work is carried out] in ἀσχολία. Indeed, many needful things must be present for one to be able to live in σχολή. For this reason it is advisable that a πόλις should be temperate and brave and capable of endurance, for, as the proverb goes, there is no leisure (σχολή) for slaves, and those who are unable to face dangers bravely are the slaves [of anyone who] attacks them. One therefore needs courage and a capacity for endurance for ἀσχολία, and love of knowledge (φιλοσοφία)[143] for σχολή one needs temperance and justice in both periods (χρόνοις), but above all when living in peace and in a condition of σχολή. For war forces men to be just and temperate,[144] whereas the enjoyment of good fortune and a condition of peaceful (μετ' εἰρήνης) σχολή makes them arrogant. Thus there is a great need of justice and temperance for those who are considered to act in the best way and to enjoy every possible good, men, for example—if there are any—such as those who live in the 'isles of the blessed', as the poets say. They will need mainly a love for knowledge, temperance and justice; and the more they live in σχολή amidst the abundance of such goods, the more they will need these qualities. This, then, clearly explains why a state that is to live happily and virtuously will have to possess such virtues. (1334a 11–36)

The idea that good fortune is potentially dangerous and a possible cause of great evils comes from traditional ethics.[145] Aristotle uses this traditional thesis to clarify—definitively, in our opinion—the focal point of our investigation. From these two texts it is clear that the happy life is conducted in σχολή and, properly speaking, the necessary activities are not part of it, though they are indispensable for securing σχολή. There are virtues such as ἀνδρεία and καρτερία, courage and endurance, that are useful in times of ἀσχολία and especially in wartime, when ἀσχολία is particularly strong. There are virtues such as φιλοσοφία (which here stands for σοφία, in the most general sense of a love for culture) which are appropriate for times of σχολή, and then there are virtues such as σωφροσύνη and δικαιοσύνη, temperance and justice, which are useful in both phases, but above all in σχολή, when people risk becoming arrogant. The happiest life, both for cities and for individuals, appears to be composed of actions in accordance with certain virtues; Aristotle sets great store by this theory, which he repeats several times. Keeping in mind the principle, repeated *ad abundantiam,* whereby the criterion of happiness is the same for the individual and the city, we can deduce the following conclusions from the chapters thus far examined:

1. it is good to develop the highest capacities we are endowed with; thus, if one is capable of theoretical reflection, one should not limit oneself to the exercise of φρόνησις alone;

2. otherwise, one limits oneself to the actualization of a lower capacity; this happens often, since not everyone can devote himself to contemplation;

3. therefore, there is no categorical imperative to contemplate, and happiness means living in accordance with all the virtues one is capable of putting into practice;

4. in the case described under point (1), one does not live to exercise solely theoretical reflection for its own sake; the life of contemplation is a complex whole that also includes the exercise of the virtues of character;

5. it is not possible, however, to exercise all the human virtues at the same time; rather, they will be activated as required by individual cases. This point leads to other, more particularized conclusions:

5.1 there are virtues that come to the fore in phases of many commitments and ἀσχολία—inevitable phases in social life, during which one does not have the leisure needed to contemplate;

5.2 but there are also ethical virtues that remain important also in periods of σχολή, and that are associated with φιλοσοφία therefore

6. in periods of σχολή some virtues are exercised for their own sake and not simply as a means for contemplation.

Of all the types of happy life, the life of contemplation is the best. The best life, therefore, does not consist of a life composed of both theory and practice, as has been thought from Arius Didimus on[146]—i.e., contemplating and at the same time taking some interest in politics; on the contrary, it consists of contemplating, and at the same time practicing the virtues of character that are compatible with the primacy of contemplation and necessarily connected with it, not as a means to an end, but as part of the harmonious realization of the philosopher's personality.

14. An Active Life

In conclusion, therefore, Aristotle does not propose a model of life in which the opposing needs of the βίος θεωρητικός and the βίος πολιτικός are mediated; it may even be doubted whether two such modes of living as these described by Aristotle can be mediated. Indeed, they are not two elements of human life, like "theory" and "practice," or "intellect" and "pleasure" in Plato's *Philebus,* which may become ingredients in a more complex whole. They are, instead, two harmonious ways of organizing goods, activities, "values" (so to speak) and ends, and in many respects they are mutually antagonistic and incompatible. Virtuous acts, in the sense of virtues of character, such as courage, generosity and affability, are part of both these modes of life, and for this reason, as we saw at the beginning, Aristotle can oscillate between two different formulations of the definition of happiness: "life in accordance with complete virtue" and "life in accordance with the most perfect virtue." Many people have found these two formulations to be incompatible, but we believe they are not.

In Aristotle it is possible to distinguish a general theory of happiness and a restricted and more prescriptive theory, which deals with perfect happiness. This latter development of the doctrine renders the general theory more specific in terms of content, but does not contradict it.

From the general and, so to speak, formal point of view, we believe that the identification of happiness with an active life lived in accordance with virtue is the most typical aspect and the most important theoretical achievement of Aristotle's ethics on the subject of happiness. Our comparison of this theory with the doctrines of the Academy has shown us that Aristotle insists greatly on the pre-eminent importance of activities as opposed to states and dispositions. Happiness is a good of the soul, and is composed of parts, which are actions in accordance with virtue: one can be more or less happy depending on the actions that one performs. In order to be carried out, actions require a series of external goods, which are useful tools. The second feature typical of Aristotle's conception of happiness, viz. the determining, though not constitutive role attributed to external goods, depends on the first. As a complex group of virtuous actions, the happy life is a set of goods that is always changing in the personal history of each single individual; and to conceive of happiness as "activity in accordance with virtue" means to link it closely to the actual life situations of each individual. An organic set of actions is strictly tied to the events of a life, even though such actions may be partly habitual, and thus relatively repetitive or often similar to one another. It is therefore much more mutable than a subjective state of mind, which may remain imperturbable and untouched by actual happenings.[147] From this point of view Aristotle's conception of happiness is very different from more "static" theories, such as those of the Academy or the Stoics, which posit that, in a certain sense, the wise man is happy no matter what happens.

Aristotle's position shows all its originality also if it is compared with more modern theories. It appears that both Kant and Hegel, though they pursue very different theoretical ends, understand happiness to be a subjective state of self-contentment, which may be at most the consequence, but not the principle, of ethical action.[148] As we have seen, the kind of active life that, for Aristotle, constitutes the happy life is not without a certain pleasure; hence Aristotle's happiness is also "contentment," but this is not its essence.

On the basis of the various remarks made by Aristotle in the course of his arguments, it is possible to analyze the components of the set of goods called "happy life." The happy life is based on internal and external necessary conditions, which stand in special relations with the actual "component parts" of happiness, i.e. virtuous actions. External conditions, such as health and material goods, stand to virtuous activity *as the means stand to the end,* and they are to be procured to the extent needed to reach the end; hence they should be neither too many nor too few, but the principle of their goodness does not lie in themselves. The internal conditions, i.e. the possession of the virtues, understood as habitual states that give rise to actions, stand to virtuous actions, roughly speaking, *as power stands to act.* Aristotle often repeats that to be happy does not mean simply to possess virtues, but to put them into practice. One who possesses virtues that he never practices is not happy, but is wasting his capabilities, like a mechanism, a tool, or even a living organism that has been perfectly conceived but has never been set in operation. There is not the same relation between virtues and virtuous acts that there is between external goods and virtuous acts: the possession of virtue is a psychological state, and a good of the soul that is, in some way, absolute; nor does it make sense to say that one must possess virtue only to the extent that it is useful for acting virtuously, since the relation between potentiality and actualization is different from that between ends and means.

To clarify this point, we must abandon the more general discourse and tackle the subject of the composition of happiness. We have seen that happiness is a "way of living," i.e. an organic whole, to which Aristotle gives the traditional name of βίος, and we have compared this βίος to the idea of a "rational plan of life" which has recently been put forward in the literature on ethics. The comparison has allowed us to determine that one of the most important consequences of interpreting happiness in terms of βίος is precisely that this distinction makes it possible to establish differing value relations between the various parts that make up the βίος, i.e. between virtuous actions; the notion of "rational plan" makes such value discriminations impossible, as such a "plan" implies the harmonious realization of all ends, which are all considered to be of equal worth.

Between happiness and virtuous actions there is neither the relation of end to means, nor the relation of "power" to "act." Virtuous actions are not the means for happiness, nor are they the concrete actualization of the human capacity to be happy. They are *the parts of happiness,* but their value—i.e., the fact that virtuous actions are goods—does not come from their "being part" of happiness. It is good to perform acts of courage, generosity and affability or to choose wisely or to contemplate the causes of reality, even if, owing to the accidents of human existence, and for any particular individual who performs them, happiness does not come from such acts.

In general, however, happiness does derive from these acts, and cannot be attained in any other way; nor would it be reasonable to exclude the possibility of reaching the supreme human good by performing virtuous acts. In our opinion, this is the meaning of Aristotle's obscure formula to the effect that virtuous acts should be performed "for their own sake and for the sake of happiness."

In every βίος there is one kind of virtuous activity that prevails over the others and, in some way, subordinates them to itself. This particular virtuous activity does not exhaust the βίος, nor is it the end of every other good activity, but it does give a distinctive trait to that particular way of life and makes it possible to judge a person who devotes himself to it, using the social institutions Aristotle calls "praise and blame." There may be bad, good or middling βίοι. The happy βίοι put into practice the human virtues. But not all virtues lie on the same plane; some are superior, others inferior; they have differing priorities and degrees of dignity, which distinguish one from another, though without reducing the inferior ones to the status of means for the superior ones. A certain, particular hierarchy of virtues is typical of human beings generally, and distinguishes them both from the lower animals and from the gods, who have different, albeit commensurable, hierarchies.

Of all human activities, those connected with rationality are the most distinctive, but they are so in a rather complex sense and the way of being "connected with rationality" is different in the various cases. There are the activities and their respective virtues that are linked to the sphere of emotions and desires; they are rational inasmuch as they are subordinated to practical reason. There are the activities of φρόνησις, which is practical and strictly linked with the sphere of desires, to which it imparts orders, gives criteria and imposes limits. Lastly there is theoretical activity, which is detached from the rest. All these activities make up the happy life, but it is not easy to organize them in such a way that they can coexist in harmony.

If the happy life is the actualization of all human capacities, it will also be the actualization of the capacity to do θεωρία and to contemplate. But the presence of the highest intellectual virtue in the happy life is not without its consequences for the other virtues and activities. Theoretical reflection, by its very nature, requires certain conditions for its existence—a certain degree of comfort and leisure time and a certain type of σχολή; it therefore imposes a particular kind of organization on the other virtues, which must somehow give way before it and limit themselves in its presence, as it is of greater dignity and worth. As we have said, this does not mean that virtues such as "affability" or "justice" become means for contemplation, but it does pose limitations on the realization of these other virtues. One will therefore have to curb one's affability in order to have leisure to reflect on first principles and contemplate basic realities. On the other hand, it makes no sense to limit one's θεωρία in order to have a more complete actualization of the virtue of affability. While a "rational plan of life" is, as we have said, an *equilibrium amongst equals,* a harmonious balancing of different goods, Aristotle's "happy life" is a *weighted equilibrium* of components that have different degrees of importance and dignity. A man realizes himself most fully if he gives the greatest play to the most worthy and laudable capacities he possesses.

This enables us to understand also why the theoretical βίος and the practical βίος are two different models of the happy life, and there can be no mediation between them, though both of them are ways of being happy, in a more or less perfect and complete way. In each of them the realization of the main activity—contemplation or the life of politics—prevents, or at least considerably limits, the realization of the activity that characterizes the opposing βίος. Whoever contemplates does not "do" politics, and vice versa. The amount of external goods needed, i.e. the indispensable means, is different in the two cases, and precisely because it is appropriate for one kind of life, it is harmful for the other. The mean of nobility, friendly relations and wealth for the life of politics is, in absolute terms, greater than the mean for the life of contemplation, and indeed would be a hindrance for such contemplation. On the other hand, the amount of external goods that is appropriate for contemplation would be embarrassing for anyone who wanted to undertake the governance of a city. Also the relation with the emotional part of the soul is different in the two cases; the philosophical life leaves relatively little room for the play of the emotions—less room, in any case, than that allowed by the life of politics: suffice it to think of the different role played by the virtue of "getting angry to the right extent" in an orator and a mathematician. The life of politics—the central part of which was occupied, in the ancient world, by war—requires great courage, whereas the life of philosophy, as Aristotle says in the *Politics,* requires mainly justice and moderation, to prevent one from becoming arrogant. This confirms what was said above: the room allowed to the various ethical virtues depends on which virtuous activity it is that characterizes the βίος.

Although, from a modern perspective, Aristotle's position may seem rather prescriptive, authoritarian and, hence, overly archaic, it is our opinion that there is something to be said on its behalf.

The model of philosophical life advanced by Aristotle, which is largely a reinterpretation of the popular appreciation of ἀπραγμοσύνη, praised by orators and poets, was not given an enthusiastic reception in Aristotle's own school, as is well-known. Dicaearchus (fr. 30 Wehrli) upheld the primacy of political life. And the interest that Aristotle's theory of happiness can hold for us today, aside from its purely historical value, is not based on the details of the model of the supremely happy life that we find in the *Nicomachean Ethics*. The defense of Aristotle's position which we mentioned before must be conducted—if at all—on a higher level of generalization. In a contemporary discussion about happiness, it may be very useful, in our opinion, to keep in mind Aristotle's idea that an individual's self-realization occurs in an active life, in which a person actualizes his or her abilities, and that happiness does not correspond to a psychological state of subjective contentment. It makes a big difference whether one conceives of happiness as a set of actions or as peaceful and inactive self-satisfaction. And, at the level of content, it seems very important to us to have at our disposal some conceptual tools with which to evaluate, and either approve or reject on the basis of relevant rational justifications, what others call the happy life, whether in theory or in real life, without needing to limit ourselves to checking the coherence and harmony of conceptions different from our own.

CONCLUSION

Aristotle describes practical knowledge, or wisdom (φρόνησις), from the standpoint of its epistemological status, as well as in terms of how it functions. With this theory he unquestionably takes philosophical discussion about human action a few steps forward, not only with regard to the philosophical debates of his own time, but also in general, theoretical terms.

He synthesizes elements coming from the tradition into a new and original position, drawing on doctrines of the sophists and the rhetors, the teaching of Plato and the debates of the Academy. It is possible to trace the sources of many of the elements in his conception, but the sense of each of them is partially modified in the Aristotelian doctrine of practical knowledge. It thus does not appear correct to give them the same value and significance they had originally.

Aristotle's main thesis is that human action is guided by a specific form of knowledge, which has its own characteristics, appropriate to the object it addresses. On the one hand, these characteristics cannot be confused with those of any other type of knowledge, but on the other they are not so totally unlike other forms of rationality as to make comparisons and explanatory analogies impossible.

As acting is (1) "doing something for something else," i.e. making movements with an end in mind, so practical reasoning is (2) "choosing one thing with another thing in mind," i.e. determining a type of future action, and initiating it. According to Aristotle, this "choosing" does not occur by chance or in a completely irrational way, at least where mature and morally sound persons are concerned; rather, it takes place on the basis of reasons and motives.

Formula (2) enables Aristotle to account for many of the features that are peculiar to practical knowledge. A choice is a program of future action, which generates a practical behavior. It is therefore related to an end and a concrete situation. The end that one proposes to reach by means of an action is actually the cause of the action, and is the principle or starting point of deliberative reasoning.

As a principle, the end is not the object of deliberative reasoning itself, but is posited by another psychic faculty, viz. ethical virtue. In reality, a man acts well because he is virtuous, not because he possesses the ability to reason in an exact and rigorous way or can deduce right ends from immutable principles or possesses a special noetic intuition of ends and ethical principles, aided by philosophical conversations held in the Lyceum or the Academy.

Ethical virtue involves the habitual possession of a state of rational balance of the emotions. It is therefore not a purely irrational element; indeed, wisdom is even a part of its definition. This is true in a twofold sense: in the determination of the end, since wisdom is the rational element that determines the mean or happy medium to be aimed at, and in the determination of the means, since wisdom specifies the general end one is trying to reach and makes reaching it feasible.

Wisdom is a form of rationality that is strictly linked with the desires and emotions; it guides the desires, i.e. the basic drives of "pursuing" and "avoiding." It does so by showing how a certain future course of action is capable of producing a desired result, and hence is good-for-something-else, even when at first sight it appears to be unpleasant, or indifferent. This does not make wisdom an irrational procedure, for Aristotle's rational desire follows the lead of reason, and does not guide it at any time in the course of its operation.

But the fact that practical wisdom is a rational form of knowledge does not imply that it is a scientific, or "philosophical" form of knowledge in the modern sense, i.e. one that can be transmitted by means of some type of completely and solely intellectual relation, such as that between master and disciple. Wisdom is the fruit of social life in all its forms, both as a part of virtue, which is the capacity to determine the ends, and as the intellectual capacity to calculate the means. It is transmitted through various social institutions: the laws of the city, family life and interaction with friends. The social functions of praise and blame, reward and punishment have the task of training the individual to pursue good ends, while practical experience of life provides each person with a series of ideas, which are valid in most cases, regarding the consequences of one's actions, and what should be done in a given situation to reach a certain objective. The practical element, that which gives rise to the action, in our interpretation is not introduced at a certain moment into practical reasoning, as some modern analyses of practical knowledge suggest, but is present from the beginning, in the constant union of reason and desire that Aristotle posits as the distinguishing feature of wisdom, as well as in the doctrine that the ends of action derive from ethical virtue.

For these reasons, wisdom cannot lead to blameworthy acts. In its definition there is an implicit reference to virtue and good ends, just as in the definition of virtue there is an implicit reference to wisdom. For the same reasons, wisdom cannot be forgotten, since it is tied to a habitual state of character and a stable disposition of desire. Again for the same reasons, it cannot be taught to one who is too young or to one who is not already well disposed, of his own free will, to act properly. As a result of social co-existence, wisdom is not handed on by Aristotle to his disciples through a reading of the *Nicomachean Ethics;* this treatise, like the *Eudemian Ethics,* is useful only to those who already possess wisdom, virtue and experience, and hence in general act correctly. These works are useful precisely because they clarify the nature of the knowledge that such people make use of, because they elevate practical reasoning from the stage of unconscious usage to that of a more conscious and monitored use, because they exhort people to behave virtuously and to pursue good ends and because they clarify, specify and redefine the ultimate end to be aimed at, i.e. the "happiness" that all people tend toward, albeit in a confused and partly inappropriate way. The relation between this treatise and its reader is like the relation that must have existed between the *Rhetoric* and a reader who was already an expert public speaker, but who, in reading Aristotle's work, saw more clearly the nature of conviction, the mechanisms used to obtain it, the comparative value of these mechanisms, the value of the various types of conviction and the different kinds of contents to be conveyed by means of it.

With reference to the lively philosophical debates in the Academy, Aristotle's treatise constituted a clear statement of his position. This consisted in the abandonment of some still "sophistical" and paradoxical positions held by Plato, and in a rediscovery of the modicum of truth contained in traditional statements.

But the importance of Aristotle's discussion does not lie wholly in his doctrines concerning the status of wisdom. His analyses of the decision-making process and of the internal mechanism of deliberation, which is a result of wisdom, are also very important. The deliberative mechanism is determined both by the epistemological status of wisdom, which involves a relation with desire, and by its end, which is to lead to action. It is therefore a radically different mechanism from that of scientific reasoning, or dialectical discussion. Nevertheless, as we have pointed out, it may be compared to them, and like them may be analyzed by means of the conceptual tool known as the syllogism.

Aristotle views deliberation and practical reasoning as an intellectual activity, which takes place in the pauses between actions, and in preparation for action; it is intended to fill a gap, created between the end and the present situation, when it is not immediately apparent how to achieve, here and now, the end that we have set for ourselves. Deliberation generally consists of an analysis of the end, which does not aim to demonstrate its goodness—that is guaranteed by the fact that it is set as an end by virtue—but rather to show its feasibility in a given context. The end, which is seen by Aristotle as a practical general judgment regarding the goodness and desirability of a future course of events, is specified, redefined and particularized by deliberation, in an activity that Aristotle sometimes calls "analysis." The outcome of the analytical mechanism is the transformation of a psychical situation wherein the agent has in mind only a universal practical premise, such as "For a hero like me it is necessary to defend my fatherland," into a situation in which the agent has in mind a practical premise sufficiently particularized that it can be carried out at once—a premise of the type "Now I shall climb over that cart and attack the enemy leader from the right." This action is desired not for its own sake, but because it produces the good result described in the universal premise; the universal premise, in and of itself, is not practical, but becomes practical only when it is specified by a particular premise. From the behavioral point of view, i.e. from the perspective of the definition of "practical knowledge," the second practical premise is the more important one, inasmuch as it alone gives rise to a course of action.

One does not always go through all the analytical steps; very often habit and experience enable us to skip many premises, but in any case it is the complete model of practical reasoning that gives rise to a chain of intermediate terms, each of which is more specific and practical than the one before, and is considered good in the light of all that has preceded it in the decision-making process. These elements are identified on the basis of experience; since human events largely occur in similar ways, experience tells us that, if we do x, it is highly probable that y will happen, or else that consequences v, y and z will ensue. On the basis of these reasonable expectations we can determine what we should do, and demonstrate in this way that we are really wise, viz. that we are not merely fine souls who have good, albeit ineffectual intentions, but are esteemed members of our society, capable of achieving the good aims we set ourselves, and securing our happiness in so doing.

In terms of content, since the concept of wisdom analytically includes the concept of "acting well," the aim of wisdom is given as being that of "behaving properly" or "acting nobly." This is not a practical end, but only a general term that sums up the distinguishing features of action (in the strong sense of the term) with respect to other kinds of practical behavior, such as the production of goods. No one ever sets out to reach the aim of "acting nobly" or of "being happy"; rather, we set out to accomplish particular actions embodying these general aims. For example, we wish to carry out actions exhibiting a specific virtue suited to the present case; or we wish to put into practice a general life program, involving certain priorities and sacrifices; or we desire to realize fully certain of our abilities and neglect others, in such a way as to give a general meaning to our existence; and so on. The sophists' argument regarding Hercules at the crossroads was drawn on by Aristotle for his idea of a general choice of way of life, one which then determines each person's individual acts, and is not combinable with other ways of living.

This choice of life is not a "given," but disciples can be exhorted to follow it. Wise men who listen to Aristotle may, from this perspective, undergo a change of mind after reading the *Nicomachean Ethics,* and may replace their current, and not completely correct, notion of happiness with a fuller and more complete idea.

In this sense Aristotle's moral doctrine is more than a mere clarification of ideas or exhortation to action; it becomes ethical teaching, the transmission of ethical contents. On this plane Aristotle's ideas now seem dated, yet even today they are not completely to be discarded. The reading of the *Nicomachean Ethics* is valuable to us as providing an authoritative opinion about how to live; this opinion is not to be embraced blindly, but it should be kept in mind, especially when we realize that we are unreflectively acting upon ethical models, value schemes, behavioral prescriptions and life choices advanced by other masters of thought, who, however distinguished they may be, are also not to be accepted without question.

AFTERWORD

I

The critical debate on the *Nicomachean Ethics* has been particularly intense during the past decade. We believe that it would be helpful to summarize some of the results of that debate on the occasion of the English translation of our essay ten years after its original publication in Italian. We will confine our remarks to discussions relating directly to the Aristotelian concept of *phronesis*.

Phronesis has been studied over the past decade both from a general theoretical point of view, in terms of its location in the Aristotelian system, and from a textual and analytic point of view, examining its exact meaning, clarifying obscurities and apparent contradictions. The more systemic approach tends to prevail in works that might be called "continental," while the more analytical and inductive approach tends to prevail in English-language contributions.

Among the major contributions we should mention especially the publication of Heidegger's 1924 lectures, including an analysis of *EN VI* (M. Heidegger, *Platon, Sophistes* [Vorlesung Wintersemester 1924–5], Frankfurt a/M 1922), and an important book by S. Broadie with a long chapter on *phronesis (Ethics with Aristotle,* Oxford-New York 1991: see Chapter IV). Moreover three collections of essays were published dealing wholly or partly with analysis of the Aristotelian conception of wisdom: one collection is Italian (A. Alberti, ed., *Studi sull'etica di Aristotele,* Napoli 1990), one is American (J. P. Anton & A. Preus, eds., *Essays in Ancient Greek Philosophy IV: Aristotle's Ethics*, New York 1991), and another is French (J. Y. Chateau, *La vérité pratique. Aristote, Ethique à Nicomaque, Livre VI,* Paris 1997). This volume was produced by a group of French scholars studying the history of the concept of "prudence," the translation often used in France for *phronesis,* particularly by those influenced by Aubenque. A. Tosel is the leader of this group; they have published several volumes on prudence and action.[1] Other interesting contributions can be found in S. G. Salkever's *Finding the Mean: Theory and Practice in Aristotelian Philosophy,* Princeton 1990, in C. D. C. Reeve's *Practices of Reason: Aristotle's N.E.*, Oxford

1992, and in R. Elm's *Klugheit und Erfahrung bei Aristoteles,* Paderborn 1996. Finally a thorough study of the *Nicomachean Ethics,* with an ample discussion of *phronesis,* comes from Argentina: O. Guariglia, *La etica en Aristoteles o la moral de la virtud,* Buenos Aires 1997.[2]

For the sake of brevity we shall gather the various contributions to the debate under three headings reflecting the points of concentration of the discussion: (a) the general philosophical issues concerning the nature of Aristotelian *phronesis* and the anthropology it presupposes; (b) the problem of the origin of the principles of wisdom; and (c) the way *phronesis* works.

II

Discussion of general philosophical issues concerning *phronesis* inevitably involves the problem of the origin of the principles of *phronesis* and how it works, but we will delay a more detailed discussion of those issues just a bit.

The debate about the forms of reason, started by Gadamer in the 1960s with a reassessment of Aristotelian *phronesis,* continued in the 1990s but with greater prudence. Pierre Aubenque has continued to compare Aristotelian practical reasoning to Heidegger's thought and to the philosophical reflections deriving from Gadamer's hermeneutics, like the Italian "pensiero debole."[3] However, many authors point out that the comparison between Gadamer's hermeneutics and Aristotelian *phronesis* is the wrong way to go. *Phronesis* is not self-sufficient knowledge (Berti); it is not opposed to science as is hermeutics (Salkever); it cannot count as a third way between Kant's formalism and ethical empiricism (Ricoeur).[4] Therefore we can say that during the last decade of the twentieth century the importance of *phronesis* as a model of philosophical thinking in general has been reconsidered, after the enthusiasms of the 1970s, when some philosophers proposed Aristotelian practical reason as a solution for the impasses and crises of modern rationality. Some scholars underlined the incongruities and problems inherent in Aristotelian *phronesis,* while others attempted a mixture of Kantian and Aristotelian ethics, something very hard to achieve, in our opinion.[5]

Heidegger interprets Aristotelian ethics as a "Phenomenology of Dasein," that is, a descriptive theory of moral behavior, rather than prescriptive. Action and reflection on action are a way of being in the world and, in Heidegger's reading, the Aristotelian theory is more concerned with the authenticity of action than with its excellence in respect to given values or in reference to an autonomous moral law.

Less generally, Berti and Salkever are among those who point out that *phronesis* must derive its principles from some other discipline. They identify different disciplines on which *phronesis* would depend—Berti names practical philosophy, and Salkever "social science." On closer inspection we observe that almost all those who assert that *phronesis* acquires its principles from a superior science seem to say that this derivation makes the practical principles clear, not that it dictates the principles to wisdom.[6] On the other hand, some still think that *phronesis* is an absolutely autonomous form of knowing that establishes its own principles by itself.

At any rate the debate about the relation between the book called *Nicomachean Ethics* and the *phronesis* described in it, the primary focus of thinking about Aristotelian ethics in the 1960s, seems partly solved. Nowadays nobody thinks with Hardie that Aristotle's ethical treatises are an outcome of the practical intellect,[7] and a consequence is that Aristotle's methodological prescriptions for practical reasoning cannot any longer be applied to *EN* itself. The *Nicomachean Ethics,* both a *methodos* and a *pragmateia,* follows the rules of construction valid for any other Aristotelian treatise. That clears up a major source of confusion about Aristotle's analysis of practical knowledge. The theoretical study of ethics does not have its own peculiar methodology, different from that of the study of nature,[8] but rather it applies common Aristotelian procedures, like dialectic and analysis by final causes, to human behavior, in much the same way as they are applied to investigations in biology.[9]

III

The most rigorous debate during the 1990s concerned the origin of the ends pursued by wisdom. Everyone agrees that *phronesis,* as the capability of grasping concrete ways and means of achieving an end on the basis of deliberation, must have a certain knowledge of the end itself. It's a matter of fact that one cannot decide which way to go if one does not know where one is headed. But the question is this: does *phronesis* itself establish practical ends, or does it acquire them from a superior faculty or discipline? This question is of course also relevant to determining the importance of the overall Aristotelian concept of *phronesis.* If it is simply a capacity for determining means to an end, then it cannot be a kind of reason able to establish ends; but in that case Aristotle's concept of wisdom would prove to be useless for solving a major issue in contemporary philosophical debate, namely how to establish the ends for action. As Chateau observed, on this issue Aristotelian texts are quite ambiguous; every point of view can find textual support.[10]

Some people argue that *phronesis* does not establish ends,[11] others maintain the opposite.[12] In the middle are some who assert that the ends of *phronesis* are given by *nous,* and the relationship between *phronesis* and *nous* can be understood in two ways: either *phronesis* is related to *nous* as *episteme* is, or as *sophia* is.

In the former case *nous* would be separate from *phronesis* and superior to it,[13] in the latter *nous* would be internal to *phronesis*.

It is not always easy to understand which position is taken by those who posit the existence of a *nous* having as object practical first principles. Some writers compare the procedure by which practical ends lead to induction, the procedure described by Aristotle in *Posterior Analytics* II.19. In the case of practical knowledge the role of experience would be played by *ethismos,* the habit of acting rightly. *Ethismos* establishes a kind of practical *epagoge,* and an intellectual intuition of principles is the outcome of this *epagoge*. Thus *phronesis* would be external to its practical *nous* as *episteme* is external to theoretical *nous*. Among those who maintain this interpretation, Tuozzo claims that *EN* does not say explicitly that *phronesis* gets its principles from *nous,* but that such a theory is clearly established in *Posterior Analytics* II.19. Reeve, on the other hand, speaks about a totally empirical origin of practical principles: in his opinion they derive from experience and not from dialectic. The only function of dialectic is therefore to make clearer the universal judgments founded on experience.[14]

Other scholars seem to make *nous* a part of *phronesis;* in that case, Aristotle's wisdom would be composed of a reasoning part, with the task of calculating means, and an intuitive part, with the role of perceiving the end. In support of this interpretation they cite some passages in *EN* where it is said that *phronesis* is both *aisthisis* and *nous*.[15] But the interpretation of these passages is rather controversial; many other interpreters, some of them well known, hold that the kind of *nous* that is related to *phronesis* is not concerned with establishing ends, and is able only to interpret the concrete cases in the light of an already established end. According to this reading, the object of practical *nous* would be the so-called second premise that states what is to be done here and now, not a universal notion of human good.[16]

The arguments of those who observe that *phronesis* is a part of ethical virtue seem much sounder. They deduce that when Aristotle affirms that virtue gives the ends, he is not talking about a habit of completely irrational desire, but is alluding to the kind of desire that complies with reason, described in *EN* I.13. These scholars point out that Aristotle says only that *phronesis* acquires its ends from moral virtue.[17] This sort of statement is repeated several times in *EN,* but is usually disregarded by the interpreters who think that moral virtue is an excellence only of the irrational part of the soul, and is unsuited for founding the first principles of human action. In opposition to this reading the interpreters we are talking about now observe that *phronesis,* in determining the measure of the right mean that is an end has something to say about the end itself. Therefore it is not correct to identify Aristotle's position with Hume's emotionalism,[18] because virtue of character is not a completely irrational state.

We must also cite the position of those who, like Berti, underline the function of practical philosophy in establishing the end: even if ends are *de facto* assimilated as habits, their theoretical foundation is given by a practical philosophy that is, in Berti's view, identified with the content of Aristotle's *Nicomachean Ethics.* The practical end, in this interpretation, is identified with the theory of human good and happiness presented in *EN* I and X. These are notions that can be firmly established only by way of an extensive theoretical discussion, and not by simple insight.[19]

Aristotle never says how the precepts about human good and happiness presented in Books I and X of *EN* should be connected to the description of the working of practical knowledge found in the other books of his *Ethics*. He simply tells us that his analysis is practical, and is meant to make people good. In our opinion, his analysis of wisdom is not directed toward the students in the Lyceum; he does not want to give them suggestions to be put into practice immediately. He is only describing the characteristics that people recognize as wise, and by means of this description he proposes a model of behavior to his readers. Wise persons like Pericles, though good, have no great philosophical preparation. We believe that Aristotle believed there to be considerable agreement between his own notion of happiness and the ends *de facto* pursued by *phronimoi*. But that optimistic point of view is never presented overtly.

There are interpreters who think that practical ends come from the *ethos* of the *polis*. Among them is Owens, who observes that in a cyclical concept of history the practical principles are eternal, and can be transmitted by education and assimilated as habits. This reading is in line with Heidegger's principle: *doxa* is the body of *phronesis.*[20] We thus must deal with the issue of the content of supreme practical principles. In fact many contemporary interpreters have tried to solve the problem of the origin of practical principles by making them totally devoid of informational content. According to this interpretation, the practical principle is simply "act well"; deliberation and *phronesis* are given the job of deriving how to act from this empty universal. Interpreters who take this line, both English-language like Broadie, and German, like Heidegger, Bubner, and Elm,[21] point out that for Aristotle the end of virtuous acting is the virtuous acting itself, *eupraxia,* and nothing more. *Eupraxia,* according to Broadie, seems to be the fruit of virtue and character alone. That is odd, and must be underlined: how can a virtue of a part of the soul that is irrational, but capable of obeying reason, give to *phronesis* this abstract universal end as a practical principle? Broadie thinks that in the practical realm what really matters is specifying this end; deliberation and wisdom see this end in the light of real situations, give it flesh and blood so to speak, and hand it over to us.[22] Thus according to Heidegger the capacity of *nous* to see the practical extreme as project and object of an action is not a pure technical ability to apply a general rule to a single case, but it is a specifically human way of "being in the truth."[23] We shall discuss Heidegger's notion of truth a little later. This interpretation gives maximum weight to Aristotle's statements according to which there is a methodological inversion between practical and theoretical knowledge tied to action: in practical knowledge the particular is more important than the universal, and what to do is more important than why. From this point of view the problem of the origin and foundation of the universal practical principle loses importance, because *praxis* is considered to be a law unto itself, and the universal principle becomes merely a linguistic formula of the autonomy of *praxis*. The reading of Aristotle that we are describing sets itself as the antipodal opposite of the interpretations described at the beginning. They assimilated the procedure of *phronesis* to the procedure of *episteme,* as described in the *Posterior Analytics,* and made universal premises the focal point of knowledge. Heidegger and others, on the contrary, concentrate all their attention on the second premise, and on the intuition of the individual case. In this sense Leszl's observations about the ambiguities of Aristotle's distinction between practical and theoretical knowledge grasped a real difficulty. It is difficult to imagine that Aristotle did not ascribe a fundamental importance to his theory of happiness, in *EN* I and X, and that he did not think that, however the *phronimos* gets his first principles, reading or listening to the philosopher's lectures can help him grasp firmly and consciously the criteria of his behavior. In other words, Heideggerian interpretations do not justify the universal and prescriptive content of the first and last books of the *Nicomachean Ethics.*

IV

While there is a great variety of opinions on the issue of principles, there is a wide agreement among interpreters in characterizing *phronesis* as practical knowledge. On this, the main differences concern the stress on one aspect or another. Berti and Besnier emphasize that the *phronimos* must be good and virtuous. Such goodness is the real *sich Erschliessen,* to be open to Being through *praxis,* the very nature of Dasein according to Heidegger.[24]

Phronesis brings about an agreement of reason and desire that finds expression in good deliberation. Practical truth features this agreement between the intellective faculty and the emotions. It would be more accurate to say that reason in the practical field is "dipped in desire"; if we do not have the right desires, reason cannot even start its analytical job.[25] The agreement of reason and desire depends on the object: the same thing is judged both good and desirable, contrary to Hume's argument, that claims that the two faculties have different objects.[26] Some think that the practical syllogism is a part of logic, and try to interpret it using analytical tools that indicate both a "causative implication" and "desire transmission from premises to end."[27] Others interpret the practical syllogism as a metaphor or pattern of thinking that is not part of the realm of logic.[28]

Against those who try to interpret the conclusion of the practical syllogism as a proposition, many scholars reaffirm that the conclusion of the practical syllogism is an action, and not a judgment about what is to be done. This suggests that Aristotle left logic behind with his practical syllogism. In any case, as Besnier underlines, the practical syllogism can have just one premise (we think that it is the second, e.g.: "this brew is healthy"), and therefore it is not a scientific syllogism.[29] Many scholars think that the end of deliberation consists in formulating an action project to which desire adheres.[30] Since this project can be formulated as a singular proposition in the future tense (e.g., "killing Caesar will bring freedom"), it can be analyzed in terms of *De interpretatione* 9 and its understanding of the truth of statements about contingent futures. That would cohere with the Aristotelian idea that practical judgments, though valid for the most part, can be false in individual cases.

The notion of "practical truth" has been analyzed by almost all contemporary scholars, and many have emphasized the differences between practical and scientific truth. Heidegger in particular, as we have already said, uses a concept of truth close to our own concept of "authenticity," a sort of full expression of oneself in the world.[31] For others, truth and authenticity in acting consist in faithfulness to a clear and coherent vision of human good, and in judging correctly actions in the light of the end.[32] To conclude, we may say that the notion of truth applied to *praxis* in Aristotle is not the correct application of a general moral precept to a single case. It is finding a coherent expression of the nature of the agent, the wise man rationally bent on acting well and achieving practical success.

NOTES

Chapter One

1. H. von Arnim (1927).

2. Von Arnim (1927), p. 27.

3. Von Arnim (1927), p. 5.

4. I. Düring (1968), pp. 202–232, especially p. 224, and E. Berti (1977), pp. 177 ff. have insisted on this point. There is mention of the discussion we shall examine here in P. Aubenque (1963), pp. 117–118 and 141.

5. Von Arnim (1927), p. 5.

6. Von Arnim (1927), pp. 5 and 24.

7. In fact, it is said that φρόνησις is the most scientific science of all (119b 32) and, on the other hand, that it governs the use of force (118a 8). A similar position is found in the *Protrepticus,* fragments 12–13 (Ross), while Xenocrates (fragments 6–7 Heinze = 84–85 and 254 Isnardi Parente) already makes a distinction between theoretical φρόνησις, practical φρόνησις and σοφία, which is different from both, as is made quite clear by Gauthier (1958–1959), II, p. 467 and M. Isnardi Parente (1981), *ad. l.* On the comparison between the *Protrepticus* and Xenocrates, cf. also E. Berti (1961), p. 485.

8. Cf. IV 3, 124a 10–14.

9. Cf. *top.* 144a 11, and E. Berti (1977), pp. 183–185.

10. Alex. Aphrod. *in Aristot. top. comm.*, p. 308, 8ff. (Wallies).

11. Cf. J. Brunschwig (1967), p. LVII note 4. A. Zadro (1974), p. 419, holds that here Aristotle wants to deny that φρόνησις can be both a science and a virtue.

12. G. Colli (1955), p. 971, seems to understand here the words τὸ ὡσαύτως ἔχον ἴδιον, which would further clarify the text. However, it seems to us to be understandable even in its present state, since, if one posits that *a* is proper to *c, b* cannot be so, and hence not even *a,* which behaves in the same way as *b.*

13. Ross suggests the reading: "it will not be the property of another virtue (ἄλλης ἀρετῆς) to be the science of evil," but this does not appear to square with the general meaning of the passage. Moreover, the emendation is suggested in a rather doubtful manner.

14. Cf. V. J. Verdenius (1968), pp. 34–35, containing a summary of previous positions.

15. Something which is "proper to" a thing is that which, while it does not express

the essence, belongs only to the thing in question, and may be predicated instead of it (I 5, 102a 18–19).

16. Cf. M. Soreth (1968), pp. 43–45. In a recent article (Barnes, Brunschwig, Frede [1990]) some friends objected to the present interpretation that from it the conclusion would follow that no predicate is a *proprium* (p. 86). I do not see how this could be: my interpretation is not: "If A has the same relationship (whatever it is) to B and C, neither B nor C can be proper to A," but: "If we suppose (κεῖται) that B is proper to A, and that it has to A the same relationship that C has to A, and C is not proper to A, then B is not proper to A."

17. von Arnim (1927), p. 25.

18. A. von Fragstein (1974), p. 385, and Woods (1982), p. 169.

19. Like most commentators, I am following the correction made by F. Dirlmeier (1963), *ad* 1246a 27: τοῦτο ἢ < ᾗ > αὐτὸ ἢ αὖ κατὰ συμβεβηκός.

20. Von Fragstein (1974), p. 359.

21. P. Moraux (1971), p. 264, rightly refers to the example of the doctor who can use his knowledge for ill. Cf. also *de an.* III 9, 433a 4–6.

22. 1246b 4; ἀλλ' ἐπεί, to be understood as in Plat. *Eutyphr.* 94b 5, and not as a positive statement made by Aristotle, who is not here expressing his point of view, but rather taking as a hypothesis the point of view of the Platonists (cf. P. Moraux (1971), p. 263; von Fragstein [1974], p. 359; Woods [1982], p. 170. It does not seem necessary to emend ἀλλ' ἐπεί to ἀλλ' εἴπερ (von Arnim [1927], p. 28) or to ἀλλ' ἔτι εἰ (A. Kenny [1978], p. 185).

23. P. Moraux (1971), p. 263.

24. Von Fragstein (1974), p. 359.

25. P. Moraux (1971), p. 264.

26. P. Moraux (1971), p. 265; von Fragstein (1974), p. 362; A. Kenny (1978), p. 186.

27. A. Kenny (1978), p. 187, correctly observes that the meaning does not change much, since ἄγνοια on the object of wisdom is ἄνοια.

28. Lines 1246b 15–18 are particularly difficult to interpret, owing to the presence of gaps and very doubtful readings. Here we largely follow the interpretation of Moraux and Woods, reading at lines 16–17: δῆλον ὅτι, κἂν ἐν μὲν τούτῳ ἀρετή, ἐν δὲ τῷ λόγῳ ἄγνοια ᾖ < ἡ > ἑτέρα μεταπείθεται.

29. 1246b 17: the emendation of τὸ δικαίως to τ' ο< ὐ > δικαίως has been suggested by Jackson and generally accepted.

30. Here there is a gap in the text that it is difficult to fill in, but the sense of the argument seems fairly clear.

31. 1246b 33: Susemihl suggests emending the manuscript text (αἱ ἄλλου ἕξεις) to αἱ τοῦ ἀλόγου ἕξεις A. Kenny (1978), p. 187, correctly observes that the emendation clarifies the text, though it is not indispensable.

32. C. J. Rowe (1971), pp. 73–92, and (1977), pp. 63–72, has maintained that Aristotle does not see any essential difference between theoretical and practical thought in *EE*, and that this explains why he uses the term φρόνησις to indicate both types of thought. However, he does not discuss this Chapter VIII 1. Now, if ἐπιστήμη is a form

of theoretical thinking—which seems undeniable—it does not seem exact to maintain that here no essential difference is posited between theorizing and practical thinking; it seems more consistent with the contents of this chapter to ascribe to Aristotle the kind of division of virtues and forms of knowledge given in *EN* VI.

33. Cf. Gauthier (1958–1959) II, pp. 451–452.

34. Von Arnim (1927), p. 30.

35. Cf. also *EE* II 1, 1220a 5 ff., and 4, 1221b 27–32.

36. In *EN* I 13, 1102a 23–32, and also in *EE* II 1, 1219b 32–34, it is said that it is not important, in a treatise on ethics, to define exactly whether the soul is really composed of a rational part and an irrational part, or if these two parts are to be separated only logically. The most recent commentators have emphasized this statement, against the evolutionary interpretation of Nuyens (1948) and Gauthier (1958–1959). Cf. W. F. R. Hardie (1968), pp. 68–73; C. Lefevre (1978), pp. 19–20; and see, more generally, C. Lefevre (1972).

37. Cf. J. A. Stewart (1892) II, pp. 9–11; on the contrary, L. H. G. Greenwood (1909), pp. 22–24, maintains that here the ἐνδεχόμενα ἄλλως ἔχειν, things which can also be otherwise, correspond to τὰ ὡς ἐπὶ τὸ πολύ, things which happen in most cases, since the other part of the ἐνδεχόμενα ἄλλως ἔχειν, which are τὰ ἀπὸ τύχης, the things that depend on fortune, are not an object of knowledge. The objects of physics fall among those things "whose principles cannot be otherwise," and not among those things that happen in most cases.

38. Cf. Burnet (1900), p. 253. Aristotle's greatest innovation with respect to Plato's vocabulary is not so much the fact that here he gives a practical meaning to the faculty called λογιστικόν, the calculating part, since even in Plato this faculty has, among other things, the task of calculating the good for an individual; cf. *resp.* IV 439D. The difference lies rather in the fact that for Aristotle it is not necessary to know the idea of good in order to make practical calculations, whereas such knowledge is necessary in Plato's *Republic.* Moreover, Aristotle introduces a purely contemplative intellectual faculty, τὸ ἐπιστημονικόν, the "scientific" faculty, which leaves only the field of praxis to the λογιστικόν. Later, in a further contrast with Plato, the λογιστικόν is even identified with the δοξαστικόν. On this point cf. pp. 43 ff.

39. Cf. *EE* II 1, 1218b 37–38, and Gauthier (1958–1959) II, pp. 443 and 449.

40. Cf. also *EE* II 4, 1221b 29–30.

41. Cf. *EE* I 5, 1216b 3–25.

42. Cf. *EN* III 4: the error is caused because pleasure deceives, and makes one think that the pleasant is good, and the unpleasant bad (1113a 33–b 2). A careful analysis of this idea of practical truth is found in L. Ruggiu (1979), pp. 50–53: the moment of practicality, he maintains, is present right from the first moment of affirmation and negation.

43. A. Kenny (1979), p. 92, correctly holds that the understood subject is τὸ εὖ.

44. Cf. Gauthier (1958–1959) II, pp. 444 and 446, where he tends to emphasize the apparent contradictions in the texts. The translation of lines 1139a 32–33 proposed by Gauthier, "le calcul, celui qui calcule les moyens pour obtenir une fin," seems to us to be overdetermined. Hardie (1968), p. 224, gives a better translation: "reasoning or a rule having an end in view." On this point, see also below.

45. Cf. XII 7, 1072a 27–30: "of these (the object of desire and the object of thought) the former are the same thing, since, on the one hand, the object of passion is the apparent good, and on the other, the object of rational desire is the true good. We desire something because it seems to us to be (such-and-such); it does not seem to us to be (such-and-such) because we desire it, since rationality is the principle." With regard to the priority of reason over desire mentioned in this passage, see below. Cf. Chapter 2, §§ 2 and 3.2.

46. In our view, desire and reason are fused together in every choice (προαίρεσις), which is always a single act. The choice can be viewed both as the union of reason and desire, and as the union of φρόνησις and ethical virtue. The two perspectives do not completely overlap, since the definition of "intellect" contains no reference to the concept of "desire" and vice versa; hence their combination is considered a mixture, a coming together of elements that work together though each one maintains its own properties. In the second case, this is not true. Both φρόνησις and ethical virtue contain a reference to the other in their definitions, and cannot be completely themselves without the other; indeed, in some way they are fused together (1144b 27). For a contrary opinion, cf. Cooper (1975), pp. 62 and 63.

47. The comparison of *EE* VIII 1 and *EN* VI 12–13 shows that by ἕξις Aristotle here means ethical virtue, and not merely any good or bad quality of character. Indeed, he always describes the best case, that of the good overall functioning of practical reasoning, and not inferior cases; hence the good choice is the one that is directed at the true good, and not at an apparent good. A modern mentality may also be interested in the applicability of this theory to other cases, and to its ability to describe any choice whatsoever. But when Aristotle speaks of εὐπραξία, he certainly means a praiseworthy behavior (ἐπαινετόν), and hence virtuous action, in the Greek sense of the term.

48. As we have seen in the scheme outlined above, there are two cases (1) and (3), in which reason and desire agree, in the one case on a good end, and in the other on a bad end. Consequently, some critics have maintained that it is not sufficient for intellect and desire to agree in order for a good choice to be made (cf. Greenwood [1909], pp. 175–176, followed by A. Kenny [1979], pp. 92–94). On the other hand, Aristotle is here talking about προαίρεσις σπουδαία (1139a 25–26). In our opinion, Aristotle wishes to show, in opposition to Plato, that, given a good choice, there must be an emotional, non-rational, ethical element in it, and that it is not merely a scientifically exact process of reasoning.

49. The whole discussion is summarized in Gauthier (1958–1959) II, pp. 147–149. His grammatical argument is not quite as strong as it appears.

50. Greenwood (1909), p. 168; Joachim (1951), p. 165.

51. On the meaning of this expression, cf. Chapter 3, § 2.3.

52. Hardie (1968), p. 224, has pointed out some passages in Book VI where it is possible to understand λόγος as "rule," but this interpretation is rather doubtful.

53. Cf. D. J. Allan (1952), p. 162; Hardie (1968), p. 212; O. Gigon (1975), pp. 102–103; Kenny (1979), p. 100 note 3; for a contrary opinion, see Rowe (1977), pp. 113–114.

54. Cf. E. Zeller-R. Mondolfo (1966), p. 59 note 140.

55. Cf. 1142b 21 ff.

56. Cf. Stewart (1892) II, pp. 1–4.

57. Burnet, Joachim and Greenwood all maintain, though in different ways, that the subject of *EN* VI is both the determination of the criterion of ethical virtue and the examination of all the dianoetic virtues; Dirlmeier holds the same position, but with an accent on the interest in dianoetic virtues; Gauthier, on the one hand, accepts Zeller's position, while on the other he considers *EN* VI 1 and 2 to be two general introductions to Book VI, of which one is older and the other more recent, in conformity with the genetic approach; Rowe basically restates Zeller's position.

58. On this point the chapter entitled "Moral Insight and Desire," in T. Engberg-Pedersen (1983), pp. 160–187, is excellent.

59. Burnet (1900), p. 261: Aristotle refers to concrete cases to justify his return to a sense of φρόνησις that is different from that of Plato, i.e. theoretical and not exclusively practical. For the history of the term, cf. Gauthier (1958–1959) II, pp. 464–469. The long discussion provoked by W. Jaeger's analysis (1923), pp. 106 ff., 321 ff., 578 ff., is well-known. Jaeger held that in the *EE* Aristotle was still using the term in a sense close to that found in Plato. The most recent discussion of this is in the two works by C. J. Rowe (1971) and (1977), with bibliography.

60. Here Aristotle is applying a dialectical procedure theorized in *top.* VI 9; cf. Von Fragstein (1974), p. 224.

61. Aristotle here takes over some elements of an Academic definition, handed down to us in [PS.] Plat. *def.* 411D 4: "φρόνησις: capacity (δύναμις) of producing, by itself, human happiness; science (ἐπιστήμη) of good and evil; disposition (διάθεσις) on the basis of which we distinguish what should and should not be done," making some changes typical of his thought: instead of ἐπιστήμη + δύναμις ποιητική (science + a "technical" application), we have a particular form of a practical rational procedure, deliberation (βούλευσις), which in Aristotle's opinion is typical of practical knowledge.

62. A brief characterization of ἐπιστήμη, in clear opposition to φρόνησις, is given by Aristotle in VI 3. Here Aristotle insists on the character of necessity that is proper to scientific knowledge, on the eternity and necessity of its objects, on the fact that it can be transmitted by instruction alone, and that it starts from better known principles, derived by induction (to which is added νοῦς cf. VI 6), and lastly that it has fulfilled its function when the subject firmly possesses (πιστεύει) the principles and what is derived from them. All these characteristics are opposed to those of φρόνησις, which is not necessary, regards objects that are neither eternal nor necessary, is not transmitted by instruction alone, does not draw its principles from a combination of induction + νοῦς, and does not exhaust its task in the generation of a πίστις.

63. F. Dirlmeier (1956), p. 450, maintains that the quotation of Pericles' name is made in an explicit polemic against Plato; it corresponds to the definition of ethical virtue given in *EN* II 6, whereby the φρόνιμος is the model to be followed in making one's choices. The habit of pointing to a living person as a παράδειγμα to be emulated is rather common also in the oratory of the time; cf. Isocr. *ad Nic.* 31, *Nic.* 37, *paneg.* 39. In this way one avoids the inevitable lack of precision that exists in attempts to apply a

universal rule to an individual case, and one finds a living criterion of choice. On this point cf. Chapter 1, P. Aubenque (1963), pp. 37–41 and G. Bien (1972).

64. Burnet (1900), p. 269.

65. Dirlmeier (1956), p. 455.

66. Only things that have an identical τὸ εἶναι share all possible predicates, *phys.* III 3, 202b 15–16; the difference between wisdom and politics does not lie in the subjective habitual state, nor in the logical structure of reasoning, but in the object to which they are applied. This does not mean that they are two absolutely distinct (ἕτερον ἁπλῶς) forms of knowledge, or that they are numerically distinct, as appears from *top.* V 4, 133b 31–35. For the meaning of the expression τὸ εἶναι ταὐτόν, cf. M. Mignucci (1985), pp. 66ff.

67. We accept the most probable interpretation; in relation to it, the text has been emended in various ways: ὡς <περὶ> τὰ καθ' ἕκαστα (Rackham) or ὡς τὰ καθ' ἕκαστα (γνωρίζουσα understood) (Dirlmeier). For a different opinion, cf. Gauthier (1958–1959) II, p. 499.

68. It is, in fact, the ultimate step in a deliberative analysis and constitutes an "act" of the assembly that issues it. Cf. Burnet (1900), p. 271; Dirlmeier (1956), p. 456.

69. We understand the comparison in the sense that particular politicians apply the laws established by legislators, just as manual laborers apply the directives of the master builders and "architects" (ἀρχιτέκτονες) who possess τέχνη.

70. Gauthier (1958–1959) II, pp. 498–499, shows the logical difficulties of the text. There are attempts to regularize the division in Stewart (1892) II, p. 64; Dirlmeier (1956), p. 457; von Fragstein (1974), pp. 232 and 233, modifying it in various ways.

71. And in fact it is introduced by terms like δοκεῖ, b 29 and λέγουσιν, b 28.

72. Cf. III 4, 1006b 2–5.

73. In *pol.* I this is spelled out, in the sense that one should pursue one's own economic interests not with a view to increasing one's οἶκος as much as possible, but in order to provide oneself with the leisure to take part in the political and philosophical life (7, 1255b 35–37).

74. The subject of the distinction between praxis and production is one of those that most clearly highlights the differences between two exegetical traditions that are today of fundamental importance, such as that in English and the German "rehabilitation of practical philosophy." H. G. Gadamer (1960), pp. 373 ff., O. Gigon (1973), p. 71, and R. Bubner (1974), pp. 62–63, all find one of the greatest reasons for Aristotle's "modernity" in the radical opposition he is said to have set up between technique and praxis. Instead, authors such as J. L. Ackrill (1965) and D. Charles (1984) have exerted themselves in discussing Aristotle's distinction, proposing counterexamples (such as: Can fixing my fence to do a favor to my neighbor be really described as "two" processes, viz. a production, consisting in the creation of a fixed fence, and an act, consisting in doing a favor to my neighbor, linked together by a relation of means to end? Or is it not rather the same process, seen from two different points of view? And if this is so, what remains of Aristotle's distinction?) The article by T. Ebert (1976) sees the limitations of Aristotle's distinction, but it seems to us to be too radically critical.

75. Gauthier (1958–1959) II, p. 474, finds this doctrine an expression of Aristotle's

optimism. To us this seems rather strange: if in φρόνησις there is an element of goodness and a very obvious element of effectiveness, why is it that one cannot say that someone is wiser, more prudent or more virtuous than another, who is also wise, prudent and virtuous? Moreover, the possibility which is here denied is apparently admitted in *EN* II 9, 1109b 18–23.

76. Cf. *metaph.* 981a 30–b 5: "[manual workers] act without knowing what they are doing, in the same way as some inanimate things produce effects, i.e. just as fire burns. For inanimate things produce effects owing to a certain nature inherent in them, while manual workers act out of habit." Higher-level craftsmen are undoubtedly given more consideration, but they are never held in very great esteem. See: G. Vattimo (1961); M. Isnardi Parente (1966), pp. 60 ff.

77. After writing this book, we read the study by M. Nussbaum (1986), who examines just this point quite extensively, paying special attention to the opinions of the tragic poets. This is an important work, which poses a basic and too often neglected question, and whose conclusions we largely share. However, the ethical opinions of the tragic poets are not the only traditional ideas on practical knowledge that should be considered in evaluating Aristotle's position, which seems to us much more "assertive" and "masculine" than Nussbaum thinks.

78. As regards practical reasoning, both the explanatory and the normative aspects of Aristotle's theory have been well described by G. Even-Grandboulian (1976).

79. At line 1107a 30, I read κενώτεροι, following Grosseteste, and not κοινότεροι, as Bywater does.

80. I.e., practical ends, which are the principles of knowledge of the man of action, as well as being the object of the philosopher's discourse.

81. Cf. mainly W. Hennis (1963); H. Kuhn (1965); A. Müller (1971); G. Bien (1972); J. M. Cooper (1975), pp. 68–71; O. Höffe (1979). For Italian authors, cf. L. Ruggiu (1973) and E. Berti (1978).

82. On this function of dialectics, cf. G. E. L. Owen (1961) and E. Berti (1972).

83. For the dialectical nature of this procedure, cf. *top.* 105a 10–19.

84. This subject is very clearly discussed by R. Bubner (1974), Chapter I.

85. In the *Analytics* Aristotle stresses the fact that there is a science not only of what is necessary, but also of what is ὡς ἐπὶ τὸ πολὺ it uses, either partly or totally, premises that are "by and large" valid, and reaches similarly valid conclusions. Cf. *a. pr.* I 13, 32b 5 ff.; 27, 43b 32 ff.; *a. po.* I 30; II 12, 96a 8 ff.

86. Cf. M. Mignucci (1965), p. 98; (1969), p. 300; (1975), pp. 585 ff., esp. 594; (1981), pp. 201–203.

87. In the practical sciences, the principle is the given and the individual case; cf. *EN* 1095b 6; 1098a 33–b 3.

88. I read, following Ross: τὰ δὲ δι' ἐπαγωγῆς ἐκ τοῦ ὁμοίου.

89. Cf. Andoc. III 2, 29, 32; Lys. XIX 62, XXV 23; Din. I 33; Eurip. fr. 811 N3.

90. "[Example] differs from induction both because the latter shows that the first term inheres in the middle term starting from an examination of all individual cases, and

because it (induction) does not connect the syllogism to the minor extreme, whereas example does so connect it and does not make its demonstration starting from all the individual cases" (69a 16–19). In the field of deliberation, a complete and rigorous induction, such as that required by Aristotle in the *Analytics* for the natural sciences, seems not to be possible. By connecting the reasoning to the minor extreme and to the practical situation at hand (should we make war on the Thebans or not?), the example is a useful tool for deliberation and deliberative rhetoric. It is only by coming back down to the particular case that an example addresses itself to the practical end of reasoning, while induction remains at the level of a universal proposition, being therefore linked to the end of theoretical reasoning, which is the formulation of true, universal and necessary scientific judgments

91. Cf. O. N. Guariglia (1978), pp. 67 ff.

92. This point is well illustrated by W. D. Ross (1923), pp. 188–190, and by W. F. R. Hardie (1964–1965), pp. 40–41.

93. Instead, in 1106b 24–35, quoting the Pythagoreans and Plato's *Republic* 445C, Aristotle maintains that whoever errs is blamed and whoever behaves correctly is praised, but that it is easier to make mistakes, because error comes in many guises and while there is only one correct behavior, it is difficult to hit the mark. In our opinion, this view is revised in the above-quoted passages, which present Aristotle's standard opinion, an opinion found also in *metaph.* 993a 30–b 7.

94. As to the meaning to be given to this term, "perception" (αἴσθησις), see Chapter 3 below.

95. Aristotle states that the mean regards passions and actions, and not actions alone. Here an action is considered to be the external manifestation of an emotional state that determines it; cf., for this point, Urmson (1973), pp. 224–226, who rightly distinguishes between the Aristotelian theory of the mean and the doctrines of the *aurea mediocritas,* according to which one must choose, in every circumstance, a middle way, and feel a mediocre and measured emotion. Aristotle himself observes that, in a sense, virtue is an extreme (1107a 6–8 and 23); cf. Hardie (1964–1965), pp. 37–38. For a rather critical examination, and a rather negative judgment, of this doctrine of Aristotle's, see W. D. Ross (1923), pp. 185–190. Urmson and Hardie are reacting against Ross in the essays cited in this note.

96. Cf. Devoto-Oli (1971), *s. v.*

Chapter Two

1. The best analyses of this chapter are those by von Fragstein (1974), pp. 118 ff.; A. Kenny (1979), pp. 81 ff.; F. Dirlmeier (1963), pp. 309 ff.; V. Décarie (1978), pp. 118 ff.; M. Woods (1982), pp. 162 ff.

2. Tὸν λόγον the correction ὁ λόγος suggested by von der Mühl (1909), p. 12, is not acceptable. Cf. Décarie (1978), p. 116.

3. *Il.* IV 323; IX 440–443; XIII 726–734; XVIII 252; XIX 218.

4. Cf. Woods (1982), p. 184.

5. Cf. pp. 9–10.

6. This idea is very much present in Plato's dialogues, and influences his ethical theory in particular; in those texts it is easy to find the elements necessary to construct a hierarchical series of ends of human action, and then attribute to the philosopher the knowledge required to correctly determine the ultimate aim, and hence the right choice on every occasion. In the *Lysis,* the first philosophical text where the distinction between ends and means appears, Plato says that if something is considered "good" or "friendly" in view of something else, it is the latter that is the cause of goodness in the former and that, moreover, it is necessary to proceed through the series of final causes until a term is found in view of which all other things are said to be "good" or "friendly." Cf. also *Gorg.* 467C-468D and *leg.* 962B, where it appears that knowledge of the ends of the πόλις is entrusted to the night council. A similar position can be found in Aristotle's *Protrepticus* (fr. 11 Ross), while the *Topics*—logically, given the nature of the treatise—deal with some distinctions and difficulties: (1) what is desirable for its own sake is better than what is desirable for the sake of something else; (2) of these, what is closer to the end is more desirable; (3) of ends, what is the end of an entire life is more desirable; (4) sometimes, however, what is a means for a lofty end is preferable to what is an end at a low level. For a discussion of these distinctions, cf. the essays of O. Gigon (1968) and C. De Vogel (1968).

7. VII 13, 1331b 26–38: the good consists of two different things: positing the end correctly and finding the actions that lead to one's aim. These two things may or may not be in agreement. It is possible to have correct ends and means, or ineffective means for good ends, effective means for bad ends, or ineffective means for bad ends.

8. This translation has the defect of encouraging confusion between the "mean," which, as we shall see, is an end, and the "means." This confusion is not possible in Greek, where the expressions τὰ πρὸς τὸ τέλος and τὸ μέσον are different. Contemporary criticism has emphasized the fact that the expression τὰ πρὸς τὸ τέλος does not indicate only the external means to an end, but also the causal conditions, the steps that lead to it, the necessary and/or sufficient conditions of the end, the definitions of it in given conditions and so on. Cf. L. H. G. Greenwood (1909), pp. 47 and 79–80; W. F. R. Hardie (1968), pp. 255–257; R. Sorabji (1973–1974), pp. 108–109; D. Wiggins (1975–1976), p. 32; J. M. Cooper (1975), p. 19; A. Kenny (1979), p. 149. This seems to go rather in the sense of Aristotle's position, even if passages such as *pol.* VII 8, 1328a 28–33 say that there is nothing in common (κοινόν) between ends and means. For a discussion of this latter passage, cf. p. 124.

9. Ποιεῖ. We therefore follow the interpretation of von Fragstein (1974) and Woods (1982), as against Dirlmeier (1983) and V. Décarie (1978): "renders correct" and not "makes" or "determines."

10. Cf. *EE* II 10 1226b 10, 1227a 11; *EN* 1151a 17, *EN* VII 8 1151a–17 ff.

11. Cf. Dirlmeier (1963), p. 305.

12. Cf. Woods (1982), p. 166.

13. Cf., for example, Plat. *Gorg.* 465Aff.; Isocr. *antid.* 180 ff.; for Aristotle, the passage cited in note 8. On the subject there is a vast bibliography; we should at least mention the classic essays by W. Jaeger (1957) and G. E. R. Lloyd (1968). Much material is

also found in W. Fiedler (1978). For a criticism of these comparisons, see the essay by G. E. M. Anscombe (1965).

14. Νοήσεως, understood correctly as "Gedankenreihe" by Dirlmeier (1963), *ad l.*, and not simply "thought" as opposed to "action."

15. Not all commentators believe that here the term μέσον signifies "mean," and they often give differing translations: "middle term" (Fortenbaugh), "intermédiaire" (Décarie).

16. The text of line 38, οὗ αἰτία ἡ ἀρετή, τὸ προαιρεῖσθαι οὗ ἕνεκα, has been emended in various ways, but Dirlmeier (1963) and von Fragstein (1974), *ad l.*, have successfully defended the manuscript reading. "Choosing of the what-for" is, in this context, in apposition to "virtue" (cf. *EN* 1106a 3–4); the words "the what-for" do not express the object of the choice, but the end for which one chooses, as Aristotle makes clear immediately afterward.

17. W. D. Ross (1923), p. 191.

18. Cf. Gauthier (1958–1959) II, pp. 446–448 and O. Höffe (1971), pp. 135–137.

19. P. Aubenque (1963), pp. 119–124, divides the meaning of προαίρεσις, which is the choice of an action in view of an end, into (1) the ability to fix an end for the choice; (2) the ability to choose the means. Obviously, in this way, in sense (1) προαίρεσις becomes the locus of moral responsibility in the modern sense (we judge someone on the basis of his choice of ends) and, in sense (2), προαίρεσις becomes the mere technical ability to find the right means, and is morally neutral. This has the consequence that, when Aristotle says that one does not choose the ends, but what leads to the end, and that "for this reason" people are judged by the choices they make, Aubenque remains "etonné" and accuses the author he has studied of being incoherent: "la suite des idées est ici peu rationelle[. . .] parfaitement inintelligible [. . .] synthèse maladroite et peu cohérente." We do not agree. On the contrary, we think the remarks of A. R. Mele (1981) are correct.

20. It must not have sounded so strange to the ancients, as for example to Cnemus, Brasidas and the other Spartan admirals, whose speech to the troops is reported in Thuc. II 87, 3, or to Odysseus in Homer (*Il.* XI 401–410 and XXII 92–130). In Thucydides the correct γνώμη coincides with virtue (in this case courage); in Homer θυμός chooses both ends and means. The Homeric heroes do not clearly distinguish between the two things, and in general their deliberations regard the complex set of ends and means. But there are also instances of deliberation that seem to regard only means, as in the case of Odysseus in *Od.* VI 141–147.

21. Ends are not the object of deliberation (*EN* 1112b 4; *rhet.* 1362a 18) nor of choice (*EN* 1111b 26–27) nor of φρόνησις (*EN* 1144a 8–9 and 1145a 4–6); there is a passage in which it would appear that Aristotle states the opposite (*EN* 1142b 31–33), but its interpretation is doubtful and controversial. Those who maintain the opposite often give the impression of fighting against Aristotle's texts; sometimes they are forced to pretend that these passages are of no value, or to consider them only imprecise expressions, as for example Loening (1903), pp. 75–76. The fact that at times Aristotle seems to refer to a προαίρεσις of ends—as in the passages collected, with considerable generosity, by W. D. Ross (1923), pp. 192 and 295, notes 37–39—is not sufficient reason to deny what

we have stated here. Often Aristotle uses philosophical terms in a colloquial way and in accordance with current usage, without respecting the definitions he himself has given; but in the determination of his ethical doctrine more weight should be given to those passages in which a concept is explicitly discussed and defined, rather than to those wherein the corresponding term is used in a colloquial way. For a very long time this question was central to the discussion of Aristotle's ethics. Loening (1903) collects and discusses all the nineteenth-century criticism. The most important contemporary contributions are those by P. Aubenque (1965); W. W. Fortenbaugh (1974); J. Rist (1983); for an opposite point of view to the one expressed here, see J. M. Cooper (1975), pp. 63–64; T. Irwin (1978); A. R. Mele (1983). W. F. R. Hardie (1968), pp. 386–387, is more doubtful.

22. As far as we know, Loening (1903), pp. 16–26, is the one who best illustrates this point.

23. There is a good commentary on this passage in the recent book by T. Engberg-Pedersen (1983), pp. 175–181.

24. Cf. Theogn. vv. 435–438 (discussed in PLAT. *Men.* 95E); Pind. *nem.* III 40–42; these poets maintain that the virtue innate in noble men is sufficient for acting well. The Sophists add διδασκαλία to virtue; cf. Protag. fr. 3 D.-K.; Prod. fr. 2 D.-K.; Socrates in Xenoph. *mem.* v. 6, 13; Dissoi Logoi, VI 11; in general see K. J. Dover (1974) III, B 2, pp. 175–186.

25. Cf. also A. Kenny (1979), p. 124.

26. This is acknowledged also by F. Dirlmeier (1956), p. 559. However, he denies that it represents an advance, because in his view there is no progress in ethics.

27. The problems of the rationality of ends in Aristotle, of his presumed emotionalism and of the comparison between Aristotle and Hume are dealt with in the recent works by T. Irwin (1975), pp. 567–568, and D. Charles (1984), especially Chapter IV, pp. 161–196. Irwin adopts basically the same position as Loening (1903) and hence, as we shall see, he makes desire depend on reason; Charles, more correctly, maintains that reason is determined by a structure of desire that is prior to it. In our opinion the two elements do not stand in a relation of prior to posterior; rather one must speak of the simultaneous action of desire and reason, as we shall try to demonstrate in the rest of the chapter.

28. As is maintained by Loening (1903), p. 75; Cooper (1975), pp. 62–63.

29. D. Wiggins (1975–1976), pp. 34–35; J. M. Cooper (1975), pp. 15 f.

30. My interpretation is contrary to the viewpoint maintained by Cooper (1975), p. 14.

31. What "depends on us" is a part of the "human world," which, in its turn, is a part of "what may also occur otherwise." The delimitation of this field is a preliminary condition for the identification of a logical structure peculiar to decision making; still, the delimitation is not free, but answers to "how things stand." In this sense, the boundary line separating what depends on us from the huge mass of things that may or may not be does not depend on choice, or on "taking possession"; on the contrary, it is only after a prudent and sensible man has recognized which events depend on him—events which, in most cases, occur "for the most part"—that he can reasonably commit

himself to making a choice. For a criticism of Aristotle's position on this point, cf. E. Severino (1980), pp. 361–369. On "precision" and "for the most part" in Aristotle's ethics, see the monograph by D. Kurz (1970).

32. Some remarks on this point are to be found in H. G. Ingenkamp (1981); cf. also *EN* VI 9 1142 32 ff., for which see Chapter 4.

33. The specification "after a meal" is absent in line 94b 9, but is added immediately afterward, in line 11, and repeated in lines 12 and 14.

34. Cf. O. Höffe (1971), p. 135; D. Wiggins (1975–1976), p. 38; T. Engberg-Pedersen (1983), p. 173; D. S. Hutchinson (1986), p. 100.

35. The impossibility met with in this case is not caused by the fact of setting oneself contradictory aims, which is an eventuality Aristotle makes no mention of here; rather, it is a factual and historical impossibility, linked to the development of technology and human abilities. For the distinction, cf. Severino (1962), pp. 215–224.

36. Aristotle likes to express the relation between deliberation and desire in the form of a dialogue, wherein desire "listens to," "obeys" or "rebels against" the dictates of reason. But this is a metaphorical way of speaking. More precisely, as we shall see in Chapter 4, the analysis carried out by deliberation makes a future state of affairs appear to be either good or bad, and hence to be sought or shunned. Thus desire, in Aristotle's scheme of things, functions as a cognitive element in the structure of human action, but the knowledge peculiar to desire consists only in a way of perceiving a mental image, as reactions of appetition and avoidance occur with every perception. There is, instead, no propositional content, no λόγος, that is transmitted by deliberation to desire and accepted by the latter, as is suggested by E. Severino (1980), pp. 371–380, and by D. Charles (1984), pp. 84–96.

37. From this standpoint, our interpretation differs from that contained in the book by R. Loening (1903), which is still a very valuable study. Loening seems still to be partly influenced by the results of nineteenth-century criticism and by the hunt for contradictions typical of that period (cf. pp. 7 note 13, 12–13, 14–15, 17). His is the merit of having recognized the essential connection between desire and λόγος in Aristotle's conception of practical knowledge, and of having expressed this point with the greatest clarity. See pp. 54, 55, 68, 70–71, 89 and, especially, 83, where he writes: "[virtue and wisdom] stehen überhaupt nicht im Verhältis von Voraussetzung und Folge, *vielmehr schliesst jede dieser beiden Tugenden begrifflich die andere bereits in sich*" (italicized in the original). However, within this essential relation he posits a dependence of ethical virtue on wisdom; they are said to be related to each other like father and son or king and subject (cf. pp. 59, 66, 83, 84, 89), and in this we disagree with him. In fact, he (under the influence of Zeller and other nineteenth-century critics; cf. note 52) is afraid of having to admit a vicious circle in Aristotle, if he acknowledges the reciprocal determination of wisdom and ethical virtue that is clearly stated in Aristotle's works. Loening claims that the dependence of ethical virtue on wisdom lies in the fact that, according to Aristotle, "practical reason" [*sic!*] recognizes the end as desirable (*begehrbar*, p. 17) and, being endowed with a force of its own (p. 63), imposes this object on desire, which takes it as a good and a desirable object, thus giving rise to movement (p. 18). This interpretation clashes with a whole series of passages in Aristotle's *EN* VI and *de an.* III 10; Loening gives the impression

of struggling in vain against these passages (pp. 72, 74, 75), or of interpreting them in an untenable way (cf. p. 86, where he maintains that μετὰ τοῦ ὀρθοῦ λόγου, 1144b 27 means "auf *Grund* der richtigen Vernunft als seiner *Ursache*"). In our opinion, the point where Loening moves farthest away from Aristotle is in positing a "practical reason" of a vaguely Kantian type, which has the task of directing human action, and to which desire is added as a necessary but not essential complement. Instead, for Aristotle, a purely rational judgment about a good is never practical, but is a mere theoretical judgment, which becomes practical only if it is combined with desire that obeys reason; cf. Chapter 1 and the conclusion of this chapter. The well-known essay by D. J. Allan (1953) limits itself, in the words of its author, to summarizing Loening's positions.

38. This passage poses two problems: is Aristotle, perhaps, here talking about a type of deliberation that does not have a choice as its end—a kind of deliberation that comes after the choice, as maintained by G. E. M. Anscombe (1965), p. 62? And is the ἑτέρα δύναμις in line 22 perhaps δεινότης and not φρόνησις, as maintained by T. H. Irwin (1978), pp. 262 and 268 note? We believe we can answer both questions in the negative. As for the first question, it seems to us that the object of deliberation is something that is to be done here and now, i.e. an action that, if nothing prevents it, is immediately put into practice by means of the choice. There is thus no room for further deliberation after the choice. For a discussion of Anscombe's interpretation, cf. also W. F. R. Hardie (1968), p. 181. As for the second question, it seems clear to us that the terms in which Aristotle expresses himself in *EE* 1227b 37–1228a 2 and in *EN* 1144a 20–22 point in both cases to φρόνησις indeed, a δεινότης that has good principles is precisely φρόνησις. A. Kenny (1979), p. 103, correctly notes that the passage should be read in context, which aims to show the utility of φρόνησις it is for this reason that the correctness Aristotle speaks of is that of a choice made for the right end, in opposition to what was said in 1144a 13–16, where mention is made of those who, whether out of ignorance or by accident, as for example in obeying others, do good actions. On this point see also Loening (1903), p. 43.

39. Cf. von Fragstein (1974), p. 251; Joachim (1951), p. 218.

40. Cf. J. Burnet (1900), p. 284 and note 24, where reference is made to *metaph.* 1046a 36ff.

41. This point has been emphasized by F. Dirlmeier (1956), p. 469, and Hardie (1968), p. 387. See also the *Theaetetus,* 176C–177A.

42. We interpret this passage in conformity with Greenwood (1909), pp. 205–206, i.e. making δεινούς the genus of which φρονίμους and πανούργους are the species.

43. As suggested by Loening (1903), p. 58; the right interpretation is in Gauthier (1958–1959) II, pp. 551–552, and in O. Höffe (1971), p. 96.

44. 1114a 31–b 13, a passage that is clearly meant as a polemic against Plat. *resp.* 518c–d, where the grasping of practical principles is compared to a "kind of vision."

45. For the texts of Aristotle regarding "natural virtue," cf. F. Dirlmeier (1937), p. 356; (1956), pp. 470 f.

46. I follow the interpretation of Greenwood, Ross and Dirlmeier; for an overview of the many ways of interpreting the expression ὁμοία οὖσα, b 13, cf. the comment by Gauthier (1958–1959) II, p. 554.

47. Cf. A. Kenny (1974), p. 188, and H. G. Ingenkamp (1980).

48. The author of the *Magna Moralia* expounds this point as follows: "for this reason Socrates was not right in affirming that virtue is λόγος, giving as his reason that it is totally useless to face dangers and to do just things without knowing what one is doing, and without choosing in accordance with λόγος by such arguments he incorrectly maintained that virtue is λόγος" (1198a 10–14).

49. The identification with the Academics is already found in J. Burnet (1900), p. 286. A similar polemic against Aristotle's Academic contemporaries is found in *top.* I 11, 104b 35–105a 2. The argument is different, but the expressions are similar.

50. The author of the *Magna Moralia* continues: "but today's thinkers say more rightly: 'to perform noble actions in conformity (κατά) with correct λόγος is said to be virtue; but even such people do not speak correctly." J. A. Smith (1920) made a thorough analysis of this passage, but he erred in stating that the opinion in conformity with which virtue is κατὰ λόγον is attributed by Aristotle to Socrates. Instead, it is attributed to Aristotle's contemporaries, whose position is opposed to that of Socrates. We are not convinced by Smith's interpretation, reiterated by Hardie, whereby in lines 1144b 26–28 the expression μετὰ τοῦ ὀρθοῦ λόγου indicates an inferior degree of cohesion between λόγος and virtue with respect to that indicated by the expression κατὰ τὸν ὀρθὸν λόγον; the context (οὐ μόνον . . . ἀλλ') decidedly points to the contrary of what they maintain. On this point, cf. also J. M. Rist (1983).

51. Loening (1903), p. 82, mentions this passage, but does not give it the importance it deserves, and considers it only an abridged and imprecise version of Aristotle's position.

52. Cf., e.g. E. Zeller-R. Mondolfo (1966) II/6, p. 72.

53. The author of the *Magna Moralia* continues as follows:

> but these people do not speak rightly either. In fact, one could perform just actions without having made any choice, and without being aware of the noble actions, by only acting out of an irrational desire, or one could perform actions correctly in accordance with ὀρθὸς λόγος: I mean, when one acts as correct λόγος would dictate. But all the same such an action would not be praiseworthy. It is better [to say], according to our definition, that [virtue] is the impulse (ὁρμή) to act nobly, accompanied by (μετὰ) λόγος, given that such a [habitual state] is virtue and is praised. (1198a 16ff.)

Here the point seems to be mainly linguistic in nature: the particle κατά could express a kind of conformity with the dictates of reason that is not the result of choice, but accidental, whereas the particle μετά expresses a necessary connection between desire and reason.

54. Cf. 1144a 1–3, as we shall see in Chapter 4.

55. This passage poses two problems: what are the terms referred to by ᾗ μέν . . . ᾗ δέ (line 5) and how is one to interpret the expression ποιεῖ πράττειν (line 6)? As regards the first question, μέν and δέ, taken in their normal usage, ought to refer to the choice and to ethical virtue. Hence the passage ought to mean the opposite of what has been said so far, and that is, that the choice is responsible for the end, and that ethical virtue

is responsible for the means. To make the passage fit with the rest of the chapter, we must understand μέν and δέ as being arranged in chiasmus; there are other examples in *EN* of such an arrangement (cf. A. Kenny [1979], pp. 104–105). As for the second question, Gauthier (1958–1959) II, p. 150, understands ποιεῖ πράττειν as "fait faire," and the translation is acceptable, provided that it is not intended to deny that ethical virtue determines the end, as Aristotle has taken pains to repeat several times up to this point. In our opinion, Aristotle wants to lay stress on the practical role of virtue and choice, which do not limit themselves to emitting a theoretical moral judgment, but actually cause behavior. It is for this reason that Gauthier's interpretation seems partly acceptable to us. Cf. also T. Irwin (1978), p. 268 note 16. Ramsauer's correction is not necessary; at line 5 he adds an ὀρθόν after τὸ τέλος. In reality, the verbal phrase ποιεῖ governs both τὸ τέλος and τὰ πρὸς τὸ τέλος.

56. A relation of dependence between reason and desire would seem to be hinted at in *metaph.* 1072a 27–30; but see D. Charles (1984), p. 182 note 18.

57. Cf. 1115b 17–20; 1120a 24–26, b 14–15; 1122a 34–35; 1125b 31–33, for which cf. 1126a 4–6.

58. Cf. 1115b 11–13, 20–24; 1120a 23–24; b 6–7.

59. In our opinion, T. Engberg-Pedersen (1983) modernizes Aristotle's position too much: one who acts for the sake of fine deeds is not an altruist in the modern sense, and his end is to be admired by others, in accordance with the classic Homeric model (cf., e.g. *Il.* XII 310 ff.; XIII 272–273; XVII 209–214), and not "the greatest possible satisfaction of needs in the community of humans involved as a whole" (p. 47).

60. Cf. 1121a 25–27, 1125a 18–19, 1128a 4–6.

61. Loening (1903), pp. 16 ff., expounds this point very well.

Chapter Three

1. G. E. M. Anscombe (1955), p. 58, and, perhaps in controversy with Anscombe, J. Hintikka (1974), p. 96.

2. W. F. R. Hardie (1968), pp. 249 and 256. He maintains that the application of a rule to a concrete situation "consists in the thinker's doing something, actually performing as an agent or producer (p. 240)."

3. A. Kenny (1979), p. 112.

4. For the difficulties of this demonstration, cf. M. Mignucci (1969), pp. 423–424, and J. Barnes (1981), p. 25.

5. For this whole issue, cf. the discussion by J. Barnes (1981), pp. 21–27.

6. Cf. G. E. M. Anscombe (1965), p. 67, and A. Kenny (1966), p. 66. Practical reasoning is related to syllogistic figures in J. Barnes (1977), pp. 211–217, who also gives the previously published bibliography.

7. Cf. S. G. Etheridge (1968), pp. 30 ff.; A. W. Müller (1982), pp. 130 and 147.

8. *EN* VI 7 1141b 14–21, VI 8 1142a 20–23, VII 2 1146b 35–1147a 5; *EE* II 10 1226b 23; *de an.* 434a 16.

9. 701a 10–11, 12, 23, 24–25.

10. Greenwood (1909), pp. 50–51; Joachim (1951), pp. 208–210; T. Ando (1958), p. 221; A. R. Mele (1981), p. 282.

11. A critical description of this position is found in M. Nussbaum (1978), p. 166 ff.

12. Cf. W. F. R. Hardie (1968), p. 249.

13. Cooper (1975), pp. 24 ff.

14. Nussbaum (1978), p. 205; B. Inwood (1985), Chapter I.

15. Cf. *EN* 1142a 31 and H. G. Ingenkamp (1981).

16. Gauthier (1958–1959) II, p. 197, finds that the text of *EE* is more Platonizing than that of *EN*, on account of its use of the term δόξα. But this use is identical to that found in *EN* VI. Burnet (1900), p. 125, thinks that the talk about δόξα in this context is merely a dialectical expedient to call to mind the Platonists' opinions. We feel that Joachim (1951), p. 100, is right when he says that δόξα is here considered to be "a mere intellectual activity."

17. Τοῦτο here refers to what follows; cf. von Fragstein (1967), p. 134; Woods (1982), p. 150; Decarie (1978), p. 111.

18. Dirlmeier (1963), p. 289, is right in thinking that here Aristotle does not posit the end as an object of choice, but only states that anyone who chooses to do something is aware of choosing it, and does so with an end in mind; cf. *EE* 1227b 36–1228a 18, for which see pp. 42 ff.

19. Μάλιστα. Aristotle says "especially" because there are also a δόξα and a βούλησις regarding the means, as we shall see below. Cf. also *de an.* 434a 16–21; *EN* III 3 1113a 9 ff.; III 3 1147a 25 ff.; and L. M. Regis (1935), p. 181.

20. The βουλευτικόν is both a logical, strictly rational moment, and an emotional moment, when desire is directed toward something. Cf. 1226b 13, 25–26, 33, 38. See also von Fragstein (1967), p. 137.

21. Similarly to what happens in the theoretical syllogism, where one starts either from first principles or from what can be clearly made to derive from first principles (*top.* 100a 27–29).

22. It is not clear whether the reference is to *EE* I 2 (Solomon, Dirlmeier) or to II 6 or even to II 10, 1226b 10 (Woods). The same comparison is found in *EN* 1151a 16–17, where it is said that the end is an ἀρχή, like the ὑποθέσεις in mathematics. Joachim (1951), p. 233, states that here Aristotle turns the end into what is assumed but not proved, the basis on which proofs depend; Gauthier (1958–1959) II, p. 648, agrees with him, whereas Burnet (1900), pp. 324–325, dissents.

23. Greenwood (1909), pp. 50–51, is of the same opinion.

24. Cf. also L. M. Régis (1935), pp. 81–82; Anscombe (1955), p. 74; Ando (1958), p. 178.

25. Cf. von Fragstein (1967), p. 136; Etheridge (1968), p. 33. The major premise is not the object of φρόνησις, despite Greenwood (1909), p. 51, precisely because of what is said in these texts: it points to a practical good, but is not itself an immediate practical premise.

26. Cf. F. Dirlmeier (1956), p. 481.

27. Cf. Ando (1958), pp. 226–228 and note 48.

28. This kind of imperative is already present in Homeric ethics, and is expressed very clearly, as for example in *Il.* XII, lines 315–321, where Sarpedon lists the "duties" of the archaic kings. In the poems this concept is not expressed by the verb δεῖν, whose use is more recent. Cf. Gauthier (1958–1959) II, p. 570.

29. Cf. G. Santas (1969), p. 166.

30. Cf. A. Kenny (1966), p. 178.

31. For example, in the cases of *de motu an.* just mentioned, on the basis of *EN* VII 3, we may say that major premises of the kind "I need a cloak" should be made to derive from more general premises, like that in *de an.* 434a 16–18, as for example: "whoever is in such a state needs a cloak" and "I am in such a state" (cf. 1147a 6). The more complete model of *De anima* makes it possible to explain also simplified forms of the premise, many of which would not, at first sight, fall under the definition of premises that are καθόλου or διὰ τοῦ ἀγαθοῦ, i.e. ones that are universal or that concern the good (cf. *de an.* 434a 16; *EN* 1147a 2–3; *de motu an.* 701a 23–25). For a contrary opinion, cf. Nussbaum (1978), p. 344.

32. In our opinion, here συλλογισμοί must be translated as "syllogisms," for the reasons mentioned at the beginning, and ἀρχή, the "starting point," is the major premise.

33. Cf. Hardie (1968), p. 251; Kenny (1979), p. 150.

34. Cf. Hardie (1968), pp. 252–253.

35. Hardie (1968), p. 253, maintains that one must distinguish between the description of an end and a judgment regarding how to reach the end; he finds that in *EN* III 3 the end is spoken of only in the latter sense. Furthermore, he regards the major premise quoted in *EN* 1144a 32–33 as part of formulation (A), and therefore proposes considering it as follows: "since the end is such and such a man should act in such and such ways," referring to *de an.* 434a 16–21. A. Kenny (1979), pp. 131–132, clearly links the indication of the nature of the end to an indication of the means or ways that may be used to attain it. And Aristotle himself, in *EN* III 3, defines the process by which one may identify the ways and means for reaching an end, as a ζητεῖν καὶ ἀναλύειν, the end itself (1112b 20). We shall see below that this analysis leads to a more concrete redefinition of it, and this enables us to see how to attain it here and now.

36. A. Grant (1885), p. 264.

37. D. J. Allan (1955), p. 337.

38. Cf. D. Wiggins (1975–1976), pp. 221–240; A. Kenny (1979), pp. 118–119; L. Ruggiu (1979), p. 38.

39. Gauthier (1958–1959) II, pp. 209–210.

40. Cf. Anscombe (1965), p. 68.

41. Ando (1958), pp. 234–235; Cooper (1975), pp. 62–67. Cf. Burnet (1900), pp. xxxvii-xlii; J. Dennert (1970), pp. 70–74; A. Kenny (1978), pp. 170–173, and (1979), pp. 151–152; T. Upton (1981), p. 182.

42. Ὅρος is here the "limit" of reasoning, in the double sense of ἀρχὴ τῶν ἀποδεικτῶν (1140b 32) and of a concrete case.

43. Ὁ μέν . . . ὁ δέ distinguish between two kinds of νοῦς and do not refer to the distinction between νοῦς and λόγος.

44. Here we are following the reading of Burnet (1900), p. 280; but the term understood here has been rendered in quite disparate ways: "demonstrations" (Gauthier); "questions" (Mazzarelli); "reasoning" (Kenny); "opinions" (Joachim). A comparison with *EN* 1147a 29 confirms Burnet's opinion.

45. In agreement with Bonitz (1870), p. 651b 27–28, we believe that here ἑτέρα πρότασις is equivalent to the ὑστέρα πρότασις of *a. po.* 86a 24. Kenny (1979), p. 171, suggests that ἑτέρα is to be understood as opposed to τοῦ ἐσχάτου καὶ ἐνδεχομένου, and hence is to be meant as "universal." This does not appear to be confirmed by the context and, in general, if Aristotle had wished to say that there is a νοῦς that intuits the major premise, there is no reason why he could not have said it in a clearer way.

46. Cf. Dover (1974) III. F. 3., pp. 235–236. Cf. also Burnet (1900), p. 280; Joachim (1951), p. 213; Dirlmeier (1956), p. 466. A more complex and, in general, less clear position is that of Gauthier (1958–1959) II, pp. 536–537.

47. This idea is well expressed by Greenwood (1909), p. 72; Gauthier (1958–1959) II, p. 538; H. Kuhn (1960), pp. 123–140; but especially Engberg-Pedersen (1983), pp. 205–207. He states that αἴσθησις is "awareness of some particular as having a certain role in a special context" and proposes rendering the Greek term as "contextual perception." Geometrical perception and ethical perception would therefore be two distinct species of this kind of αἴσθησις. In particular, ethical perception "grasps the particular 'in the light of' some universal, rational grasp or, more precisely, grasps it *in a rational context*" (the author's italics). This seems to be exact, although, as we shall see, it is preferable to speak of a perception of the particular in the light of the end and not of a "universal" or a "rational context," expressions which lead one to think of the application of a universal rule to a specific case.

48. J. M. Cooper (1975), pp. 28–29, has correctly pointed out that the distinction between judgments καθόλου and judgments καθ' ἕκαστον must be understood as the distinction between universal and particular judgments, and not between universal and individual judgments. This is true, but this fact depends on the very nature of actions, and the argument is not able to support the interpretation that Cooper gives of the PS. As a matter of fact, every action is, *per se,* a single event, since one performs a particular act, and not a type of act. But at the end of deliberation, when we have identified a means that is useful for the end, to be carried out here and now, we do not find a single action but rather a program of action (e.g.: "Now I offer him my hand") which is definitely identified only at the moment when the action is performed (on this point, cf. Kenny [1979], p. 134). This means that, no matter how accurately one may deliberate, one can never establish, in the choice, all the infinite particular characteristics that an act has when it happens. The minor premise, the outcome of deliberation, therefore provides us with a possible course of actions, which is useful for achieving the end, but it is still very general, although it contains some particular terms. To continue with our example, if the program of action, the outcome of deliberation, is: "Now I'll shake

Valentina's hand with a nice smile," the actual circumstances in which it occurs, as well as its meaning and success, depend on the concurrence of the agent's decision, the καιρός (the particular moment, in this case) and τύχη, which always influences human events.

49. Cf. Engberg-Pedersen (1983), p. 203.

50. Cf. *EN* II 4 1105a 28–33. Cooper (1975), p. 62, is right when he speaks of a "lived conception" of practical principles, but it does not necessarily have to derive from a form of νοῦς that intuits the ends of action.

51. For a different opinion, cf. R. Sorabji (1973–1974), pp. 126 ff. Some German commentators who wish to assimilate Aristotle's φρόνησις to forms of aesthetic judgment or immediate intuition maintain that, in an absolute sense, practical knowledge is not learned. This appears to be very different from what Aristotle affirms; for him, practical knowledge is not acquired in the same way and under the same conditions as theoretical knowledge, but in any case it is part of a heritage of doctrines, principles and prescriptions that can be transmitted from one person to another. We are here referring to H. G. Gadamer (1960), p. 363, and E. Vollrath (1977), p. 92.

52. The best recent explanation of induction in *a. po.* is, in our opinion, to be found in C. H. Kahn (1981).

53. *EN* III 3 1112a 34; VII 6 1149a 32; *EE* II 10 1226a 33; *de motu an.* 701a 25.

54. Cf. Plat. *soph.* 253A, and *Theaet.* 207A–208B.

55. The best commentary on these passages is in Woods (1982), p. 153. It does not seem to us, however, that the examples given in *EN* and *EE* are as different as Woods maintains, since the application of fixed rules to particular cases only requires that one should correctly perceive what one is doing.

56. On the meaning of this παρακούειν cf. *de. insomn.* 458b 31f.: "taking one thing for another (παροράν) and misunderstanding (παρακούειν) occur when one sees or hears something that is true, but is not what one thinks it is."

57. For an opposite view, cf. Burnet (1900), p. 314, and Gauthier (1958–1959) II, pp. 631–632, who think that here θυμός applies to a specific case a general rule of the type "such conduct is insolence, ὕβρις." But in this formulation such a "general rule" has nothing practical about it and does not indicate any good to be achieved; even Gauthier calls it an "opinion."

58. The case described here is different from that described in 1147a 32–33, for which see the Appendix to this chapter. Here we do not have an opinion to which desire is added, but Aristotle presents us with the expression of an impulse in verbal form.

59. Nussbaum (1978), p. 345, maintains that here the syllogism of ἐπιθυμία is complete. On this opinion, see below, note 82.

60. Cf. G. H. von Wright (1971), p. 140. We do not fully understand how the case mentioned by von Wright can occur. However, for Aristotle, it is clear that the objective determining an individual's behavior can only be understood by starting from what the individual in question actually does; nor does it seem admissible, in Aristotle's theory, to imagine an individual who does not arrange to achieve his desired ends if no obstacle lies in his way (*EE* 1228a 11 ff.).

61. Cf. A. Kenny (1979), pp. 133 ff.

62. Ibid., p. 137.

63. I am following the exposition of PS. Alex. *in Metaph.*, p. 491, 25.

64. We are following Jaeger's text. We have added the words between square brackets.

65. The best commentary on this passage is that of the London seminar. Cf. M. Burnyeat (1979), *ad l.*

66. Cf. E. Berti (1983), pp. 442–445, containing the previously published bibliography. See also M. Mignucci (1975), p. 283. The references to ἀνάλυσις in a geometrical sense are especially clear in *EN* 1112b 20–24 and *EE* 1227b 28–33.

67. We have given a fuller discussion of this passage in C. Natali (1987), pp. 133–139.

68. W. D. Ross (1949), p. 643, and A. W. Müller (1982), p. 77, hold that here the middle term indicates an efficient cause. A comparison with *EE* shows, instead, that in this example the efficient cause is (C) and that the middle term is the final cause of (C) and not of (A), just as, earlier in the same chapter, at 94a 25–35, term (B) is the intelligible matter of (C) and not of (A) and, at 94a 36–b 8, term (B) is the efficient cause of (C) and not of (A). The right interpretation is given in Philop. *in Anal. post.*, pp. 378 35–379 3.

69. *Logica,* S. II, C. III, B-C, in the Italian translation (2nd ed. 1968), pp. 844–856. However, Hegel takes "means" to be only what we would call the "external means," and he therefore finds that being "a means to an end" is an extrinsic determination to what the means is in itself. This objection does not seem to be valid if the means is a μέρος, a constituent part, of the end. Cf. H. Bonitz (1870), pp. 455b 32 ff., cf. *metaph.* 1035b 4–5.

70. With respect to the two formulations (A) and (B) of the major premise, in the minor premise Aristotle seems to be concentrating mainly on the problem of specifying the end, on the τοιόνδε that defines the τέλος.

71. Cf. Joachim (1951), p. 212, and Engberg-Pedersen (1983), pp. 205–207.

72. In this, Aristotle is following the current tradition, present (for example) in the description that Thucydides gives of Themistocles (I 138 3).

73. The passage 1141b 8–22, from which we have taken this example, was considered by Grant (1885), p. 264, as a general explanation of the nature of the PS. Allan does not quote this passage in his discussion of the PS, whereas D. Wiggins (1975–1976), p. 228, seems to understand the "universals" spoken of here as "questions of general policy." In our opinion, they are rather general rules of prudence, as maintained by Regis (1935), p. 181.

74. Cf. Burnet (1900), p. 272: the ultimate is the last outcome of deliberation.

75. Cf. 1110b 6–7.

76. Von Fragstein (1974), p. 236, thinks that this means: "it is opposed in διαίρεσις."

77. As color, sound, etc. Cf. Gauthier (1958–1959) II, p. 505.

78. We prefer to keep, in agreement with Gauthier, *cit.*, the expression ἐν τοῖς μαθηματικοῖς in line a 28. This expression is placed in square brackets by Bywater.

79. I read ἢ < ἡ > φρόνησις. Cf. Burnet (1900), *ad loc.*

80. For an opposite view, cf. Etheridge (1968), p. 33, and D. K. Modrak (1976), p. 384.

81. This "seeing" is the fruit of φαντασία βουλευτική on φαντασία see the essay by Nussbaum (1978), pp. 221 ff.

82. We do not agree with Nussbaum (1978), p. 345, who maintains that what is stated in lines a 25–26, where it is said that the minor premise is missing, is an unsuitable introduction to the example in lines a 28–33, since the syllogism presented in those lines is complete. But this interpretation is not authorized by the text, in which Aristotle clearly says that the lack of the minor premise is the reason (διό) why we do rapidly what we do without calculating, and that this happens when (ὅταν) we directly apply the end to the facts of the situation, given by perception, imagination or intellect. Hence in the syllogism of "drinking," the minor premise is missing.

83. Various authors have interpreted this link as the transmission from one premise to another of an element that determines the action: Ando (1958), pp. 227 and 230–231, thinks that it is "value" or "virtue"; Kenny (1979), p. 144, thinks that it is the "good"; M. T. Thornton (1982), pp. 65–67, 71–72 and 74, thinks of a "characterisation of desirability" in the presence of desire; Modrak (1976), pp. 381–382, correctly states that the PS does not lead either to a proposition that is in a certain relation with the action, or to a conclusion in the form of an imperative, but to an action, and that therefore the link between premises and conclusion must be such as to generate an action. Nussbaum (1978), pp. 187 ff., instead thinks that the premises "entail" the action, but also mentions the causal action of desire; Cooper (1975), pp. 56–57, maintains that "the conclusion of a practical syllogism is an action immediately performed," because "the major premises express the contents of decisions or occurrent appetites." We shall return to this point below.

84. We follow Bywater's text, κατὰ τὴν βούλευσιν the correction made by Gauthier (1958–1959) II, p. 206, κατὰ τὴν βούλησιν, does not render the sense of Aristotle's discourse: we (for example) desire to take a walk if, on the basis of deliberation, this seems to us a means or way to reach the end of staying healthy. The correct meaning is grasped by Burnet (1900), p. 132; Joachim (1951), p. 104; Hardie (1968), p. 102.

85. Cf. *phys.* II 3, 194b 32–195a 3. This example differs from that in *a. po.* II 11 quoted above (pp. 82–83). Here Aristotle considers three terms—an agent, a means and an end—whereas in the example of the *Posterior Analytics,* of *EE* and of *metaph.* VII 7, there are still three terms, but they are an "end," a "definition" or specification "of the end" and a "means" identified on the basis of the definition. Difficulties and misunderstandings arise when the two examples are superimposed on one another, as happens in W. D. Ross (1949), p. 642.

86. Alex. Aphrod. *in Metaph.*, p. 350, 5–18.

87. A. Kirwan (1971), p. 126.

88. In 1015b 6–7 the kind of necessity peculiar to demonstration is expressly added as being different from the kinds of ἀναγκαῖον described previously. One of them is this kind of "practical necessity," for which see J. Barnes (1977), p. 217.

89. See Alex. Aphrod. *in Metaph.*, pp. 360, 22–28, and 361, 11–13.

90. R. M. Hare (1969), now in the volume of the same name, pp. 60–62.

91. Cf. the commentary by J. L. Mackie on the essay by Hintikka in S. Körner (1974), p. 112, as well as G. Santas (1969), p. 174.

92. M. Dufour (1932), *ad l.*, distinguishes between: (1) formal condition, (2) external and necessary condition and (3) frequent condition. M. A. Grimaldi (1980), p. 125, agrees with Dufour, but understands (3) as a cause that is not necessary but useful. However, this analysis is not in harmony with the other examples in which Aristotle cites the cases of foods and gymnastic exercises as ways of attaining the end in a given situation.

93. A good discussion of this text is found in O. Gigon (1968), pp. 233–256.

94. A complete analysis of the text, accompanied by a commentary astonishingly hostile to Aristotle, is given in V. J. Oates (1963), pp. 122–130.

95. Here Aristotle speaks of measuring the means in relation to the ends pursued: it is in this sense that he can speak of a single criterion. This is different from the case of a general commensurability of goods, such as that mentioned by Plato, *Prot.* 354D–355D, and denied by Aristotle in *pol.* 1283a 3–10. In that passage Aristotle discusses political equality in relation to the doctrines contained in the treatises on ethics: "moreover, according to this reasoning, every good would be commensurable with every other good. For if some quantity were a contender [to be compared with other goods], also quantity in general would be a contender with wealth and freedom. Thus, if one thing has a given height, in the same degree as another thing has a given virtue, and if height in general is superior to virtue, then everything would be commensurable [with everything else]. Indeed, it is clear that if a certain amount of greatness is superior to something [a certain amount of virtue], then another amount [of greatness will be] equal [to that amount of virtue]." On this problem, cf. M. Burnyeat (1980), p. 91 notes 28 and 29.

96. Cf. O. Gigon (1968), p. 234.

97. For example, in the series of rhetorical ἰδέαι taught by Isocrates to his disciples. Cf. *antid.* 180–185.

98. It is a transmission of actual desire, which gives rise to an action, and is not mere "'desire' in a wide sense" (p. 170) typical of every value judgment, as maintained by R. M. Hare (1963) IX 4, pp. 228–229 and 304 note 2. For Aristotle there are evaluations unaccompanied by desire, such as those of σύνεσις. It is a source of confusion, in these contexts, to take the term "cause" in the narrow "Humean" sense. Cf. P. Ricoeur (1977), pp. 74 ff., 123 ff.

99. A summary analysis of these positions is found in Modrak (1976), p. 380.

100. Cf. A. Kenny (1979), p. 143; Mele (1981), p. 297.

101. Cf. Nussbaum (1978), p. 194; the positions of Mele (1981), p. 298, and Müller (1982), p. 156, are less clear.

102. Cf. D. Wiggins (1978–1979), p. 248; D. Charles (1984), pp. 262–263.

103. Cf. G. Patzig (2nd ed. 1963), p. 97, and M. Mignucci (1969), p. 190.

104. Cf. A. Müller (1982), pp. 300–301.

105. German "neo-Aristotelianism" departs in many ways from Aristotle's position, in which it is not possible to find an opposition between "System und Lebenswelt," between "instrumentelles und kommunikatives Handeln," between "Zweckrationalität und Wertrationalität" and so on. Cf. H. Schnädelbach (1986), pp. 17 ff. On the originality

of German neo-Aristotelianism and its progressive departure from its Aristotelian origin, see also F. Volpi (1986), pp. 933–943, and L. Cortella (1987).

106. On this problem there is a vast literature. Some of the most important books are the study by J. J. Walsh (1963), and the more recent study by N. O. Dahl (1984). Dahl summarizes and discusses all the relevant literature in English. The article by P. L. Donini (1977) should be added to his bibliography. Our intention here is only to see how the PS proposed by Aristotle works at a certain point in his investigation. For a general interpretative framework we refer to what Dahl calls the "traditional interpretation."

107. Walsh (1963), pp. 97–106 and 109, is right to link Aristotle's attitude to Socrates in *EN* VII 3 with the attitude taken by him toward Socrates in *EN* VI 13. In our opinion, in neither case is there agreement between the two philosophers; in fact, the way in which Aristotle expresses his appreciation of Socrates, as well as the words he uses, empty Socrates' position of its essential content.

108. Cf. Gauthier (1958–1959) II, p. 611.

109. Kenny (1966), p. 175.

110. See the subtitles added to the translation by Gauthier (1958–1959) I, pp. 191–192.

111. The adverb has been interpreted in different ways. Some say they do not know how to translate it (e.g. Walsh). Others interpret it in a very general sense, as "more specifically" (Cooper), or "starting from appropriate principles" (Gauthier); others think it means "starting from facts relating to (human) nature" (Hardie, Wiggins, Etheridge). The interpretation of the adverb depends on the way in which one interprets the explanation that follows. We think that here Aristotle is explaining, by means of the PS, which psychical factors cause ἀκρασία hence we interpret φυσικῶς, as do Burnet and Dirlmeier, as referring to psychology, i.e. that branch of physics that studies the human psyche.

112. The fact that here it is said that, in general, the minor premise regards particular objects, ὧν αἴσθησις ἤδη κυρία, does not mean that the minor premise of the PS provides only perceptual data such as "this is bread" or "it is well done" (*EN* 1113a 1). In actuality, the specification found here regards "particular cases" that are the object of the premise, and not the premise itself. It is possible to give information about objects that fall in the domain of αἴσθησις without limiting oneself to providing only sense-data. Moreover, at this point, the definition is intended both for the minor theoretical premise and for the practical premise; therefore it is too general to describe adequately the characteristics of the practical minor premise. As for the meaning to be attached to the term κυρία, it should be remembered that in *EN* 1139a 18 Aristotle says that three elements of the psyche are the κυρία of truth and praxis, αἴσθησις, νοῦς and ὄρεξις, but then he assigns the function of being the ἀρχή of praxis only to the latter two. Therefore the expression must be equivalent to "falls within the domain of sensation" or something similar.

113. Here, too, we are following Burnet (1900), p. 302: προτάσεις is the understood subject of the sentence and is paralleled in *de motu an.* 701a 23.

114. Donini (1977), p. 187, maintains that τοῦτο cannot indicate the concrete object that stands before the agent, and that it must be translated, or at least understood, as "this class of objects." But the τοῦτο found here is like the τοῦτο in line 1147a 31,

τοῦτο . . . πράττειν, which Donini translates as "performs . . . this action" (and not "this kind of action"). We therefore prefer to stick to the usual interpretation, whereby τοῦτο indicates a particular, feasible action, which is definitely specified only at the moment when the action is performed.

115. Obviously, this argument presupposes that the text of *EN* VII 3 is a unified whole and not a collection of contradictory passages, as Cook Wilson (1912) thought; but until an insurmountable contradiction is, without the shadow of a doubt, found in Aristotle's text, it seems to us more prudent to assume that the argument given here is a continuous and coherent whole. In this way, in fact, we will be able to learn from Aristotle some interesting and useful theoretical concepts.

116. Kenny (1966) is an exception, but we do not accept his interpretation. For a criticism of Kenny, cf. N. O. Dahl (1984), pp. 160–161, 168–169, 172–181 and note 43.

117. The most natural interpretation is one that supposes that the practical premise and the δόξα have the same subject. The solution suggested by W. D. Ross (1923), p. 214 (Methuen University Paperbacks [1964], reprint, p. 223), understands a characterization as "being x" which is different from "being sweet"; he is then forced to posit the existence of a minor premise "this is x" which is different from "this is sweet"; but there is no trace of this in the text.

118. Cf. Walsh (1963), pp. 106–109; Donini (1977), p. 186; Robinson (1955), p. 82; von Fragstein (1974), p. 286; Etheridge (1968), p. 35; Hardie (1968), p. 282; Santas (1969), p. 183; Wiggins (1978–1979), p. 249; Charles (1984), p. 119.

119. Cf. Burnet (1900), p. 302; for an opposite view, see Gauthier (1958–1959) II, p. 61.

120. Cf. Wiggins (1978–1979), p. 249.

121. Cf. 1147b 2–3: ἡ γὰρ ἐπιθυμία ἐναντία . . . τῷ ὀρθῷ λόγῳ.

122. Cf. R. Robinson (1955), p. 82.

123. Cf. Rorty (1980), pp. 271 and 283.

124. Cf. W. F. R. Hardie (1968), p. 287.

Chapter Four

1. We have translated εὐδαιμονία by "happiness" even if this traditional term has a rather different meaning than the Greek word. The English word is usually defined as meaning a "feeling of pleasure or satisfaction" (*The Shorter Oxford English Dictionary* [1956] defines it as "the state of pleasurable contentment of mind, which results from success or the attainment of what is considered good," while the *Collins Cobuild English Dictionary* [1995] defines "happy" as follows: "Someone who is happy has feelings of pleasure, usually because something nice has happened or because they feel satisfied with their life."). Such a subjective conception of happiness is far from the Greek concept. It is not possible, for an ancient Greek, to feel his heart burst with εὐδαιμονία one should rather think of the objective situation in which the individual finds himself. Ross suggests translating the term by *well-being,* which, however, lays emphasis on the idea of physical (or psychological) health. The question has been discussed in detail by J. M. Cooper (1975), p. 89, who

suggests translating it by *[human] flourishing,* and, more recently, by R. Kraut (1977), pp. 167 ff. Kraut defends the most common translation (*happiness*), for the following reasons: it is not true, he maintains, that when we, today, speak of happiness, we mean only a state of subjective and lasting contentment, and it is not true either, he adds, that Aristotle's notion of εὐδαιμονία does not include also a subjective psychological state, in addition to an objective condition. In any case, it seems to us that Aristotle's notion is rather close in meaning to what we would today call "self-fulfillment," as in the expression "to find fulfillment," which is accompanied also by a sense of joy, but which is not the experience, for a limited period of time, of a sensation of intense contentment.

2. W. F. R. Hardie (1965).

3. Cooper (1975), p. 95, rightly suggests that in Aristotle's system it is difficult to admit that one can put order in the scheme of ends and desires of an individual life, if one admits the existence of more that one ultimate end. Indeed, in that case, whenever one has to make a choice between ultimate ends, one would remain without any criterion, since in Aristotle's system such a criterion can apparently only come from a higher end that includes all the others within itself. So much for Cooper. We shall return to this point later.

4. The main contributions are those by A. Kenny (1965–1966); T. Nagel (1972); J. L. Ackrill (1974); S. R. L. Clark (1975), especially Chapter v.1.; K. W. Wilkes (1978); A. Kenny (1978), Chapter 8; T. Engberg-Pedersen (1981) and (1983), Chapter 1; M. Wedin (1981); L. Nannery (1983); this topic is not dealt with in a number of important works, such as: J. Léonard (1948), a bit outdated; J. Ritter (1956); R. Kraut (1977); P. Aubenque (1978); B. Bossi de Kirkner (1984–1985). On the comparison between Aristotle and Kant, there are now studies by N. Fischer (1983); J.-E. Pleines (1984). Obviously, all general expositions of Aristotle's ethics contain a section on happiness.

5. The later contributions by Hardie to the discussion of Aristotle's concept of "happiness" are: W. F. R. Hardie (1968), Chapter 2; (1979); and the *Appended Notes* to the second edition (1980) of his book on Aristotle's ethics.

6. Hardie (1979), p. 44; (1968), pp. 23, 35, 357.

7. Jaeger (1928), p. 580, in reference to L. H. G. Greenwood (1909), p. 82.

8. Jaeger (1928), pp. 577 ff.

9. D. den Huyl and T. R. Machan (1983).

10. Cooper (1975), pp. 116, 143, 147–148; Kenny (1978), p. 203.

11. It is unclear which passage Aristotle is referring to. Gauthier (1958–1959), *ad l.*, refers to 1098a 17. But that passage speaks of happiness in accordance with the "best and most complete" virtue, and not in accordance with "a complete virtue and life." The two conceptions are opposites, and if we accept Cooper and Kenny's interpretation, it would seem strange that Aristotle would here cite a passage containing a totally different conception of happiness. If, therefore, Gauthier's reference is exact, the two conceptions must not have seemed totally contradictory to Aristotle.

12. 1103a 2–10.

13. C. Natali (1984), pp. 58–59.

14. J. Burnet (1900), p. 3 note 3; F. Dirlmeier (1963), p. 163; Gauthier (1958–1959) II, pp. 65–66.

15. An Italian translation of this text is now available: G. Pini (1985).

16. For clarity's sake we have indicated the beginning of the various sections, adding the English terms in brackets and adding numbers to distinguish the various sections in the definition given by Xenocrates. The passages quoted here are fragments 57 Lang, 101 Isnardi Parente, 77 Taran of Speusippus; 77 Heinze, 232 Isnardi Parente of Xenocrates; 123 Gigante of Polemo. The overall structure of this account has been analyzed by H. J. Krämer (1972), pp. 199–201. Important commentaries are also found in the editions of the fragments of Speusippus and Xenocrates by M. Isnardi Parente (1980, 1981), and of Xenocrates by L. Taran (1981).

17. The terms used are rather common. Isocrates also speaks of ἀρετή and its μέρη as the best allies for εὐδαιμονία, but the meaning he attaches to the terms is much closer to common usage: they are "capacities" that are allied for the achievement of "economic well-being." It is typical of the Academy to use words taken from the ordinary language in new senses; this often happens also in Plato's dialogues.

18. H. J. Krämer (1972), p. 205; L. Taran (1981), p. 436.

19. Aristotle himself, in *top.* II 6, 112a 36–38 (= Xenocr. fr. 81 Heinze, 236 Isnardi Parente) criticized Xenocrates' attempt. Xenocrates wanted to deduce the meaning of εὐδαίμων from an analysis of the term's component parts. He therefore maintained that one who is εὐδαίμων is a man endowed with a good soul, since the term corresponds to "one who possesses a favorable demon," and for Xenocrates the soul was a man's demon. Aristotle, instead, prefers to start from the current use of the word. It is therefore not possible, in interpreting Aristotle, to refer to real or fictitious etymologies of the term εὐδαιμονία one has to start from Aristotle's interpretation and rationalization of the current usage of his time.

20. F. Dirlmeier (1963), p. 163. The doubts expressed by O. Gigon (1971), p. 110, are less convincing. There is, in actuality, no need to make a close connection between this passage and the distinction of three βίοι made in 1215a 26 ff., as Gigon would have it. Other identifications have been proposed by Décarie (1978), p. 55 (Xenocrates, Plato, Democritus, Heraclitus, Pythagoras), and by M. Woods (1982), p. 55 (Socrates, Plato and others). The manifest link between this passage and the passages that we shall discuss in the following pages seems to us to confirm Dirlmeier's interpretation.

21. ταύτης in line 1098b 31 should be referred το ἀρετήν in line b 30, as maintained by Ross, Dirlmeier and Gauthier. Among the Italian commentators, Mazzarelli has given a less good interpretation of the passage; he refers ταύτης to ἀρετήν τινα in line b 30, and translates "it is proper to a certain virtue" ([1979], p. 101), whereas Plebe and Zanatta, in their translations, refer this pronoun to the understood subject of the previous sentence, εὐδαιμονία, interpreting the passage as meaning that activity in accordance with virtue "is proper to happiness" (cf. [1973], p. 17, and [1986], p. 115); Plebe also adds the words "in our opinion" which appear to have no equivalent in the Greek text.

22. Cf. Gauthier (1958–1959) II, p. 65; Burnet (1900), p. 42. See also the *Protrepticus*, fr. 14 Ross, 80 Düring.

23. The first careful consideration of the rigorous structure of *EE* is found in the essay by D. J. Allan (1961). See also C. J. Rowe (1977), pp. 24–26; W. Kullmann (1974),

pp. 235–238; A. von Fragstein (1974), pp. 53–59; A. Kenny (1978), pp. 198–200; Woods (1982), pp. 93–96; Hutchinson (1986), pp. 40–43. There is a comparison with Plato's dialogues in J. Moreau (1971), pp. 223–229.

24. Woods (1982), pp. 93 and 95; Rowe (1977), p. 24, and Kenny (1978), p. 198, are right.

25. F. Dirlmeier (1963), p. 221, refers to *EN* 1143a 25 and 28, where ἕξεις and δυνάμεις are used indifferently; as for κινήσεις and ἐνέργειαι, it is well known that in *phys.* III and *metaph.* IX 6 Aristotle distinguishes between processes, directed toward a certain τέλος, and activities, but this distinction does not appear to be used in the passage given here.

26. In the *Ethics,* ἔργον is usually translated by "function"; here, wherever it indicates both an object and an activity, we shall translate it by "work," trying in this way to keep the ambiguity of the Greek word in this context.

27. Woods (1982), p. 25.

28. It is not enough, because one who has only ἕξεις and δυνάμεις, i.e. habits and dispositions, which he never puts into practice, e.g. because he is always sleeping, according to Aristotle does not possess a part of happiness—indeed, he is not happy at all (1219b 16–20 and a 40–b 4). But habits and dispositions are something more, because their relation with activities is like that between power and actuality (*metaph.* IX 5).

29. At line a 30, I read <τὰ ἐν> αὐτῇ, following Susemihl, in the critical apparatus.

30. I refer τῆς ψυχῆς to ἄριστον and not to ἀρετῆς, in agreement with Woods, and against Solomon, Dirlmeier and Décarie, because of the requirements of the argument.

31. On the relation between this passage and the texts of Plato, especially *Phaed.* 98B and *polit.* 287D ff., a balanced analysis of the similarities and differences is given in E. Schütrumpf (1980), pp. 20–27.

32. At line 1214b 7, I read <δεῖ> θέσται; regarding the need for interpolation, cf. O. Gigon (1971), pp. 102–103, and Woods (1982), p. 200. If one omits the δεῖ and makes θέσται depend on ἐπιστήσαντας, as does F. Dirlmeier (1963), p. 6, the passage would state a falsehood, viz. that all those who can live in accordance with their choices set themselves a single aim; this statement would then be contradicted by Aristotle immediately afterwards, in lines b 9–11.

33. O. Gigon (1971), p. 103.

34. F. Dirlmeier (1963), p. 156.

35. Woods (1982), p. 53; cf. F. Dirlmeier (1963), p. 156. See also *metaph.* VII 10.

36. For example, by W. Jaeger (1923), pp. 311 f.

37. On this point, the studies by E. E. Ryan (1961) and E. La Croce (1987) are very useful.

38. Gauthier (1958–1959) II, pp. 6–7, wonders how a hierarchical series of moral activities is possible, and Ackrill (1974), pp. 18–19, thinks that here the inferior practices stand in a relation of part to whole with the "architectonic" practice. Such objections are evidently based on the principle that praxis, as such, has no external end, and that, for it,

"acting well (εὐπραξία) itself is the end" (1140b 7). What Aristotle means, in this initial (and not very precise) treatment is made clear in 1094b 2–7: politics, the architectonic science that gives rise to actions and not products, orders and directs other sciences such as economics and rhetoric, even though they, too, do not produce material objects, but behaviors. Politics uses them, and decrees what is to be done or not done, as a king uses the valorous actions of his warriors for his higher ends. As we shall see, the fact that an act is an end in itself does not at all prevent it from also being used for something else, in another perspective.

39. Ackrill (1974), see previous note, sees in this περιέχοι ἄν the sign of an "inclusive" conception of the supreme good. But, as Alexander of Aphrodisias long ago pointed out, also the end περιέχεται (surrounds) the means (Alex. Aphrod. *in Top.*, p. 247, 10 Wallies, a passage we shall return to later).

40. Besides the commentaries of Burnet (1900), Joachim (1951), Dirlmeier (1956) and Gauthier (1958–1959), *ad l.*, there are important remarks in P. T. Geach (1958), p. 112; G. E. M. Anscombe (1957), p. 34; B. A. O. Williams (1962); A. Kenny (1965–1966); C. Kirwan (1967); W. F. R. Hardie (1968), p. 17; R. Robinson (1971), p. 191 note 8; K. Jacobi (1979); T. Engberg-Pedersen (1981); G. Seel (1981); M. Wedin (1981).

41. Gauthier (1958–1959) II, pp. 7–8; likewise Hardie (1968), pp. 16–17, and Cooper (1975), p. 93, hold that (1) is a supposition, not demonstrated by the present passage.

42. Burnet (1900), pp. xlii-xliii; Léonard (1948), p. 19; Joachim (1951), p. 21.

43. Cf. O. Höffe (1971), p. 35, and R. Bubner (1974), pp. 62 and 153; K. Jacobi (1979), p. 300.

44. Wedin (1981), pp. 247, 249 ff.; for a contrary opinion, see Ackrill (1974), p. 25.

45. *Metaph.* I 9, 990b 12; cf. Seel (1981), p. 264, and O. Gigon (1985), pp. 339–340.

46. Or, at least, the most common ones. Cf. 1095a 28–30 and *EE* 1214b 28–1215a 3.

47. After Burnet (1900), the dialectical nature of Aristotle's discussions has been pointed out by G. E. L. Owen (1961); E. Berti (1972); Cooper (1975), pp. 66 ff.; T. B. Eriksen (1976), pp. 22–30. For more recent studies, see J. Barnes (1980); M. Nussbaum (1986).

48. I read, with Woods, μάλιστα <δὲ> πρὸς ὅ.

49. Περὶ ἕκαστα, in line a 11, refers το τῶν ἐπιεικῶν in the following line.

50. Θειότερον, line a 17, considered untranslatable by von Fragstein (1974), p. 19, has been well explained by V. Décarie (1978), p. 54: it is more divine because it is more independent and does not undergo the influence of casual or biological factors.

51. The passage is rather confused: unlike most translators, I refer τῶν μέν (line 26) and τῶν δέ (line 32) to: διῃρημένων δὲ τῶν βίων (line 26), and I understand: τῶν (καὶ πρότερον ῥηθέντων) ἀγαθῶν (line 33) as meaning: "goods also mentioned before," i.e. the second type of goods.

52. Ἀλύπως perhaps refers also to the ἀοχλησία / ἀλυπία of Speusippus and not only to Anaxagoras.

53. Section 1215b 15–1216a 10 interrupts the course of the argument with a series of traditional τόποι on the fact that it is better to die than to live; cf. F. Dirlmeier (1963), p. 169. The discussion of happiness is resumed at 1216a 11.

54. Προσάπτουσιν, cf. Bonitz (1870), 643a 55–b 11.

55. The most recent investigation of the subject is that by J. C. B. Gosling and C. C. W. Taylor (1982), containing the previous bibliography.

56. This passage has been exhaustively discussed by M. Mignucci (1985), pp. 60–61.

57. This text is part of fr. 82 Heinze, 240 Isnardi Parente of Xenocrates.

58. Cf. Liddell-Scott (1940–1949), s. v.; J. H. Schmidt (1876–1886) I, pp. 40–53; P. Chantraine (1968), pp. 176–177; Cooper (1975), p. 160 note.

59. When it is applied to animals in general, the concept of βίος serves as a method of general classification of the various animal species, alongside other possible methods and criteria (cf. *hist. an.* 487a 12, 14, 16 and b 33). From this point of view, animals can be divided, for example, into ones that are solitary or living in herds or living in both ways; settled or nomadic; carnivorous, herbivorous and omnivorous; and in many other ways. The term βίος indicates the series of activities typical of an animal species, activities that center around the two functions of nutrition and reproduction. Indeed, almost all the efforts and activities of animals are directed to these ends (cf. *hist. an.* 589a 1). When dealing with rather primitive populations, also human communities can be distinguished in terms of βίος, especially with regard to the different ways of procuring food. This is the prevailing type of activity in primitive forms of βίος and makes it possible to distinguish one kind of human society from another. We thus have (*pol.* 1256b 1) the nomadic life, the life of the marauder, the hunter, the fisherman and the farmer. This subject of ways of living has been studied mainly by Jaeger (1928) and Joly (1956).

60. In *pol.* 1333a 31 the human βίος is divided into necessary and free activities (ἀσχολία / σχολή), as well as into activities of war and peace (πόλεμος / εἰρήνη).

61. Cf. Burnet (1900), p. 33; R. Hackforth (1972), p. 32, on the comparison with EN I 7.

62. On the contrary, in *pol.* I 11 Aristotle reports the attribution to Thales of Miletus of an astute scheme for getting rich.

63. The comparison with the book by J. Rawls (1971) VII/63, pp. 336 ff. is not as gratuitous as it may seem, nor is it dictated by the desire to take into account the latest publication or the most recent fashion. In reality, in many respects Rawls's premises are compatible with Aristotle's, and this explains why some authors (Cooper, Nussbaum) appeal to Rawls to interpret Aristotle, and why others, such as F.-A. Koch (1978), try to interpret Rawls from an Aristotelian perspective. Cf. also O. Höffe (1977). Nonetheless, the difference between the two theories is enormous, and the comparison may be useful mainly in clarifying two theoretical positions by showing how far apart they are.

64. I follow the interpretation of Burnet, Ross, Dirlmeier and Mazzarelli, against Gauthier and Zanatta.

65. Δι' αὐτό, according to Bywater, Burnet, Gauthier and others. One could also understand δι' ἄλλο, as do the old translators and, among the moderns, Ross and Dirlmeier. In this latter case, the text would not spell out that some of the ends-in-themselves produce the other end-in-itself, and this fact would be added only later on, at line a 34 ff., with regard to happiness.

66. Cf. Gauthier (1958–1959) II, p. 52.

67. Kenny (1965–1966), p. 28. This seems to go against what is said in *top.* 149b 37, which we shall discuss below.

68. Cf. Alex. Aphrod. *in Top.*, p. 485, 1–17. In the same sense, see A. M. Ioppolo (1974), p. 382. The essence of virtuous acts seems to be the actualization of a certain human ability. Cf. D. Charles (1984), Chapters 1 and 5.

69. Cf. J. Ritter (1956), p. 88.

70. In *Top.* pp. 246, line 27–247, line 12. For the interpretation of the verb περιέχεται, which appears in this passage, compare pp. 238, lines 1–17, and 240, line 1–241, line 28. Alexander understands "to be comprised" as meaning "to be a means for," and the reason why the virtues are not added as goods to happiness is just because they are exclusively considered as means for happiness. The example (one does not prefer health + medicines to health alone) is very clear on this point.

71. Cf., e.g. Aspas. *in Eth. Nic.*, p. 17, 3–17, and Léonard (1948), pp. 188–194, who criticizes Alexander but reaches the same conclusion.

72. I follow the text of the manuscripts, together with G. Colli (1955) and A. Zadro (1974), *ad l.* Others have felt it necessary to emend the text, as does T. Waitz (1844), p. 467, who interprets thus: "and nothing prevents some non-goods <together with goods> from being preferable to goods <that are more numerous>." W. A. Pickard-Cambridge (1928) *ad l.*, interprets as follows: "and nothing prevents some non-goods <together with> goods from being preferable." Others have understood the expression μὴ ἀγαθά as "a sum that is not a sum of goods alone"; cf. J. Brunschwig (1967), p. 157. In actual fact, such emendations are not indispensable in order for the passage to make sense, although, if we maintain the traditional text, the argument seems quite sophistical.

73. Léonard (1948), p. 54, maintains that in Aristotle the term αὐτάρκεια does not mean "independence and self-sufficiency," but only "sufficiency," in that happiness does not result in anything else, but needs external goods. In our opinion it is unlikely that αὐτάρκεια may mean only "sufficiency"; cf. *pol.* 1326b 30: "αὐταρκής is to have everything and to lack nothing." Aristotle's argument should rather be interpreted in the sense that the concept of happiness (= activity in accordance with virtue) analytically comprises the idea of "possession of a sufficient quantity of external goods" and "possession of good dispositions of the soul."

74. For a different opinion, cf. T. Engberg-Pedersen (1983), p. 11.

75. Cf. W. Kullmann (1974), pp. 231–232.

76. J. Burnet (1900), p. 34.

77. Regarding the interpretation of this passage, cf. Burnet (1900), p. 34; Léonard (1948), pp. 27–38; Joachim (1951), pp. 49–50; Gauthier (1958–1959) II, pp. 54–56; Hardie (1968), pp. 23–25 and 362–363; Kullmann (1974), p. 232; Clark (1975), pp. 14–28; M. Nussbaum (1978), pp. 81–85 and 100–106.

78. Rawls (1971) VII/61, p. 330. For a comparison between these two theoretical positions, cf. W. Charlton (1970), p. 102.

79. As is well known, Aristotle maintains that "being a man" (τὸ ἀνθρώπῳ εἶναι, *metaph.* 1007a 24–25) does not coincide either with any particular human activity—at

least at this point in the discussion—nor with the whole set of all human activities, but is to be identified, on a more general and abstract plane, with a specifically human form of life.

80. Here I am following Burnet and Cooper, *contra* Joachim.

81. A good translation is in Zanatta (1986), *ad l.*

82. Cf. Cooper (1975), pp. 145 and 148. There is a difference between *EN* and *EE* on this point, since the latter speaks of the ἔργον of the soul and not the ἔργον of man. But in the *Topics* Aristotle identifies man with his soul.

83. Wherein I read ὅτι <ταὐτὸ> τὸ ἔργον, as emended by Casaubon.

84. For the meaning of this μετά, cf. *EN* VI 8 1144b 27 (and see note 53, p. 204).

85. Burnet (1900), pp. 36–37, is right in thinking that this passage is part of Aristotle's long premise and not a duplication of the previous passage, as supposed by Bywater, who places this passage between square brackets.

86. Πλείους, here, does not indicate the many ethical virtues, as opposed to contemplation, but the two kinds of virtue of the rational soul; the word πολύς is used also for two things, cf. *metaph.* 1056b 19–27. Hutchinson (1986), pp. 54–55, is of the same opinion. For an opposite view, see Kenny (1978), pp. 203–206 and, more recently, La Croce (1987), pp. 106–107.

87. It is uncertain whether one should read "in a life that has reached maturity, and is completely developed," as maintained by Gauthier (1958–1959) II, pp. 59–60, or "in a complete life span," as would be suggested by the comparison with Herod. I, 32, or in a life composed of many activities.

88. As will be said in more detail in *EN* I 13.

89. Cooper (1975), p. 100 note 10, rightly holds that here the superlative τελειοτάτη is "by its very nature exclusionary," and means "most having the character of an end"; he states, however, that there is no reason to immediately identify this τελειοτάτη ἀρετή with σοφία and that Aristotle does not explicitly make such an identification, but is rather vague on the matter.

90. The words "produces health" are to be understood (as interpreted by Stewart, Dirlmeier and Gauthier), and not "produces happiness" (as maintained by Eustathius, Greenwood and Léonard), since, in the latter case, health would be an instrument, just as medicine is an instrument for health.

91. The text in line 1144a 6, printed by Bywater as a crux: + τῷ ἐνεργεῖν εὐδαίμονα +, can be understood, according to Burnet (1900), p. 83, as expressing the fact that whoever possesses virtue acts in accordance with it.

92. Cf. Greenwood (1909); W. D. Ross (1923), p. 221; Dirlmeier (1956), p. 469; Hardie (1968), p. 235; Cooper (1975), p. 112.

93. E.g., cf. R. Loening (1903), p. 14, who speaks of "bloßes Mittel" in this case.

94. Cf. Woods (1982), p. 185.

95. Ὅλον is to be understood here as in *EN* 1144b 3–6, examined above. See also *EE* 1219a 30 and 1220a 2–4.

96. Cf. Léonard (1948), p. 116; for Ross (1923), pp. 211 and 223, the philosopher is the happiest man but is not the only one who is happy. This position is correct, but see

also E. Berti (1979) and I. Düring (1966), p. 531. "A personal opinion," is the comment of G. E. R. Lloyd (1968), p. 218.

97. In reality, the theoretical life recommended by Aristotle in *EN* X does not exactly coincide with the life of the philosopher shut up within a school. Actually, the schools of philosophy were established for organizational purposes, as a way of ensuring that some people would have a space in which to contemplate; it was not, for the Peripatetics of the early generations, the place of choice for the philosopher's life, as it was later to become for the Epicureans. On this point see Natali (1983).

98. Besides general comments on *EN,* cf. G. Rodier (1897), whose introduction has been republished in G. Rodier (1969), pp. 177–217, and T. B. Eriksen (1976).

99. Cf. T. B. Eriksen (1976), p. 40.

100. A study of the role of νοῦς in *EN* goes beyond the limits of this book. Unlike other commentators, we do not feel it is indispensable to connect this passage with the doctrines of *De anima,* as it seems to us that what Aristotle says here can be better understood in terms of the doctrines of his purely ethical writings. For a clear treatment of the subject, see H. Seidl (1971), pp. 159–161. He rightly points out that the divinity of νοῦς, which Aristotle speaks of here, should not be understood in the sense that a part of the divine essence is present in man, but only that there is a close relationship between human and divine νοῦς.

101. Cf. Cooper (1975), p. 156: "a most curious assertion."

102. Cf. T. B. Eriksen (1976), p. 42.

103. We are here following Cooper (1975), pp. 157–160, as opposed to Gauthier (1958–1959) II, pp. 893–896.

104. A detailed survey of the competitive aspects of the popular morality of the time can be found in the recent volume by L. B. Carter (1986), pp. 1–25, in his chapter "Fame and Honour."

105. There is here a clear opposition between two excellencies: "nobility and greatness" as against σπουδή, a term that indicates "scientific seriousness, commitment, rigor"; cf. Bonitz (1870), p. 697a 48 ff. F. Solmsen (1964), p. 209, notes the different use of σπουδή in Plato, where this concept includes all activities, whether warlike or peaceful, that are opposed to amusements and other forms of relaxation (παιδιά). Cf. also p. 214, where it is shown that Aristotle replaces Plato's contrast of παιδιά/σπουδή with another pair of opposites: ἀσχολία (with intervals of παιδιά)/σχολή.

106. Eriksen (1976), p. 115, simplifies things too much, when he says that the end of the political life is to guarantee the conditions for θεωρία. The βίος πολιτικός aims at power, honor and also virtuous actions. In the case of the good legislator, he will try to see to it that his fellow citizens enjoy the greatest happiness possible under the circumstances; in the case of the best constitution, he will organize things in such a way as to encourage the exercise of the intellectual virtues. But this is only one possibility among many; it is inexact to think that one can dedicate oneself properly to the βίος πολιτικός, while having solely the aim of guaranteeing contemplation for others.

107. Cf. L. B. Carter (1986) and F. Solmsen (1964) with the previously published bibliography.

108. Cf. *metaph.* I 2 and T. B. Eriksen (1976), pp. 119–136. Aristotle's is an invitation to immortalize oneself in the course of one's life, in accordance with the Homeric tradition. It has no relation with religious doctrines or with the problem of salvation after death.

109. The expression κατὰ τὴν ἄλλην ἀρετήν has the force of an exclusion and indicates "the other virtues" (excluding contemplation), as in 1177b 29. Therefore the hypothesis advanced by Cooper (1975), pp. 166–167, is unacceptable; for Cooper this "second" kind of happy life includes both the exercise of moral virtues and contemplation. See also 1178a 22–23, where the opposition expressed by the text again suggests that here Aristotle is speaking of life according to the moral virtues, excluding contemplation.

110. Cf. T. B. Eriksen (1976), p. 148.

111. Cooper (1975), pp. 160–165, holds that one who lives the βίος θεωρητικός is not a person who combines the exercise of contemplation with the moral virtues, but one who, as he thinks that only νοῦς is his true self, considers only contemplation to be worthy of him. In this interpretation, moral actions are nothing but an instrument for furthering θεωρία and, at most, a concession the philosopher makes to the mortal part of his being. Thus they would take their place alongside external goods and those practices indispensable for survival, such as eating and sleeping. In this way the important distinction between the parts of happiness and the necessary conditions for it is lost.

112. 1178b 7–23, cf. 1177b 26–1178a 8.

113. Here, too, Aristotle appears to exaggerate, with respect to what he said in *EN* 1099b 32 ff. For the ethical and political dividing line between the animal and human worlds, cf. G. Bien (1973), pp. 117–121.

114. In terms of mode of life, it does not make much difference whether the object of θεωρία is the reality of the sublunary world or a separate reality. According to *EN* 1177a 15, θεωρία deals with noble and divine things; according to *EN* 1141a 20, 21–22, b 1–2, the things most worthy of honor are the object of the highest intellectual virtue, σοφία. Aristotle describes the objects of σοφία in *metaph.* I 1–3, and there is no reason to doubt that Aristotle is thinking, first of all, of the entities described in that text, i.e. the causes and principles of reality, including also the unmoved mover, conceived of as a cause and principle. On this point, see C. Natali (1974). For a different opinion, cf. the recent work by J. A. Dudley (1981).

115. This is another opinion that must not have been very pleasing either to Alexander or to the democratic party of Athens.

116. F. Dirlmeier (1956), p. 596.

117. Cf. Gauthier (1958–1959) I, p. 306, and the translation by Zanatta (1986), p. 1110.

118. It is a real pity that L. B. Carter (1986) limited his study to the Pre-Socratics and Plato, philosophers in whom it is not very easy to find a real position of "political Quietism," completely ignoring these very well-known passages of the *Nicomachean Ethics*.

119. Eriksen (1976), p. 34.

120. This is one of the most often discussed passages in the *EE*. The celebrated analysis by Jaeger, who found in this passage the manifesto of a "theonomic" ethics, is in

(1923), pp. 326 ff. The anti-Jaegerian polemic of von Arnim is also famous; he went to the opposite extreme and interpreted the "god" Aristotle speaks of here as being identical to the human intellect; of his various studies, let us mention only von Arnim (1924). Today the best analysis of the text is that by V. J. Verdenius (1971), pp. 285–297. See also D. J. Monan (1968), pp. 125–134; von Fragstein (1974), pp. 384 ff.; Cooper (1975), pp. 135–143; Rowe (1971), pp. 68–69; and the translation by Décarie (1978), *ad l.*

121. This is our interpretation of λόγος cf. V. J. Verdenius (1971), p. 286, and Décarie (1978), p. 223.

122. I read, following Ross, καὶ τὴν ἐνέργειαν.

123. It is not clear whether here ἕκαστον means "each element" or "each individual." Décarie (1978), p. 223, keeps the ambiguity and translates, appropriately, "chaque être."

124. I read ἑαυτοῦ, with Dirlmeier, Woods and von Fragstein.

125. Τὸ θεωρητικόν is the "contemplative faculty" (Dirlmeier, Verdenius, Woods) and not a generic theoretical-practical "cognitive faculty," as others maintain.

126. The "god" spoken of, who has no need of anything (cf. b 16) cannot be νοῦς, whose activity needs the service of φρόνησις and a certain amount of external goods (health, food, leisure), as well as internal goods (a tranquil state of mind). It is, instead, the object of νοῦς.

127. To be understood as practical wisdom and not as theoretical-practical knowledge, as maintained by Décarie (1978), p. 224.

128. I open the parentheses before διώρισθαι and not before διττόν, following von Fragstein (1974), p. 384.

129. I read ἔχει δ' οὕτω τῇ ψυχῇ, following Woods (1982), p. 221.

130. Ἀλόγου (Susemihl).

131. In *EN* 1178a 14–23 it is said that φρόνησις is linked to the passions and that the exercise of this intellectual virtue must "be subjugated," together with that of the emotional part of man, while the activity of νοῦς is separate. The position of *EN,* therefore, does not seem to differ much from that of *EE.*

132. We have put between square brackets the parts of the translated text that are implicit.

133. Ritter (1956), pp. 82–83.

134. Cf. Barker (1906), p. 88; Schütrumpf (1980), pp. 5–6, takes the statement almost literally.

135. Lord (1982), pp. 183–184.

136. Aristotle here expresses himself in the following terms: "(a life) separated from all external realities, as for example a certain kind of theoretical life, which some say is the only kind worthy of a philosopher." This sentence seems to imply that this is a conception of the theoretical life that he reports without sharing it; perhaps it is that of the *Theaetetus* of Plato.

137. Cf. E. Berti (1963), p. 20. It is not possible to speak here of a "union of theory and practice," as some do; Aristotle's position consists, instead, in the substitution of theoretical activity for the practice of politics. Newman (1889–1902), p. 337, notes that

this is not the only passage in which Aristotle uses πρᾶξις in such a broad sense. Cf. also Bonitz (1870), p. 631a 22–25. But it is the only one in which the shift in meaning is so clear and so consciously exploited.

138. Cf. Schütrumpf (1980), p. 91; F. Solmsen (1964), p. 218.

139. Schütrumpf (1980), p. 8, thinks of internal politics; Lord (1982), p. 189, suggests that the philosopher should participate in some fashion in political life as a moral example (as Socrates did), or as an adviser; Solmsen (1964), pp. 215–221, thinks mainly of "music" in the broad sense, including all the fine arts; see also Hardie (1968), p. 340.

140. *pol.* 1332a 8 = EE 1219a 38, b 2; *pol.* 1332a 20 = EE 1248b 26.

141. Newman (1889–1892), p. 441, interprets correctly: if one can achieve only the activity of the irrational part of the soul, plus that of the practical intellect, then one will have to give more importance to the better of these two.

142. I read, at lines a 32 and a 33, εἰς τὰ ἀναγκαῖα and εἰς τὰ καλά.

143. Here φιλοσοφία has the broader sense of "love for culture" in general. Cf. Solmsen (1964), p. 198. On the meaning of the term in the culture of the time, cf. W. Burkert (1960), pp. 159–177.

144. The virtues that are exercised toward one's fellow citizens, in case of danger and when everybody is, so to speak, in the same boat, are "necessary" virtues and are somehow not free, unlike pure and simple virtues (cf. 1332a 7–11), but they are not a mere appearance of virtue, as seems to be suggested, with some hesitation, by Newman (1889–1892), p. 450.

145. Cf., e.g., Herod. I 32, 1; VII 46, 4; Pind. *py.* III 80; Aesch. *Ag.* 752.

146. Cf. Gauthier (1958–1969) II, pp. 860–866, who proposed this interpretation again.

147. This point has been amply illustrated and eloquently defended by M. Nussbaum (1986).

148. Cf. I. Kant, *Kritik der praktischen Vernunft,* P. I, l. II, Chapter II/2, ed. by K. Vorländer, Hamburg (1929–39), p. 137 (= 214); G. W. F. Hegel, *Encyklopädie d. philos. Wiss.,* §§ 479 and 505. It would be very interesting to make a critical comparison between Rawls's position and the objections expressed by Hegel, in his § 479, against a representation in which happiness is the "reciprocal limitation" of impulses, but this task cannot be undertaken here. As often happens, Nietzsche clearly sees the difference between modern and ancient conceptions of ethics, and rightly argues against a conception of happiness as "self-contentment." But we would not dare to affirm that there is anything more than a distant echo between what Aristotle means by happiness and what Nietzsche is speaking of when he uses this concept. For this entire aspect of the question, there are many useful perspectives given in C. Vigna (1986) and Tatarkiewicz (1945).

Afterword

1. A. Tosel, ed., *Les logiques de l'agir dans la modernité,* Besançon (1992); *De la prudence des anciens comparée à celle des modernes,* Besançon (1995); *Formes de rationalité et phronetique*

moderne, Besançon (1995); see also the monographic issue of "Philosophie," No. 53, 1997: *L'action à l'âge classique.*

2. We shall quote other authors further in this survey. At any rate this survey does not aim to be complete: we shall quote only works we believe to be the most interesting to the best of our knowledge.

3. P. Aubenque, *Philosophie pratique et herméneutique,* in A. Tosel, *Les logiques de l'agir,* quoted, pp. 15–32, tends to link his own research on *phronesis* to Heidegger's thought although in his previous study *La prudence chez Aristote,* Paris (1963), Heidegger's influence is not quite manifest and even Heidegger himself has a different position from Aubenque on several main topics; it is a more optimistic standing on the capabilities of *phronesis.* A criticism to Aubenque is in P. Ricoeur, *A la gloire de la phronesis,* in Chateau, ed., pp. 13–14.

4. E. Berti, *Il metodo della filosofia pratica secondo Aristotele,* in Alberti, ed., pp. 23–63; see also *Phronesis et science politique,* in P. Aubenque and A. Tordesillas, *Aristote politique,* Paris (1993), pp. 435–459; Salkever, pp. 57–104; Ricoeur, pp. 13–22.

5. See W. Leszl, *Alcune specificità del sapere pratico,* in Alberti, ed., pp. 65–118; Guariglia, pp. 355–362. Leszl considers very little the difference in ends of practical knowledge in respect to physics. It is an element which explains why, though sharing some aspects, the two knowledge forms are essentially different. Like Guariglia, also J. Owens, *Value and Practical Knowledge in Aristotle,* in Anton and Preus, ed., pp. 153–155, thinks Aristotelian ethics is not self-sufficient and must be completed with elements derived from other theories and visions of the world.

6. For Berti and Salkever see the works quoted earlier; Reeve, pp. 7–66. An objection of Broadie's is then overcome: if *phronesis* gets its principles from philosophy then only the philosophers' disciples will be really wise and righteous men (Broadie, p. 199). That would be an acceptable theory for Plato but obviously not for Aristotle; but in the interpretations summarized here practical philosophy founds and brings to full awareness ethical principles already obscurely present in the minds of wise men such as Pericles and his followers.

7. W. F. R. Hardie, *Aristotle's Ethical Theory,* Oxford (1980), p. 30; a rather agnostic argument of the issue is in G. Anagnostopoulos, *Aristotle on the Good and Exactness in the Ethics,* Berkeley (1994), pp. 75–87, which sets out clearly the logical consequences of the many positions; Guariglia, pp. 33–102, when speaking of Aristotle's "practical reason" cannot seem to tell the two levels clearly; it is uncertain if he is speaking about the *Nicomachean Ethics* or *phronesis.*

8. Owens, pp. 143–148, correctly points out that the modern distinction between fact and value is not valid in Aristotle and that, for him, "good" is an universal object, like any other object of science. Similarly Salkever, pp. 57–60, criticizes all attempts to compare practical Aristotelian philosophy—he defines it as a "social science"—to the philosophical positions of the early twentieth century, which wanted to give to social sciences a method distinct from the procedures of natural sciences, a method based on intuition and empathetic understanding.

9. Compare E. Berti, *Le ragioni di Aristotele,* Rome-Bari (1989), pp. 113–152; Reeve, pp. 39–43; Broadie, p. 184.

10. J.-Y. Chateau, *L'objet de la phronesis et la verité pratique,* in Chateau, ed., pp. 185–188.

11. Berti, *Il metodo,* p. 35; Leszl, pp. 88–89; Ricoeur, p. 21.

12. Guariglia, pp. 292–298; Chateau, pp. 193–194 and 254–255.

13. Leszl, pp. 88–89.

14. T. M. Tuozzo, *Aristotelian Deliberation Is Not of Ends,* in Anton and Preus, eds., pp. 204–205; Reeve, pp. 58–61 and 97.

15. P. Schollmeier, *Aristotle on Practical Wisdom,* "Zeitschrift f. philosophische Forschung" 43, 1989, pp. 124–132; R. B. Louden, *Aristotle's Practical Particularism,* in Anton and Preus, pp. 172–174; Reeve, p. 60. This thesis was held earlier by J. M. Cooper and T. H. Irwin.

16. Heidegger, pp. 156, 163–164; Broadie, pp. 243–244; Elm, pp. 217–218, 281–282; Ricoeur, p. 21.

17. Leszl, pp. 74–75; Broadie, p. 247.

18. D. K. W. Modrak, *Aristotle on Reason, Practical Reason, and Living Well,* in Anton and Preus, eds., pp. 188–190; Broadie, p. 215; Guariglia, p. 309.

19. Berti, *Il metodo,* quoted, pp. 36–50, 63.

20. Heidegger, p. 55; cf. Owens, pp. 153–154.

21. It is interesting to observe how, beyond the sort of usual opposition between "Anglo-Saxon" and "Continental" philosophies, one can find common positions among the most representative philosophers of the two schools. We can observe a similar case in respect to the interpretation of Aristotle's *Physics:* compare S. Waterlow's (Broadie), *Nature, Change and Agency in Aristotle's* Physics, Oxford (1988); and M. Heidegger's essay *Von Wesen und Begriff der* physis, *Aristoteles'* Physik *B. 1* (1939), now in *Holzwege,* Frankfurt am Main (1976).

22. Broadie, pp. 218–219 and 227–232.

23. Heidegger, pp. 138, 148–150, 163–164.

24. Heidegger, pp. 129–131 and 163–164; Berti, *Il metodo,* quoted, p. 59; B. Besnier, *Le rôle du chapitre 5 dans le sixième livre (Ethique à Nicomaque, VI 5),* in Chateau, ed., pp. 83–85.

25. Heidegger, pp. 49–50; Owens, pp. 150–151.

26. Broadie, pp. 215–216.

27. P. Gochet, *Le syllogisme pratique d'Aristote,* in A. Motte and J. Denooz, *Aristotelica secunda,* Mélanges . . . Rutten, Liège (1996), pp. 117–129; however, we can ask ourselves to what point a syllogistic inference involving a causal entailment is still a logical structure and not a template to describe a practical inference.

28. Chateau, p. 248.

29. Besnier, p. 84.

30. Broadie, p. 218; Chateau, pp. 246–247.

31. Heidegger bases all his argument on the concept of practical truth: however, see particularly pp. 21–27 and 163–164; see also Broadie, pp. 219–225; A. Leandri, *L'action et la verité (Ethique à Nicomaque VI, 2),* in Chateau, ed., pp. 52–53.

32. Salkever, pp. 105–116; Chateau, pp. 233, 255–260.

TEXTS CITED

AA. VV. *Aristotelismo veneto e scienza moderna,* Padua, 1983.

AA. VV. *Autour d'Aristote,* Recueil d'études . . . offert à Mgr. Mansion, Louvain (Belgium), 1955.

AA. VV. *Kephalaion,* Studies . . . De Vogel, Assen (Netherlands), 1975.

Ackrill, J. L. "Aristotle's Distinction Between Energeia and Kinesis," in R. Bamborough (ed.), *New Essays on Plato and Aristotle* . . . (1965), pp. 121–141.

———. "Aristotle on Eudaimonia" (1974), now in A. O. Rorty (ed.), *Essays on Aristotle's Ethics* (1980), pp. 15–34.

Adorno, F. *Platone. Dialoghi politici,* Turin, 1953–1954.

Alfieri, V. E., and M. Untersteiner (eds.). *Studi di filosofia greca,* Bari (Italy), 1950.

Allan, D. J. "Aristotle's Account of the Origin of Moral Principles" (1953), now in J. Barnes et al., *Articles on Aristotle.* 2 (1977), pp. 72–78.

———. "The Practical Syllogism," in *Autour d'Aristote* (1955), pp. 325–343.

———. "Quasi-mathematical Method in the Eudemian Ethics," in S. Mansion (ed.), *Aristote et les problèmes de Méthode* (1961), pp. 303–318.

———. *La filosofia di Aristotele* (1952), Ital. trans., Milan, 1973.

Ando, T. *Aristotle's Theory of Practical Cognition,* The Hague, 1958, 1971–1973.

Anscombe, G. E. M. *Intention,* Oxford, 1957.

———. "Thought and Action in Aristotle" (1965), now in J. Barnes et al., *Articles on Aristotle.* 2 (1977), pp. 61–71.

Aphrod, Alexandr. *Aristotelis Metaphysica comm.* M. Hayduck (ed.), (C. A. G., I), Berolini, 1891.

———. *Aristotelis Topicorum comm.*, M. Wallies (ed.) (C. A. G., II/2), Berolini, 1891.

Arnim, H. von. "Die drei aristotelischen Ethiken," Sitzungsberichte der Akademie der Wissenschaften in Wien, philosophisch-historische Klasse. 202–2, Vienna (1924).

———. "Das Ethische in Aristoteles' Topik," Sitzungsberichte der Akademie der Wissenschaften in Wien, philosophisch-historische Klasse. 205–4, Vienna (1927).

Aspas. *In Aristotelis Eth. Nic. comm.*, G. Heylbut (ed.), (C. A. G., XIX/1), Berolini, 1899.

Aubenque, P. *La prudence chez Aristote,* Paris, 1963.

———. "La prudence aristotélicienne porte-t-elle sur la fin ou sur les moyens?" *Rev. ét. grecques* 78 (1965), pp. 40–51.

———. "Die Kohärenz der aristotelischen Eudaimonia-Lehre," in G. Bien (ed.), *Die Frage nach dem Glück* (1978), pp. 45–57.

Bamborough, R. (ed.). *New Essays on Plato and Aristotle,* London, 1965.

Barker, E. *The Political Thought of Plato and Aristotle,* London, 1906.

Barnes, J. "Aristote dans la philosophie anglo-saxonne," *Revue Philos. de Louvain* 75 (1977), pp. 204–218.

———. "Proof and the Syllogism," in E. Berti (ed.), *Aristotle on Science: The "Posterior Analytics"* (1981), pp. 17–60.

Barnes, J., et al. (eds.). *Articles on Aristotle, 2: Ethics and Politics,* London, 1977.

Barnes, J., J. Brunschwig, M. Frede. "Le propre de la prudence," in *Hérmeneutique et ontologie,* Hommage à P. Aubenque, Vrin, Paris, 1990, pp. 79–96.

E. Berti, *La filosofia del primo Aristotele,* Padua, 1961.

———. *Il "De re publica" di Cicerone e il pensiero politico classico,* Padua, 1963.

———. "La dialettica in Aristotele" (1972), now in *Studi aristotelici* (1975), pp. 108–133.

———. *Studi aristotelici,* L'Aquila (Italy), 1975.

———. *Aristotele dalla dialettica alla filosofia prima,* Padua, 1977.

———. "Ancient Greek Dialectics as Expression of Freedom of Thought and Speech," *Journ. of Hist. of Ideas* 39 (1978), pp. 347–370.

———. "Storicità ed attualità della concezione aristotelica dello Stato," *Verifiche* 7 (1978), pp. 305–358.

———. *Profilo di Aristotele,* Rome, 1979.

———, (ed.). *Aristotle on Science: The "Posterior Analytics,"* Padua, 1981.

———. "Differenza tra il metodo risolutivo degli aristotelici e la 'resolutio' dei matematici," in *Aristotelismo veneto e scienza moderna* (1983), pp. 435–457.

Bien, G. *La filosofia politica di Aristotele* (1973), Ital. trans., Bologna, 1985.

———. "Die menschlichen Meinungen und das Gute. Die Lösung der Normproblems in der Aristotelischen Ethik," in M. Riedel (ed.), *Reahbilitierung der praktischen Philosophie (1972–1974),* pp. 345–371.

———. (ed.) *Die Frage nach dem Glück,* Stuttgart-Bad Cannstatt (Germany), 1978.

Bonitz, H. *Index aristotelicus,* Berlin 1870, repr. Graz (Austria), 1955.

Bossi de Kirchner, B. "El concepto Aristotélico de eudaimonia," *Ethos* (Buenos Aires), 12–13 (1984–1985), pp. 247–283.

Brunschwig, J. *Aristote. Topiques,* text established and translated Paris, 1967.

Bubner, R. *Azione, linguaggio e ragione* (1974), Ital. trans., Bologna, 1985.

Burkert, W. "Platon oder Pythagoras? Zum Ursprung des Wortes," *Philosophie, Hermes* 88 (1960), pp. 159–177.

Burnet, J. *The Ethics of Aristotle,* London, 1900.

Burnyeat, M. "Aristotle on Learning to Be Good" (1980), in A. O. Rorty (ed.), *Essays on Aristotle's Ethics* (1980), pp. 69–92.

Burnyeat, M. (ed.). *Notes on Book Zeta of Aristotle's Metaphysics*, Oxford, 1979 (mimeographed).

Camerer, L. *Praktische Klugheit bei Herodot*, diss. Tübingen (Germany), 1965.

Carter, L. B. *The Quiet Athenian*, Oxford, 1986.

Chantraine, P. *Dictionaire étimologique de la langue grecque*, Paris, 1968.

Charles, D. *Aristotle's Philosophy of Action*, London, 1984.

Charlton, W. *Aristotle's Physics I, II*, Oxford, 1970.

Clark, S. R. L. *Aristotle's Man*, Oxford, 1975.

Colli, G. *Aristotele. Organon*, Introd. trans. and notes, Turin, 1955.

Cooper, J. M. *Reason and Human Good in Aristotle*, Cambridge (Mass.) and London, 1975.

Cortella, L. *Aristotele e la razionalità della prassi. Una analisi del dibattito sulla filosofia pratica aristotelica in Germania*, Rome, 1987.

Dahl, N. O. *Practical Reason, Aristotle and the Weakness of the Will*, Minneapolis, Minn., 1984.

Decarie, V. *Aristote. Ethique à Eudème*, Introd. trans. notes and indices, Paris-Montréal, 1978.

Defourny, M. *Aristote. Etudes sur la "Politique,"* Paris, 1932.

Dennert, J. *Die ontologish-aristotelische Politikwissenschaft und der Rationalismus*, Berlin, 1970.

Derenne, E. *Les procès d'impieté intentés aux philosophes à Athènes au Vme et au IVième siècles avant J. C.*, Paris-Liège (France), 1930.

Detienne, M. "En Grèce archaique: géometrie, politique et société," *Annales E. S. C.* 20 (1965), pp. 421–441.

Detienne, M., and P. Vernant, *Le astuzie dell'intelligenza nell'antica Grecia* (1974), Ital. trans., Rome-Bari, 1978.

Devoto, G., and G. C. Oli, *Dizionario della lingua italiana*, Florence, 1971.

Dirlmeier, F. "Die Oikeiosis-Lehre Theophrasts'," *Philologus* Suppl. 30–31 (1937).

———. *Aristoteles. Nikomachische Ethik*, trans. and comm., Berlin, 1956.

———. *Aristoteles. Eudemische Ethik*, trans. and comm., Berlin, 1963.

Donini, P. L. "Incontinenza e sillogismo pratico nell'Etica Nicomachea," *Rivista Critica di Storia della Filosofia* 32 (1977), pp. 174–194.

Dover, K. J. *La morale poplare greca nell'epoca di Platone e di Aristotele* (1974), Ital. trans., Brescia (Italy), 1983.

———. "The Freedom of the Intellectual in Greek Society," *Talanta* 7 (1976), pp. 24–54.

Dudley, J. A. *Gott und Θεωρία bei Aristoteles. Die metaphysische Grundlage der Nikomachischen Ethik*, Bern (Switzerland), 1981.

Dufour, M. *Aristote. Rhetorique*, text established and translated, Paris, 1932.

Düring, I. *Aristotle in the Ancient Biographical Tradition*, Göteborg (Germany), 1957.

———. "Aristotle's Use of the Examples in the Topics," in G. E. L. Owen (ed.), *Aristotle on Dialectic* (1968), pp. 202–232.

———. *Aristotele* (1966), Ital. trans., Milan, 1976.

Engberg-Pedersen, T. "For Goodness' Sake: More on Nicomachean Ethics" I vii 5, *Archiv f. Gesch. d. Philos.* 63 (1981), pp. 17–40.

———. *Aristotle's Theory of Moral Insight,* Oxford, 1983.

Eriksen, T. B. *Bios theoretikos. Notes on NE X 6–8,* Oslo, 1976.

Etheridge, S. G. "Practical Syllogism and Necessity," *Philologus* 112 (1968), pp. 20–42.

Even-Grandboulian, G. "Le syllogisme pratique chez Aristote," *Et. Philos.* unnumbered (1976), pp. 57–76.

Fiedler, W. *Analogiemodelle bei Aristoteles,* Amsterdam, 1978.

Finley, M. I. *La democrazia degli antichi e dei moderni* (1972), Ital. trans., Rome-Bari, 1973.

Fischer, N. "Tugend und Glückseligkeit. Zu ihrem Verhältnis bei Aristoteles und Kant," *Kant-Studien* 74 (1983), pp. 1–21.

Fortenbaugh, W. W. "Aristotle's Conception of Moral Virtue and Its Perceptive Role," *Trans. Amer. Philol. Assoc.* 95 (1974), pp. 77–87.

Fragstein, A. von. *Die Diairesis bei Aristoteles,* Amsterdam, 1967.

———. *Studien zur Ethik des Aristoteles,* Amsterdam, 1974.

Gadamer, H. G. *Verità e metodo* (1960), Ital. trans., Milan, 1972.

Gauthier, R. A., and J. Y. Jolif, *Aristote. L'Ethique à Nicomaque,* Introd. trans. and comm., Paris-Louvain, 1958–1959, 2nd ed. 1970.

Geach, P. T. In *Journal of the Philosophical Association* (1958), 112.

Gigon, O. *Problemi fondamentali della filosofia antica* (1959), Ital. trans., Naples, 1984.

———. "Aristoteles. Topik" iii 1–3, in G. E. L. Owen (ed.), *Aristotle on Dialectic* (1968), pp. 233–256.

———. "Das Prooimium der Eudemischen Ethik," in P. Moraux-D. Harlfinger, *Untersuchungen zur Eudemischen Ethik* (1971), pp. 93–134.

———. "Theorie und Praxis bei Platon und Aristoteles," *Museum Helveticum* 30–31 (1973), pp. 65–87, 144–165.

———. "Phronesis und Sophia in der Nikomachischen Ethik des Aristoteles," in *Kephalaion* (1975), pp. 91–103.

———. "Die Eudaimonia im ersten Buch der Nikomachischen Ethik," in J. Wiesner (ed.), *Aristoteles Werk und Wirkung* (1985) I, pp. 339–365.

Gladigow, B. *Sophia und Kosmos,* Hildesheim (Germany), 1965.

Gosling, J. C. B., and C. C. W. Taylor, *The Greeks on Pleasure,* Oxford, 1962.

Grant, A. *The Ethics of Aristotle,* London, 1885.

Greenwood, L. H. G. *Aristotle. Nicomachean Ethics Book Six,* Cambridge, 1909.

Grimaldi, M. A. *Aristotle, Rhetoric I. A Commentary,* New York, 1980.

Groningen, B. A. van. *Theognis. Le premier livre,* edited with comm., Amsterdam, 1966.

Guariglia, O. N. *Quellenkritische und logische Untersuchungen zur Gegensatzlehre des Aristoteles,* Hildesheim-New York, 1978.

Hackforth, R. *Plato's Philebus,* Cambridge, 1972.

Hardie, W. F. R. "Aristotle's Doctrine that Virtue Is a 'Mean'" (1964–1965), now in J. Barnes et al. (eds.), *Articles on Aristotle*. 2 (1977), pp. 33–46.

———. "The Final Good in Aristotle's Ethics," *Philosophy* 40 (1965), pp. 277–295.

———. *Aristotle's Ethical Theory*, Oxford, 1968, 2nd ed., 1980.

———. "Aristotle on the Best Life for a Man," *Philosophy* 54 (1979), pp. 35–50.

Hare, R. M. *Libertà e ragione* (1963), Ital. trans., Milan, 1971.

———. *Practical Inference*, London, 1971.

Hegel, G. W. F. *Scienza della logica* (1831), Ital. trans., Rome-Bari, 2nd ed. 1968.

Hennis, W. *Politik und praktische Philosophie*, Stuttgart (Germany), 1963, 2nd ed. 1977.

Henrich, D., et al. (eds.). *Die Gegenwart der Griechen im neueren Denken*, Festschrift Gadamer, Tübingen (Germany), 1960.

Hintikka, J. "Practical vs. Theoretical Reason. An Ambiguous Legacy," in S. Körner (ed.), *Practical Reason*, pp. 82–102.

Höffe, O. *Praktische Philosophie. Das Modell des Aristoteles*, Salzburg (Austria), 1971.

———. "Ethik als pratische Philosophie. Die Begründung durch Aristoteles," in *Ethik und Politik. Grundmodelle und-probleme der praktischen Philosophie*, Frankfurt am Main, 1979, pp. 38–83.

Humphreys, S. *Anthropology and The Greeks*, London, 1978.

Hutchinson, D. S. *The Virtues of Aristotle*, London and New York, 1986.

Huyl D. den, and T. R. Machan. "Recent Work on the Concept of Happiness," *American Philosophical Quart.* 20 (1983), pp. 115–134.

Ingenkamp, H. G. "Erkenntnisverb durch stochazesthai bei Aristoteles," *Hermes* 109 (1981), pp. 172–178.

———. "Das Fundament stochastischen Verhältnis nach Aristoteles," EN vi13, *Rheinisches Museum* 123 (1981), pp. 41–50.

Inwood, B. *Ethics and Human Action in Early Stoicism*, Oxford, 1985.

Ioppolo, A. M. "La dottrina stoica dei beni esterni e i suoi rapporti con l'etica aristotelica," *Rivista Critica di Storia della Filosofia* 29 (1974), pp. 363–385.

Irwin, T. "Aristotle on Reason, Desire and Virtue," *Journ. of Philos.* 72 (1975), pp. 567–578.

———. "First Principles in Aristotle's Ethics," *Midwest Stud. Philos.* 3 (1978), pp. 252–272.

Isnardi Parente, M. *Techne. Momenti del pensiero greco da Platone a Epicuro*, Florence, 1966.

———. *Speusippo. Frammenti*, Naples, 1980.

———. *Senocrate-Emodoro. Frammenti*, Naples, 1981.

Jacobi, K. "Aristoteles' Einführung des Begriffes 'eudaimonia' im I Buch der 'Nikomachischen Ethik,'" *Philos. Jahrbuch* 86 (1979), pp. 300–325.

Jaeger, W. *Aristotele. Prime linee di una storia della sua evoluzione sprituale* (1923), Ital. trans., Florence, 1935, 4th ed., 1968.

———. "Genesi e ricorso dell'ideale filosofico della vita" (1928), Ital. trans. in appendix to *Aristotele* (1935), pp. 559–617.

———. *Paideia iii* (1947), Ital. trans., Florence, 1959.

———. "Aristotle's Use of Medicine as Model of his Ethics," *Journ. Hell. Stud.* 77 (1957), pp. 54–61.

Joachim, H. H. *Aristotle. The Nicomachean Ethics, A Commentary,* Oxford, 1951.

Joly, R. *Le thème philosophique des genres de vie dans l'antiquité classique,* Brussels, 1956.

Kahn, C. H. "The Role of Nous in the Cognition of First Principles in Posterior Analytics ii 19" in E. Berti (ed.), *Aristotle on Science* (1981), pp. 385–414.

Kenny, A. "Practical Inference," *Analysis* 26 (1965–1966), pp. 65–75.

———. "Aristotle on Happiness" (1965–1966), now in J. Barnes et al. (eds.) *Articles on Aristotle,* 2 (1977), pp. 25–32.

———. "The Practical Syllogism and Incontinence," *Phronesis* 11 (1966), pp. 163–184.

———. *The Aristotelian Ethics,* Oxford, 1978.

———. *Aristotle's Theory of the Will,* London, 1979.

Kirwan, G. "Logic and the Good in Aristotle," *Philos. Quart.* 17 (1967), pp. 97–114.

———. *Aristotle's Metaphysics Books Gamma, Delta, Epsilon,* Oxford, 1971.

Koch, F.-A. "Gerechtigkeit als Gedankenexperiment. Rawls und Aristoteles," *Zeitschr. f. philos. Forschung* 32 (1978), pp. 239–253.

Körner, S. (ed.). *Practical Reason,* Oxford, 1974.

Krämer, H. J. *Arete bei Platon und Aristoteles,* Heidelberg, 1959, Amsterdam, 2nd ed. 1967.

———. *Platonismus und hellenistische Philosophie,* Berlin and New York, 1972.

Kraut, R. "Two Conceptions of Happiness," *Philos. Review* 88 (1977), pp. 167–197.

Kuhn, H. "Der Begriff der Prohairesis in der Nikomachischen Ethik," in D. Henrich et al. (eds.) (1960), *Die Gegenwart der Griechen in neueren Denken,* pp. 123–140.

———. "Aristoteles und die Methode der politischen Wissenschaft," *Zeitschrift für Politik* 12 (1965), pp. 101–120.

Kullmann, W. *Wissenschaft und Methode,* Berlin and New York, 1974.

Kurz, D. *Akribeia. Das Ideal der Exaktheit bei den griechen bis Aristoteles,* Göppingen (Germany), 1970.

La Croce, E. *La doctrina del bien en Aristoteles,* diss. Buenos Aires, 1987.

Latte, K. "Der Rechtsgedanke im archaischen Griechentum," *Antike und Abendland* 2 (1946), pp. 63–76.

Lefevre, C. *Sur l'évolution d'Aristote en psychologie,* Louvain (Belgium), 1972.

———. "Sur le statut de l'âme dans le De anima et les Parva naturalia," in G. E. L. Owen and G. E. R. Lloyd (eds.), *Aristotle on Mind and the Senses* (1978).

Leonard, J. *Le bonheur chez Aristote,* Brussels, 1948.

Librizzi, C. *La morale di Aristotele,* Padua, 1960.

Liddell, H. G., and R. Scott, *A Greek-English Lexicon,* Oxford, 19409.

Lloyd, G. E. R. *Polarity and Analogy,* Cambridge, 1966.

———. "The Role of Medical and Biological Analogies in Aristotle's Ethics," *Phronesis* 13 (1968), pp. 68–83.

———. *Aristotele* (1968), Ital. trans., Bologna, 1985.

Loening, R. *Die Zurechnungslehre des Aristoteles,* Jena (Germany), 1903.

Lord, C. *Education and Culture in the Political Thought of Aristotle,* Ithaca, N.Y. and London, 1982.

Luzac, J. *Lectiones atticae,* Leiden (Netherlands), 1809.

Maddalena, A. "L'umano e il divino in Erodoto," in V. E. Alfieri and M. Untersteiner, *Studi di filosotia greca* (1950), pp. 57–84.

Mansion, S. (ed.). *Aristote et les Problèmes de Méthode,* Louvain-Paris, 1961.

Marasco, G. "I processi di empietà nella democrazia ateniese," *Atene e Roma* 21 (1976), pp. 113–131.

Mazzarelli, C. *Aristotele. Etica Nicomachea,* Introd. trans. and paraphrase, Milan, 1979.

Mele, A. R. "Choice and Virtue in the Nicomachean Ethics," *Journ. Hist. Philos.* 19 (1981), pp. 405–423.

———. "The Practical Syllogism and Deliberation in Aristotle's Theory of Action," *New Scholasticism* 55 (1981), pp. 281–316.

———. "Aristotle on the Roles of Reason in Motivation and Justification," *Arch. f. Gesch. d. Philos.* 66 (1983), pp. 124–147.

Mignucci, M. *La teoria aristotelica della scienza,* Florence, 1965.

———. *Aristotele. Gli analitici primi,* Trans., introd. and comm., Naples, 1969.

———. *L'argomentazione dimostrativa in Aristotele,* Padua, 1975.

———. "ὡς ἐπὶ τὸ πολύ et nécessaire dans la conception aristotélicienne de la science," in E. Berti (ed.), *Aristotle on Science* (1981), 173–204.

———. "Puzzles about Identity. Aristotle and his Greek Commentators," in J. Wiesner (ed.), *Aristoteles' Werk und Wirkung* (1985) I, pp. 57–97.

Mikkola, E. *Isokrates. Seine Anschauungen im Lichte seiner Schriften,* Helsinki, 1954.

Modrak, D. K. "Aisthesis in the Practical Sillogism," *Philosophical Studies* 30 (1976), pp. 379–391.

Monan, D. J. *Moral Knowledge and its Methodology in Aristotle,* Oxford, 1968.

Moraux, P. "Das Fragment viii1. Text und Interpretation," in P. Moraux and D. Harlfinger (eds.), *Untersuchungen zur Eudemischen Ethik* (1971), pp. 253–284.

Moraux P. and D. Harlfinger (eds.), *Untersuchungen zur Eudemischen Ethik,* Berlin, 1971.

Moreau, J. "Telos et arete d'après EE ii1, et la tradition platonicienne," in P. Moraux and D. Harlfinger (eds.), *Untersuchungen zur Eudemischen Ethik* (1971), pp. 223–230.

Mühl, F. von der. *De Aristotelis Ethicorum Eudemiorum auctoritate,* Gottingae, 1909.

Müller, A. W. *Autonome Theorie und Interessedenken,* Wiesbaden (Germany), 1971.

———. *Praktisches Folgern und Selbstgestaltung nach Aristoteles,* Freiburg-Munich (Germany), 1982.

Nagel, T. "Aristotle on Eudaimonia" (1972), in A. O. Rorty (ed.), *Essays on Aristotle's Ethics*, pp. 7–14.

Nannery, L. "The Problem of the Two Lives in Aristotle's Ethics: the Human Good and the Best Life for a Man," *Intern. Philos. Quart.* 21 (1983), pp. 277–293.

Natali, C. *Cosmo e divinità. La struttura logica della teologia aristotelica*, L'Aquila (Italy), 1974.

———. "Problemi organizzativi di alcune scuole filosofiche ateniesi," *Hermes* 91 (1983), pp. 52–69.

———. "Virtù o scienza? Aspetti della φρόνησις nei *Topici* e nelle *Etiche* di Aristotele," *Phronesis* 29 (1984), pp. 50–72.

Newman, W. L. *The Politics of Aristotle*, Introd., essays and notes, Oxford, 1889–1902.

Nussbaum, M. *Aristotle's De motu animalium*, Text, trans. comm. and interpr. essays, Princeton, N.J., 1978.

———. *The Fragility of Goodness. Luck and Ethics in Greek Tragedy and Philosophy*, Cambridge, 1986.

Nuyens, F. *L'évolution de la psychologie d'Aristote*, Louvain (Belgium),1948.

Oates, W. J. *Aristotle and the Problem of Value*, Princeton, N.J., 1963.

Oncken, W. *Die Staatslehre des Aristoteles*, Leipzig (Germany),1875.

Owen, G. E. L. "Τιθέναι τὰ φαινόμενα," in S. Mansion (ed.), *Aristote et les problèmes de Méthode* (1961), pp. 83–103.

———. (ed.) *Aristotle on Dialectic. The Topics*, Oxford, 1968.

Owen, G. E. L., and G. E. R. Lloyd (eds.), *Aristotle on Mind and the Senses*, Cambridge, 1978.

Patzig, G. *Die aristotelische Syllogistik*, Göttingen (Germany), 1959, 2nd ed. 1963.

Peretti, A. *Teognide nella tradizione gnomologica*, Pisa (Italy), 1953.

Pini, G. *Clemente Alessandrino. Gli Stromati. Note di vera filosofia*, Milan, 1985.

Pleines, J.-E. *Eudaimonia zwischen Kant und Aristoteles*, Würzburg (Germany), 1984.

Rackham, H. *Aristotle, The Nicomachean Ethics*, text, introd. trans. and notes, Cambridge, Mass. and London, 1934, repr. 1994.

Rawls, J. *Una teoria della giustizia* (1971), Ital. trans. Milan, 1982.

Regis, L. M. *L'opinion chez Aristote*, Paris-Ottawa, 1935.

Ricoeur, P. *La semantica dell'azione* (1977), Ital. trans., Milan, 1986.

Riedel, M. *Rehabilitierung der praktischen Philosophie*, i-ii, Freiburg im Breisgau (Germany), 1972–1974.

Rist, J. "An Early Dispute about Right Reason," *Monist* 66 (1983), pp. 38–49.

Ritter, J. "Felicità e vita civile" (1956), Ital. trans., in *Metafisica e Politica* (1983), pp. 50–93.

———. *Metafisica e Politica* (1969), Ital. trans. Casale Monferrato (Italy), 1983.

Robinson, R. "Ends and Means and Logical Priority," in P. Moraux and D. Harlfinger (eds.), *Untersuchungen zur Eudemischen Ethik* (1971), pp. 185–194.

———. "Aristotle on Akrasia" (1955), now in J. Barnes et al. (eds.), *Articles on Aristotle. 2* (1977), pp. 79–91.

Rodier, G. *Aristote. Ethique à Nicomaque livre x,* Paris, 1897.

———. *Etudes de philosophie grecque,* Paris, 1969.

Rorty, A. O. (ed.),"Akrasia and Pleasure: Nicomachean Ethics Book 7," in A. O. Rorty (ed.), *Essays in Aristotle's Ethics* (1980), pp. 267–284.

———. *Essays on Aristotle's Ethics,* Berkeley, Calif., 1980.

Ross, W. D. *Aristotele* (1923), Ital. trans., Milan, 3rd ed., 1982.

———. *Aristotle's Prior and Posterior Analytics,* Oxford, 1949.

Rowe, C. J. "The Meaning of φρόνησις in the Eudemian Ethics," in P. Moraux and D. Harlfinger (eds.), *Untersuchungen zur Eudemischen Ethik* (1971), pp. 73–92.

———. *The Eudemian and Nicomachean Ethics: a Study in the Development of Aristotle's Thought,* Cambridge, 1977.

Ruggiu, L. *Teoria e prassi in Aristotele,* Naples, 1973.

———. *La scienza "ricercata." Economia politica e filosofia. Studi su Aristotele e Marx.* Treviso (Italy), 1979.

Rummel, E. "Isocrates' Ideal of Rhetoric. Criteria of Evaluation," *Class. Journ.* 75 (1979–1980), pp. 25–35.

Ryan, E. E. *The Notion of Good in Books Alpha, Beta, Gamma and Delta of the Metaphysics of Aristotle,* diss. Univ. Gregoriana, Copenhagen, 1961.

Santas, G. "Aristotle on Practical Inference, the Explanation of Action, and Akrasia," *Phronesis* 14 (1969), pp. 162–189.

Schmidt, J. H. *Synonimik der griechischen Sprache,* Leipzig (Germany), 1876–1886.

Schnädelbach, H. "Was ist Neuaristotelismus?," *Information Philosophie* 14 (1986), H. 1, pp. 6–25.

Schütrumpf, E. *Die Analyse der Polis durch Aristoteles,* Amsterdam, 1980.

Seel, G. "Wert und Wertrangordnung in der aristotelischen Guterlehre," *Arch. f. Gesch. d. Philos.* 63 (1981), 253–288.

Seidl, H. *Der Begriff des Intellekts (νοῦς) bei Aristoteles,* Meisenheim am Glan (Germany), 1971.

Severino, E. *Studi di filosofia della prassi* (1962), Milan, 2nd ed., 1984.

———. *Destino della necessità,* Milan, 1980.

Smith, J. A. "Aristotelica," *Classical Quart.* 14 (1920), pp. 19–22.

Snell, B. *Leben und Meinungen der Sieben Wiesen,* Munich, 1934.

Solmsen, F. "Leisure and Play in Aristotle's Ideal State," *Rheinisches Museum,* 107 (1964), pp. 193–220.

Sorabji, R. "Aristotle on the Role of Intellect in Virtue," *Proceed. Aristotelian Soc.* NS 74 (1973–1974), pp. 107–129.

Soreth, M. "Zu Topik E 7, 138a 8–20," in G. E. L. Owen (ed.), *Aristotle on Dialectic. The Topics* (1968), pp. 43–45.

Stark, R. *Aristotelesstudien,* Munich, 1963, 1972.

Steidle, W. "Redekunst und Bildung bei Isokrates," *Hermes* 80 (1952), pp. 257–296.

Stewart, J. A. *Notes on the Nicomachean Ethics of Aristotle,* Oxford 1892.

Susemihl, F., and R. D. Hicks, *The Politics of Aristotle,* Text, introd., analysis and comm., London, 1894.

Taran, L. *Speusippus of Athens,* Critical study, text, comm., Leiden (Netherlands), 1981.

Taylor, A. E. *Plato. The Sophist and the Statesman,* Transl. and introd., Folkestone and London, 1972.

Tracy, T. *Physiological Theory and the Doctrine of the Mean in Aristotle,* Paris and The Hague, 1969.

Upton, T. "Aristotle's Moral Epistemology: the Possibility of Ethical Demonstration," *New Scolasticism* 56 (1981), pp. 169–184.

Urmson, J. O. "Aristotle's Doctrine of the Mean," *Amer. Philos. Quart.* 10 (1973), pp. 223–230.

Vattimo, G. *Il concetto di fare in Aristotele,* Turin, 1961.

Verdenius, V. J. "Notes on the Topics," in G. E. L. Owen (ed.), *Aristotle on Dialectic. The Topics* (1968), pp. 22–42.

———. "Human Reason and God in the EE," in P. Moraux and D. Harlfinger (eds.), *Untersuchungen zur Eudemischen Ethik* (1971), pp. 285–297.

Vigna C. (ed.). *Teorie della felicità,* Abano (Padua), 1986.

Vogel, C. J. de. "Aristotle's Attitude to Plato and the Theory of Ideas, according to the Topics," in G. E. L. Owen (ed.), *Aristotle on Dialectic* (1968), pp. 91–102.

Vollrath, E. *Die Rekonstruktion der politischen Urteilskraft,* Stuttgart (Germany), 1977.

Volpi, F. "La riabilitazione della filosofia pratica e il suo senso nella crisi della modernità," *Il Mulino* 34 (1986), No. 6, pp. 928–949.

Wedin, M. "Aristotle on the Good for Man," *Mind* 90 (1981), pp. 243–262.

Wehrli, F. *Hauptrichtungen der griechischen Denkens,* Zürich-Stuttgart (Switzerland-Germany), 1964.

Wersdörfer, W. *Die φιλοσοφία des Isokrates im Spiegel ihrer Terminologie,* Leipzig (Germany), 1940.

Wiesner, J. (ed.). *Aristoteles Werk und Wirkung,* Festschriften P. Moraux, I, Berlin and New York, 1985.

Wiggins, D. "Deliberation and Practical Reason" (1975–1976), now in A. O. Rorty (ed.), *Essays on Aristotle's Ethics* (1980), pp. 221–240.

———. "Weakness of the Will, Commensurability, and the Objects of Deliberation and Desire" (1978–1979), in A. O. Rorty (ed.), *Essays on Aristotle's Ethics* (1980), pp. 241–266.

Wilkes, K. W. "The Good Man and the Good for Man in Aristotle's Ethics" (1978), in A. O. Rorty (ed.), *Essays on Aristotle's Ethics* (1980), pp. 341–358.

Williams, B. A. O. "Aristotle on the Good. A Formal Sketch," *Philos. Quart.* 12 (1962), pp. 289–296.

———. *Ethics and the Limits of Philosophy* (1985), Ital. trans., Rome-Bari (Italy), 1987.

Wright, G. H. von. *Spiegazione e comprensione* (1971), Ital. trans., Bologna, 1977.

Woods, M. *Aristotle's Eudemian Ethics Books i, ii and vii,* Oxford, 1982.

Zadro, A. *Aristotele. I Topici,* introd., trans. and comm., Naples, 1974.

Zanatta, M. *Aristotele. Etica Nicomachea,* introd. trans. and comm., Milan, 1986.

Zeise, H. "Der Staatsmann. Ein Beitrag zur Interpretation des platonischen Politikos," *Philologus* Suppl. 31/3 (1938).

Zeller, E., and R. Mondolfo, *La filosofia dei Greci nel suo sviluppo storico,* ii/6, Ital. trans., Florence, 1966.

Zuccante, G. *Aristotele e la morale,* Florence, 1929.

INDEX OF GREEK TERMS

INDEX OF NAMES

(the names of Aristotle and Plato have not been included, on account of their frequent appearance)

INDEX OF PASSAGES CITED

SUBJECT INDEX